SOCIAL THEMES

PRENTICE-HALL, INC.
Englewood Cliffs, N.J.

BENJAMIN GORMAN

University of Florida

SOCIAL THEMES

PRENTICE-HALL SOCIOLOGY SERIES

Neil J. Smelser, *Editor*

Current printing (last number): 10 9 8 7 6 5 4 3 2 1

C-13-819599-4
P-13-819581-1

Library of Congress Catalog Card No.: 72-142382

PRENTICE-HALL INTERNATIONAL, INC., London
PRENTICE-HALL OF AUSTRALIA, PTY. LTD., Sydney
PRENTICE-HALL OF CANADA, LTD., Toronto
PRENTICE-HALL OF INDIA PRIVATE LIMITED, New Delhi
PRENTICE-HALL OF JAPAN, INC., Tokyo

PREFACE

If I could do anything I wanted to do, I might spend the next couple of years traveling around the world or lolling on the beach. Sooner or later I would get bored by this sort of thing and would return to my present activity: discovering things about society. Human society is exciting, and coming to understand it is an exciting activity. I am almost addicted to this particular activity. I am a socioligist.

Most of you who read this book will not be sociologists, but you will live your entire life in society; and if you too are not excited by society, you are missing a very great part of your life. In a fashion that you can understand without being a sociologist, therefore, I have tried to present some solid sociological understandings about society. I hope that the book retains the excitement, that it stimulates as well as informs. If it fails, the fault is not with the subject.

This book is not an introduction to sociology. Such an introduction would lean heavily on substantive research findings within the field, would make the reader cognizant of the major scholars within the discipline, and would exhibit a comprehensive coverage of the entire range of subject matter. One of the major functions of this book is to persuade the reader that the study of such an introduction can be both intrinsically and extrinsically rewarding. Another function is to introduce the reader to society.

Whenever the alternative arose, I tried to concentrate more on how society operates than on how sociologists study it. This approach implied a relative absence of technical terms, quantitative data, footnotes, and other trappings of professional scholarship. I do not mean to sell these things short; most of the better understandings of society come from professional scholarship in sociology. This book is derived almost exclusively from these understandings, but it translates them from sociological terminology to everyday discourse and focuses them on the challenging issues of our time and our society.

By limiting footnotes, I have also limited the opportunities to acknowledge my just debts to people who have had an influence on this book. Most of my ideas are not new; they are borrowed. Sometimes they are combined and altered in such a way that their original owner might not recognize them or want to claim them. Other ideas have achieved such currency that the original ownership is diluted or in question. Still, I feel more debts than even the most exhaustive footnotes could cover, and so I take this opportunity to credit everyone who recognizes something of himself in this book, and to apologize for anything he may have lost in the translation.

Specifically, I must mention: Howard Becker, Howard S. Becker, Daniel Bell, Reinhard Bendix, Joseph Bensman, George Benz, Peter Blau, Wilbur Bock, Michael Bohleber, Milburn Bolin, Leonard Broom, Theodore Caplow, Lewis Coser, Emile Durkheim, Munro Edmonson, Amitai Etzioni, E. E. Evans-Pritchard, William Fink, Erving Goffman, Joyce Gorman, Bill Harrell, Carl Hempel,

Lew Hendrix, Robert Keohane, William Kolb, Thomas Ktsanes, Weston LaBarre, Richard Larson, Forrest LaViolette, Gerhard Lenski, Gerald Leslie, Marion Levy, Jr., Robert Lystad, Karl Marx, Em McElderry, Scott Miyakawa, John Mogey, Wilbert Moore, S. F. Nadel, Talcott Parsons, William Pendleton, A. R. Radcliffe-Brown, Leonard Reissman, Daniel Selakovich, Neil Smelser, Maurice Stein, Samuel Stouffer, Sara Sutker, Solomon Sutker, James Tarver, Daniel Thompson, Ralph Turner, Herman Turk, Joseph Vandiver, Max Weber, Florian Znaniecki, and hundreds of students (some of whose names I remember). Some people on this list I have known personally, others only through their writings. They are all my teachers.

CONTENTS

SOCIAL THEMES

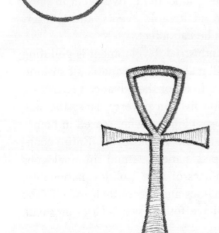

1 UNDERSTANDING SOCIETY

Life is problematic. You may die before you finish reading this paragraph, or your health may be radically improved. You may become richer or poorer or more or less loved. Although this instant is unlikely to be so dramatic, dozens of events that are occurring will come to have an impact on your life. You may have little or much control over them, be deeply influenced or not at all; but as an individual actor, a conscious and purposive

1

one, you will seek some outcomes and make an attempt to avoid others.

You base your behavior on your understanding of the problematic aspects of life. You drive carefully on slippery pavement; you bank your surplus money; you are considerate of your friend. By such behavior, you hope to prevent loss of life, wealth, and love. Your success depends on your awareness of impactful events and your understanding of the principles on which they operate. To avoid becoming a highway fatality you must appreciate the need for traction between wheel and road and have some practical driving skills. This kind of knowledgeable intervention renders some of life's situations less problematic.

Most of the effects worked on anyone's life are worked through contacts with other people. Man lives in a social and physical world, but the impact of the social upon him far outweighs the physical. The problematic aspects of life are primarily social ones, yet it is precisely the social world about which man displays the greatest unawareness and ignorance.

You know more about matters related to the preservation of life and health (primitive physics, chemistry, and biology) than you know about preserving wealth (primitive sociology and economics) or friendship (primitive sociology and psychology).

PROBLEMS IN SOCIETY

The contemporary world is full of problematic social issues: little and big. Some of these enmesh the individual in ways he is powerless to resist. Others trap only the unwary. In either case, it behooves the individual to become a knowledgeable and active agent in these affairs, to move sensibly with the unalterable events, and to exert pressure shrewdly on those events he can affect.

We all live in a world where industrial development is polluting the air and water at a rate that will make them incapable of sustaining life for many more generations. In all of the advanced countries, a sizeable portion of the population lives in poverty, lacks the skill and opportunity to escape, and raises children who, reared in homes with these conditions, will perpetuate the vicious cycle. Entire countries, the so-called underdeveloped nations, stand in analogous circumstances. The virulent prejudices of race, politics, nationality, and religion reinforce these inequalities and create their own. In the last five years, over fifty nations have fought wars—large or small, foreign or domestic. Military fingers around the world hover over their atomic buttons. Millions of people pursue their personal visions of the good life with drugs, artistic expression, free speech, free sexuality, bombs, or strange dress. Other millions strive to suppress them. Seldom have the tensions between an orderly state and personal liberty been so clear. People are bearing more offspring than the world can support. Events with the scope of these affect us all.

Other problems strike only one person, or a few. But if the same occurrence repeats itself, if the same fate occurs frequently, its impact is more general and its source clearly societal. In the United States, on the day you read these words, fifteen hundred youths will drop out of high school. Sixty people will commit suicide. Three million people, most of whom are willing and able to work, will be unable to find jobs. Four thousand women who don't want babies will find out they are pregnant. Nineteen thousand people will be arrested for serious crimes. Almost two thousand divorces will be granted, more than half of which will break homes in which there are children. Three and a half million old maids will pass another day in loneliness, frustration, bitterness, or whatever other condition may overtake old maids. Thirty people will be murdered. Sometime this week, one of these will be a child murdered by a parent. Forty thousand sixteen-year-old girls will go without a date tonight, when they wanted one badly. More than a million friendships will be seriously ruptured. Three thousand people will be admitted to mental institutions.[1]

Each of these conditions and many more similar ones demonstrate the validity of the opening statement of this book: Life is problematic.

The preceding has also shown that the focus of these problematic issues is in social life. Every action of every individual is aimed, consciously or unconsciously, at the resolution of one or another of these problems. The guides to action are desired outcomes and an implicit and fuzzy understanding of the principles of operation of

[1] All of these figures are as sound as such estimates can be. They still vary from moderately precise to terribly wild. The figure on unwanted pregnancies, for instance, was based on illegitimate births, over-reproduction (excess of children ever born over a figure based on married womens' statements concerning how many children they would like to have, adjusted for age-cohort), intentional abortions, births less than nine months after marriage, and estimated misspacings. These were adjusted downward for overlap and extraneous intruding causes, summed and adjusted upwards for pregnancies less than full term. Additionally, most of these estimates are based on yearly averages and may be inaccurate as incidence undergoes a weekly or yearly fluctuation. If you are reading this on a Saturday in July, for instance, the number of murders will be higher, the number of mental institution admissions lower, than on a Wednesday in November.

the social world. The person bases his behavior on some assumptions concerning how this behavior will affect his prospects. Notions about social reality are central to human life. Humans have always developed and elaborated such notions. Despite this attention, the notions have remained little more than that; they are mostly inaccurate. Our attempts to guide our behavior more sensibly, to bring outcomes more nearly in accord with our desires, to reduce the problematic aspects of life, depend most directly on acquiring a better understanding of the workings of the social world.

MISUNDERSTANDING SOCIAL LIFE

The oldest, most obvious, and most widely-used understandings of social life are those labeled folk knowledge. All people live their entire lives in human company. It is not then surprising that they develop insights, understandings, and rules-of-thumb concerning the operation of human society. Some of these understandings are dim and unarticulate, some are private. Many are reduced to epigrammatic dimensions and communicated widely through the population.

All men are brothers.
Birds of a feather flock together.
It is easy to despise what you cannot get.
I get by with a little help from my friends.
East is East, and West is West, and never the twain shall meet.
Opposites attract.
Absence makes the heart grow fonder.

For any social situation, an explanation can be found; for any new problem, a guide to behavior exists. Folk knowledge suffers from no shortage of axioms. In fact, the problem is precisely the opposite. Whatever happens, folk knowledge offers an explanation. But folk knowledge is not knowledge at all; it is a form of self-delusion that may give the individual a feeling of security. It may offer a pretense of rationality in decision making, for it contains elements of truth (if every possible interpretation is placed on an event, at least one of them is surely correct), but it offers no device for determining which truth is applicable.

In the absence of effective answers, folk knowledge is not simply ineffective and therefore useless, it is actively harmful. The false sense of truth lulls the individual to a complacency that keeps him from seeking better, more useful answers.

Folk knowledge begins with human experience; this is a proper start. But the ways of generalizing from that experience are not orderly, the attempt to cover every possible contingency is too exhaustive, and the testing of accuracy is nonexistent. If we wish effective interpretations of social life we must look elsewhere.

Theological answers present themselves as a candidate, but they also fail the effectiveness test. Theology is strong where folk answers are weak. It offers explanation that is not a jumble of disconnected notions. Rather, all explanation is hinged to, and revolves around, a few central principles. There is a rationality and orderliness to this kind of explanation, but theology is weak in the one area where folk knowledge is strong. Theology does not draw its substance from everyday experience. The central principles from which it draws are nonempirical in origin and hence nonexperiential or derived from a very special sort of experience. This is not to say that all theology is false, but simply to note that its core is in a world other than the social one we are trying to explain. When theology attempts to explain this world on the basis of principles derived from another one, it strays beyond its proper boundaries. The "job" of theology, in effect, is to explain things that cannot be explained in any other fashion. The nature of theology is such that it constantly violates this precept.

The nature of the soul, good and evil, life after death, and other such problematic issues are timelessly in the domain of theology. Everyday-experience answers to these questions will never be demonstrably satisfactory. Theology begins with these but extends their principles to cover other unexplained problems. The unexplained, as opposed to the inexplicable, may vary from time to time and place to place. In the absence of any experiential understanding of astronomy, then, it is perfectly satisfactory for theological principles to be extended to provide astronomical explanation: The story of Apollo's fiery chariot may serve until something better comes along. But when something better does come along, theology should retreat. Theology should recognize that giving up the fiery chariot need not cast doubt on the ultimate reality of Apollo. Historically, such recognition and retreat has been uncommon.

The faith of Apollonians in the fiery chariot was undeterred by Egyptian astronomical observation. The Catholic church's Bible-inspired belief in a fixed earth as the center of the universe did not founder on Galileo's evidence of rotation and orbit.

But neither Ptolemy's, Galileo's, Keppler's, Newton's, nor Einstein's insights tell us whether the earth should orbit the sun or whether this orbit should be larger or smaller. Such questions are irrevocably moral. If, on moral grounds, we decide in favor of a larger orbit, we then enter the problematic area of life, as I am using the terms here. Having decided to alter the orbit, we would more effectively achieve that end through conversance with Newton's three laws of motion than through conversation with Apollo. Theological answers here are a siren call to ineffectuality.

Theology, after all these years, has pretty well removed itself from the realms of physics and astronomy. It still hangs on in the life sciences, as in the remaining resistance to the theory of evolution and in the definition of "life" in heart transplants. In the social arena, theology holds stubbornly without sign of retreat. At the problematic level and with a virtually complete neglect of experiential foundation, it is a bar to understanding.

A third source of understanding is art. Literature is the main entry, but visual and musical forms also pretend to offer understandings. The limitations of art as explanation of reality are not so easily pinpointed as are those of folk knowledge or theology. Some artists rest their work solidly in experience. Some tie theirs more firmly to theological vision. Some present a tightly worked logic. Others overwhelm us with a mass of loosely connected vignettes. George Bernard Shaw criticized Shakespeare as a feeble thinker and an ignorant man. He went on to say that Shakespeare's work would endure forever because Shakespeare had an unequalled dramatic power of expression. Shaw, of course, considered Shaw a powerful thinker and a learned man. Yet if his work lives forever, and I suspect it might, it will be because he, too, had great ability at dramatic expression. Here is the nub of the problem with art as explanation: its ability to convince us varies more with the skill of the artist than with the merit of the explanation.

SCIENCE AS UNDERSTANDING

Among those claiming to offer explanation of life's problematic aspects, this leaves only science. In urban-industrial societies, the acceptance of scientific answers is nearly complete as far as the physical and biological sciences are concerned. In fact, science is often over-accepted. The cautions I offered in my discussion of theology are ignored or swept aside. People expect science to separate good from bad as surely as it separates true from false. They expect it not only to provide answers but also to determine which are the important questions. Science cannot do these things. Any faith so placed in it converts science to another sort of theology.

What science can do, and do better than any competitive approach, is determine and describe the operations of the world and suggest the possible effects of certain actions on the world. That is what science is about. If people on some other grounds can decide what outcomes are desired, their chances of obtaining them will be increased by attention to scientific principles. Science, properly used, offers guides to action in the problematic aspects of life. This is a utilization of science, not the operation of science. Science is the derivation of explanation. If the explanations happen to be useful, and ultimately many will, benefits appear for the actors involved. These benefits—increased achievements of desired ends, avoidance of undesired outcomes, efficiency in intervention—are by-products of science, rewards for scientifically selecting means.

Science is a special way of arriving at explanations of the world. These explanations rest ultimately in experience, in evidence from the world that can be seen, heard, smelled, felt, tasted. Scientists attempt to codify, simplify, and generalize these explanations, and to test them once more against evidence. Wresting evidence from the world may sometimes involve rigorous pursuit of an esoteric logic. Codification, simplification, and generalization—the derivation of explanation—usually requires brilliant insight and sharp rationality. Often a special language, perhaps a mathematical one, will be required to express these explanations with precision. Some of these features of science will be discussed further in Chapter 12.

Few of us possess scientific skills and facilities. We can nonetheless avail ourselves of scientific explanation without being scientists. We can learn and accept simplified versions of the explanation and use these as guides to action. We can place ourselves in the hands of scientists and technicians for specialized services. To do so is not to be a scientist but simply to use science to reduce the problematic aspects of human life and of social living.

No person, whatever his capabilities, is able to understand the world. It is too large, too diverse, too complex. Nobody lives long enough or can observe or absorb enough to acquire knowledge of everything. Science, therefore, depends on a division of labor. The world is divided into chunks that are small enough, hopefully, for the attainment of understanding. This division is for purposes of efficiency, so that more understanding results from each investigative effort. The best sort of division is then one that also offers greatest efficiency, and so let us test several ways of dividing the world against the yardstick of efficiency.

The world could be divided into space-time chunks. A scientist could then specialize in the Western Hemisphere since 1800 or, more narrowly, in Pennsylvania between 1940 and 1950. Such division and specialization cannot offer increased efficiency. Pennsylvania during the 1940's contained most of the kinds of things, in almost as bewildering complexity, as are found in the whole world. Our specialist would still need to know about clouds, rocks, birds, people, viruses, silicates, atomic nuclei, weeds, speech patterns, and the many other elements of the world represented in that time and place. This collection is little reduced in variety from that of the whole world for all time.

A second form of division is the sorting of the objects of the world into classes and the development of a specialty for each class. Objects are characterized by their properties or qualities. If objects are generally labeled with nouns, their qualities are all the adjectives that could be applied to them. The simplest class would be all objects sharing a single quality. Sample classes would include soft-things, green-things, rough-things, symmetrical-things, conceptual-things, heavy-things, living-things, and shiny-things. You may now notice that the earlier space-time categorization is only a special form of categorization by quality. Pennsylvanian-things is a class just like any other. Any quality class presents the same inefficiencies as does a space-quality class: the class still contains too great a diversity for understanding. A softologist, for instance, would need expertise on cotton, mud, mattresses other than orthopedic, women, answers that turn away wrath, demineralized water, sponges, India's foreign policy, music *pianissimo*, new grass, and the entire variety of other things soft.

We can reduce the variety somewhat by considering complex classes. Pennsylvania-1940-things is such a class. The classification is restricted to objects possessing more than one attribute in common. Soft-Pennsylvania-1940-things would narrow the membership and decrease the variety still further. We could go on, adding other qualities as criteria.

If the set of qualifying criteria is selected appropriately, we will end up with sensibly homogeneous classes. Most nouns represent such classifications and designate classes of objects that would not serve too badly as a basis for a division of labor for science. Humanology, rockology, atomology, and so forth, would be appropriate names for the resulting disciplines. Still, the rockologist would have an unwieldy subject matter. He would need to know the specific gravity of rocks with particular compositions. He would need to know the conditions under which they were formed. He would need to know the effect of certain acids on their chemical composition. He would need to know their resiliency when polished round and bounced against one another on a smooth table covered with green felt. He would need to know the conditions under which they were likely to be thrown through embassy windows. He would be little better off than a softologist or Pennsylvanianologist.

Classification—grouping objects in terms of their similarities—has a logical appeal but does not result in an efficient division of labor for science. We must look for boundary lines not based on similarities.

Objects may be considered as "going together" by reason of *relationship* rather than *similarity*. A collection of related objects is called a *system*. A small system might, then, include one rock, the man who is throwing it, the embassy window through which it passes. Rock, man, and window are dissimilar but are also involved with one another in the cause-and-effect chain. The man and window are physically enmeshed with each other only through the agency of the rock. The rock's passage through the atmosphere would be unlikely without the action of the man who throws it, and the configuration of the window is changed by the passage of the rock through it. This small system illustrates the basic properties of all systems: member-units and relationships between them.

There are additional relationships extending beyond this system. If we look for relationships between this system's units and other units outside the system we can find them. The window came from a glass factory. The man had some lunch. If we begin tracing all such relationships we will soon be no better off than if we had stuck with classes. This difficulty arose when we stopped attending to the system and the relationships among the objects in the system and focused instead on the objects themselves. Our investigation of classes should have warned us to be wary of focusing on objects. Let's stick to relationships.

The relationships among man-rock-window may be seen as political ones. In this case, we will want to look for further political relationships extending beyond this system. We will want to inquire into the ambassador's response to having his window broken. We will want to know the political associations of the rock thrower. We will want to examine international relations between the state in which the incident occurs and the one the embassy represents. But no matter how far we extend, we have a homogeneously political system, one explicable in political principles; understanding is relatively simple.

If the man-rock-window relation is seen as a physical one, we could extend our compass to take in only other physical relationships and build a different explanation, a physical explanation of a physical system. Concentration on relations rather than objects reveals that man-rock-window is a system that can be viewed from several relational perspectives or is even several different systems.

Whichever view of this multiple nature we take, this little system is contained within several distinct larger systems. The larger systems, such as physical and political, may share this mini-system in common but are distinguished from each other in terms of different unshared component units as well as different types of relationships. Several kinds of systems may jointly occupy a space and possess commonly involved units, but the relational nature of the occupancy and possession is different. Moreover, the world is made up of systems, most of which have subsystems, many of which are themselves part of some larger system. There are systems within systems within systems within systems. Each level may be analyzed on its own or seen as part of the larger system.

In the scientific division of labor, the trick is to expand to include enough levels to yield a significant subject matter and to stop soon enough to have a manageable subject matter.

Finally, a number of independent systems, systems that have little or no relationship binding one to the other, may each have internal relationships so similar to the others that their principles of explanation are identical. To do the same work over, under another disciplinary label, would be foolish. The physical relationship of man-rock-window may then be seen to belong to the same class as a duck lighting on thin ice. The two small systems have no binding relations, but the relations within each depend on understanding impact, velocity, tensile strength, and other such explanatory concepts. Lumping such similar systems together yields the basis for the scientific division of labor: The world is divided into classes of systems; each specialty defines a class of systems and concentrates its efforts at explanation.

Broadly speaking, physics deals with matter-and-energy systems, biology with life systems, and so forth. Further specialization leads to fields like entomology (limited to life systems within the insect class of living things) and enzymology (limited to the class of enzyme systems within life systems). Generally, fields like the second are preferable to the first, because its definition leans more surely on the systemic approach to the division of labor. Any field that is unable to claim a systemic subject is likely to be nonscientific, or to be scientific inefficiently.

One final caution is related to the warning I issued earlier about a theological acceptance of science. While granting the expertise of a scientist with regard to explanations of the subject-matter system that is his specialty, you need not give him more than that. Physicists' opinions on politics and political scientists' opinions on nuclear fall-out are no better than baseball stars' opinions on razor blades. Razor blade companies pay large sums of money to insure that we hear the judgments of athletes concerning their blades. However silly the notion, it sells blades. I remind you of this because we all stand some-what in awe of the recent technical accomplishments flowing from the natural sciences. We have a serious tendency to translate this into awe of the natural scientist and his judgment and to accept that judgment in problematic social issues. Remember that the natural scientist earned his deservedly high reputation for expertise in physical matters by concentrating his attention on physical systems. He has, therefore, had less time to study social systems, and, if anything, he should be somewhat less knowledgeable about social systems than the rest of us, who could devote time to their study.

SOCIOLOGY: THE SCIENCE OF SOCIETY

For social answers, go to scientists whose inquiry focuses on social systems.

Social systems are a special kind of system and are held together by distinctive relations. The main units in social systems are human actors. They are not the only units; when our rebel picked up the rock it became a part of a social system. Many other kinds of objects may enter social systems incidentally, but human actors predominate. Similarly, social relations are the relations that characterize social systems. These relationships are between humans or larger units in which humans are components. Any social action is affected by other actors within the system; this effect is the substance of social relations.

A married couple engaged in conversation exemplify the operation of a small and simple social system. One speaks; the other responds. To explain a particular comment by the husband, we might need to take into account the following: the husband's belief about the general nature of the situation and the conversation; what the wife just finished saying; how the husband interprets this as a response to his previous comments; what the husband thinks the wife expects him to say; the kinds of things he believes she will think of him for saying it; how the husband expects the wife to respond to what he says. Clearly, these many contingencies mark a social relationship.

Even these factors will not provide sufficient explanation for the husband's comment. It might also be helpful to know the relationship between this couple and their children or parents, the nature of the institution of marriage in their country, their occupations, incomes, educations, religious orientations, political activity, and so on. The utility of these factors as explanation indicates the presence of relational bonds extending beyond the husband-wife-conversation social system. That little social system is contained within several levels of larger systems.

As we explore new sets of relations extending out from our couple, we will occasionally be able to draw another set of boundaries and define another system. Then, pursuing more relations that extend beyond these new boundaries, we will note that the new unit is a subsystem of some still larger system. Ultimately we may reach a point where only a relatively small portion of the relations violate the boundary, where the system stands nearly independent. Such social systems are labeled *societies*. Societies are social systems which are not subsystems of some larger social system. Social action in societies can be substantially explained on the basis of relationships within their own boundaries.

Although societies are an interesting type of system, they are no different from other social systems except in the matter of independence. The relationships within a society's subsystems are also the relationships of the society. No different explanatory principles are needed. The scientific specialty that deals with one must deal with the other.

Sociology is the general science of social systems, and sociologists attempt scientific explanation of these systems.

The argument of this chapter can be contained in a few sentences. Life is problematic. If the individual actor understands the world he may be able to reduce its problematic aspects. Most of the problematic issues are social. The best available explanations of the social world are to be found within sociology. Therefore, every person should acquire at least a modest familiarity with the field of sociology.

This will not be a cure-all. No matter how soundly an action program might be based, there will remain some irreducible problematic areas. Sociology is certainly subject to all the limitations mentioned earlier for science generally. (The validity of any scientific explanation is limited to one special sort of system. Science cannot provide moral or motivational instructions.) Also, because sociology is a science, it is directed at explanation for its own sake. Sociologists seek orderly statements about the world that are compatible with the evidence. They are, like any other scientists, really engaged in a puzzle-game with nature. Questions they ask and answers they get are not perfectly adapted to the problematic orientation.

Further, sociological explanations of the social system are weak compared to most other scientific fields' explanations of their systems. I do not believe this implies that sociology is a weak science. I defined science in terms of activities and goals, and sociology meets this definition as well as most other disciplines. But our activities so far have resulted in less solid accomplishment of these goals. Perhaps this is so because some of the other sciences got started earlier than sociology. Perhaps it is because sociology has not attracted its share of brilliant practitioners. Perhaps it is because we have not yet hit on precisely the questions that will yield the best answers. There is probably some truth in each of these reasons. Primarily, though, I believe the difficulty lies in the system studied rather than in the discipline itself. If social systems are more problematic for individuals regarding action, why should they not also be more problematic for scientists regarding explanation? It may simply be that, being a social animal, I am prejudiced, but I believe social systems are more complex than molecular systems or other nonsocial systems. I believe that under the rubric of society more kinds of relationships join more kinds of units in more complex systems. Whatever the reasons, I can assure you that when you look to a chemist for explanations about molecules and to a sociologist for explanations about groups, you will get much more precision and validity from the former.

If you could then choose to live in a molecule you would have no need for sociology. You can't. Sociology's answers may not be much, but they're the best you can get. This chapter began with a recitation of problems ranging from the merely painful to the lethal, from those affecting individuals to those affecting humanity. If man is to become in any degree master of his fate, if he is to mitigate in any way the problematic aspects of his existence, sociology must play a part. The field must be more fully developed by professionals and more closely studied, used, and respected by amateurs.

FURTHER READING

For this chapter and for every chapter, I have arbitraily limited the list to ten book-length items. This practice implied the omission of many worthwhile works. The alternative—exhaustive listing of every item that bears on the topic—leaves the reader with little guidance and an inordinately long shopping list. This way, if you sample these volumes and don't like what you find, you can blame me rather than chance.

Problematic Issues

Freeman, Howard and Norman Kurtz, eds., *America's Troubles: A Casebook in Social Conflict.* Englewood Cliffs, N.J.: Prentice-Hall, 1969.

Klapp, Orrin E., *Collective Search for Identity.* New York: Holt, 1969. Available in paperback.

Rosenberg, Bernard, Israel Gerver, and William Howton, eds., *Mass Society in Crisis.* New York: Macmillan, 1964.

Science and Explanation

Chase, Stuart, *Guides to Straight Thinking with Thirteen Common Fallacies.* New York: Harper, 1956.

Huff, Darell, and Irving Geis, *How to Lie with Statistics.* New York: Norton, 1954. Available in paperback.

Shapley, Harlow, Samuel Rapport, and Helen Wright, eds., *New Treasury of Science.* New York: Harper, 1965.*

Snow, C. P., *The Two Cultures and a Second Look.* London: Cambridge University, 1964.*

Sociology and Social Systems

Berger, Peter, *Invitation to Sociology: A Humanistic Perspective.* Garden City, N.Y.: Doubleday, 1963. Anchor paperback.

Inkeles, Alex, *What Is Sociology? An Introduction to the Discipline and Profession.* Englewood Cliffs, N.J.: Prentice-Hall, 1964. Available in paperback.

Radcliffe-Brown, A. R., *A Natural Science of Society.* New York: Free Press, 1957.*

*Recommended only for those who want to know a great deal more and are willing to put out the concomitant effort.

THE DEVELOPMENTAL PERSPECTIVE

2 BIO-SOCIAL DEVELOPMENT

One of the standard questions that philosophers and scientists ask in trying to understand a thing is "How did it come to be?" The answer to this question tells much about "What it is." This chapter and the next deal with the becoming of two different things, biological man and the societies he operates; but the two evolutions are not unrelated.

The following story overlooks much of the technical detail that would be found in a competent introduction to anthropology and resolves differences in interpretation among scholars in the field by emphasizing one view to the exclusion of all others. What is left is plausible; it is consistent with the known evidence; it is likely to be easily reconciled with new findings. If it oversimplifies, if it should prove to have inaccuracies, it is because it focuses on the tune rather than the lyrics.

THE MAMMALIAN HERITAGE

Once upon a time, a hundred million years or so ago, there were some small, rat-or-hedgehog-like creatures who wandered around the world looking insignificant, an insignificance that made these animals scarcely worth killing. The only other advantages that they had were advantages only when seen in retrospect; they offered a portent for future utility without providing much of an edge for survival then. These potential advantages were placental nutrition and live birth, mammary nutrition after birth, and warm-bloodedness, features that represented variations from standard reptilian design. It is the reptiles, from small lizard to great dinosaur, which were then the dominant form of land-dwelling life.

The placenta is a membrane filter that permits close association between the circulatory systems of mother and unborn offspring. It serves as a lifeline to the offspring, which is, in effect, a parasite, lacking any direct contact with the outside world. The functions that relate body cells to that world—breathing, eating, and waste-dispersal—are performed for the offspring by the mother. Theoretically, this system could go on forever, with the fetus absorbing oxygen and nutrients from the mother's bloodstream and passing off carbon dioxide and poisonous by-products into it by means of the placental middleman.

Embryonic reptiles, in contrast, must operate in the closed-system environment of the egg. Whatever materials are to be used in growth and development must be stored in the egg at the time of formation; wastes must likewise be stored in the egg as they are produced. The problems are similar to those of men in a space capsule, only more severe; at least the astronaut can throw some of his garbage overboard.

The significance of all of this is that it takes time to manufacture a sophisticated product. Reptile development, racing the clock, is necessarily simple. Placental embryos take longer in development and become much more complex, particularly in their nervous systems, sensory apparatus, and brains.

Warm-bloodedness is actually a misnamed characteristic. It might more properly be called "constant-temperature-bloodedness." All animals consume carbohydrate fuels, breathe in oxygen, and survive by combustion. They are, therefore, heat-producing engines. Mammalian innovations allow a thermostatically controlled retention or dissipation of this heat in order to maintain a stable body temperature, regardless of environmental fluctuation. All this is accomplished by variable metabolism (alterations in the rate of heat production), hair (insulation), skin pores (adjusting the surface area available for heat radiation), variable capillary diameter (redistributing heat internally), and sweat glands (surface evaporative cooling).

Reptiles, then, are not necessarily cold-blooded; rather, they are the same temperature as their surroundings. For their fishy ancestors, adjustment was no real problem, because the temperature fluctuations of water are relatively small and gradual. It presents more severe difficulties to an atmosphere dweller. First, as temperatures approach the freezing point, body functioning virtually ceases. With seasonal variations in climate, this implies several months of dormancy. The difficulties of adjusting to this kind of cycle handicap the reptile in his struggle for survival, even in the absence of competition from others, and would probably have doomed the large reptiles in the course of time. When a warm-blooded competitor was introduced, the problems multiplied. It is highly probable that the seemingly-insignificant early mammal played a part in the demise of the dinosaur by depleting reptile food supplies during the reptile's dormant period, and even by feeding on reptiles and their eggs. If a dinosaur could think, imagine how mad it would have made him to lie there helpless in the cold, while something not 1/100,000 his size gnawed a hole in his stomach.

A second and more important advantage of stable body temperature follows from the fact that the sophisticated nervous system, sensory apparatus, and brain, made possible by placental nutrition, could not be supported in a wildly fluctuating temperature environment. The most elaborate and sensitive heating, air-conditioning, filtering, and dehumidifying equipment is used in physics laboratories, control-systems locations, and computer centers. This controlled environment is not meant for the comfort of the humans who operate those machines, but for the maintenance of a stable atmosphere necessary for the delicate and precise operation of the machines themselves. Mammals similarly pamper their brains and nerve endings with their own stable-temperature body systems and thus maintain the complex and sophisticated structures that placental development produces.

Mammalian nursing, like the other features mentioned above, is a profound biological miracle. Its social implications are more profound and more miraculous. It binds together, in a relationship of mutual dependence for a considerable period of time, two organisms of the same species. Prior to the era of the rubber nipple and mashed bananas in a jar, mother's milk was the only food source upon which young mammals could readily survive; eating appears to be a pleasure-filled and drive-reducing activity, even for the very young; one side of the dependence has been established. The other side is frequently overlooked. Mothers need their newborn, as much as their newborn need them. Lactation without release is uncomfortable. To say that mother love begins with an ache in the breast, or when the little one tugs at her heartstrings, may, with allowance for euphemism and anatomical fuzziness, be correct enough. Research on the feeling of dairy cows for their farmer or his milking machine is clearly indicated. In any case, mothers and their newborn do stay together for a relatively large portion of their lives and the sociability of mammals begins here.

This intense association between a young and a mature member of the same species makes social learning much more important for mammals than for animals of any other type. The young can, and almost automatically do, acquire some of the benefits of the lifetime of experience gained by the mother. The possibility of an increased intelligence has been suggested previously; with these conditions it becomes a benefit. Social animals have more opportunities to learn more things and those with better brains are in a position to exercise this option.

Constant body temperature, placental development, and mammary glands—the innovations of the mammals—imply sociability and intelligence. On the basis of these traits, the mammals expanded in numbers and kinds. They did well enough to invade a variety of different environments and to adapt themselves to a variety of different conditions. Their competitive advantages and the problems of reptiles discussed earlier left mammals heir to the world, the dominant animal form for the past fifty million years. Some—whales and porpoises—went back to the sea and are doing well in competition with their fishy ancestors. Bats, although a pretty poor imitation bird, give our group at least some airborne representation. Others diversified and occupied deserts, swamps, forests, and plains: all of the earth's varied habitats. Mammals developed enormous variability in locomotion, diet, sensory utilization, and in other ways. Some took to the trees. When they did so, they were still small, insignificant, rat-or-hedgehog-like creatures. Some, like squirrels, developed bark-penetrating claws and a series of related adaptations to their new environment. Others, more conservative, kept to the more primitive post-reptilian paw and simply wrapped it around branches and hung on. They are the ones to watch.

LOOK, UP IN THE SKY . . .

A paw that could wrap around a branch, that could grasp, clench, open, manipulate, was a hand. It could be used for grabbing things other than branches. One of the earlier uses to which it was put was in grasping and tearing food. One hesitates to say it, but evolution proceeded on a hand-to-mouth basis. The most casual inspection of a bear or hog, animals with diets similar to ours, will show their muzzles to be radically different in construction from that of man. If, in the interest of scientific experimentation, you were to broil a steak, toss it on the lawn, plant all four of your "feet" firmly on the ground, and then try to eat that meat, the reason for these differences would be quickly apparent. You and all of your tree-grasping relatives lack the pointed, protruding muzzle, the holding, tearing, cutting, and grinding teeth, and the powerful jaw muscles that are demanded in this sort of endeavor. They were made unnecessary by the development of the hand, which allowed its possessor to tear his food into little chunks and shove it into his mouth.

The other feature on the forward face of your model bear or hog is his nose. This, too, became relatively useless for a tree dweller. A sense of smell operates as stray molecules of an object waft through the air and are sniffed into the nose. It registers when these molecules rest on the membrane passages inside the nose. The greater the area of these passages, the more sensitive the sense of smell. The hog may not smell good, but you don't smell well. He has a bigger nose, and consequently more surface area of nostril passages, than do you. Such long noses are useful if the sense of smell is of assistance in finding food or avoiding danger. The molecules that are worth smelling are, for the most part, heavier than air and are found on or near the ground. Hunting animals "track" with their long, efficient noses near the ground. At tree height such sensory ability became irrelevant, and a long nose relatively useless.

That things are useless and can disappear does not, in evolution, mean that they will. If the miniaturization of the nose and jaw is to be explained, it must be explained in terms of survival advantages; the fact that there are no disadvantages to miniaturization is not enough.[1] At this point in the commentary, it has been shown that tree-dwelling mammals with relatively small noses and jaws could have survived as well as those with larger structures. Given the variability that marks the mechanics of genetics in a sexually reproducing population, all animals, whether long-nosed or short, heavy-jawed or more delicate, could be expected to have lived side by side. What yet remains is to show selective factors working against those with large protruding muzzles, conditions that caused animals bearing them to die sooner and leave, on the average, fewer offspring to pass their characteristics on to succeeding generations. Sight was one of these factors.

The sense of sight has been important from the time of fishes. It helped animals to know what was in their perceptual environment, and in what direction. But as long as the perception was accomplished with one lens, it did not really provide an accurate cue concerning how far away an object was. This datum was not of critical importance to a ground dweller. If, for instance, he recognized an object as food, he ran in the proper direction until he caught it. For a tree dweller, who was leaping or swinging from branch to branch, distance became a matter of life or death. He could not start a leap with the slapstick intention of leaping until he got there. He needed, in survival terms, depth perception. This he could achieve by replacing single-lens vision with dual-lens vision.

When two eyes focus on an object, they register slightly different views of the same object, because the eyes themselves are located in different positions. The closer the viewer is to the object, the more different will these two pictures be; the magnitude of difference helps assess distance. The facial structure of most ground-dwelling animals placed a wall between the two eyes, and such animals perceived one-half of the world with each eye; the two seldom, if ever, focused together. When this muzzle became shorter, both eyes were brought to the front of the face, and stereoscopic, depth-perceiving vision resulted. The advantages of such a spatially precise sense

[1] What is said here with regard to these characteristics is, of course, just as true of other evolutionary changes mentioned throughout this chapter. The argument will not be repeated at every juncture but must be understood to apply.

began with jumping or swinging in trees, but did not end there. Coupled with the splendidly manipulable hand, the utility of this sense broadened; hand-eye coordination developed; an animal of such mechanical virtuosity and variability found a higher intelligence more adaptive.

Intelligence has been discussed in terms of the increased sophistication of nerve and brain design that came with body air conditioning and placental development. The adaptive advantages of such intellect have been shown to follow from hand, eye, and opportunities for social learning. Alterations in the design of the brain also increased intelligence. The foreward portion is more directly related to learning and insight than other areas and was increased at their expense. The surface is more efficient than the interior, and so added surface without increased volume came with a complex wrinkling and folding known as convolution.

Still, there were some engineering problems that placed a severe limit on the increase of intelligence.

1. Raw brain size, at least up to some limit not then approached, is crudely but directly proportional to intellectual capacity.

2. This increase cannot be accomplished simply by increasing the size of the animal, for a portion of the brain must be devoted to "housekeeping" functions for the body. The larger the body, the larger the segment needed. Despite his radically larger brain mass, an elephant is not much brighter than a rat; their marginal surpluses beyond reflex and sensation are roughly similar. Real improvement can only come with an increase in brain weight–body weight ratio.

3. Brains are delicate instruments and must remain encased within the protection of the skull, as they have been since the beginnings of fishes.

4. The head size of any species is limited by the size of the head of the newborn of that species. Platelike bones, such as those of the skull, are structurally incapable of the same degree of growth as are such linear bones as femurs. The growth limitation can be softened, but not eliminated entirely, by devices such as sutured skulls, with expansion joints between the plates, joints which do not calcify until some time after birth. This accounts for the almost grotesquely misproportioned and oversized heads of infants.

5. The size of heads of newborn is limited by the size of the pelvic opening and birth canal of the adult female.

6. An indelicate increase in pelvic opening and related body structure without a corresponding and self-defeating increase in overall body size would leave adult females immobile and inviable.

The contingencies of the above six points seem to set a boundary for brain–body ratio, but there are loopholes, and the ground for finding them is implicit in the evolutionary sequence already outlined. One possibility is to devote a larger portion of overall head space to brain. This was feasible with the reduction of nose and jaw already noted. The archaic heavy jaw also required for its operation powerful muscles that were attached to, and pulled against, heavy and roughened bone structures at the cheek, temple, brow, and upper head regions. More delicate muscles operated with lighter, smoother holding surfaces; the massiveness of the whole head's bony structure was reduced. A thinner container, without change in outside dimensions, held more. Brain size increased without a concomitant increase in head size.

The new type of brain that emerged was bigger—and better. Animals bearing that brain could learn more, more rapidly, than any other kind of animal. This gain was accompanied by a loss in material already "known." Pre-imprinted reflex or instinct material almost disappeared. A brain with this capacity rendered its bearer capable of a greater variety of behavior, and such flexibility increased survival potential and placed a further premium on social learning.

Meanwhile, adaptations to tree dwelling and interlocked echoes of these adaptations were occurring in portions of the anatomy other than the head. A freely-moving, radially jointed shoulder developed and fed into the hand-eye-mechanical facility-intelligence chain. Ultimately, using the two forward arms and swinging from branch to branch superseded leaping as the standard form of locomotion for some varieties. This implied a radically different posture; the swinger hung below the branch with his two hands, while the leaper remained basically quadrupedal atop the branch. The latter, like his terrestrial and even aquatic ancestors, lived with his backbone parallel to the horizon, while the former assumed a vertical posture.

The backbone of the quadrupedal ground dweller was an arch. It was the ideal architectural form for supporting weight in the directions from which its stresses came. The internal organs of such animals hung down from the backbone as neatly as laundry on a line. Shifting this system ninety degrees worked no harm on the back itself, because hanging down required no supportive strength (Fig. 2–1). An arch could do it; so could a rope. But the organs presented a different picture. Still suspended on only one end, they tended to fall down on each other, and so the transitional ape must have had serious problems with ruptures. Several internal structural adjustments—in diaphragm, rib cage, and supporting ligatures—were

24

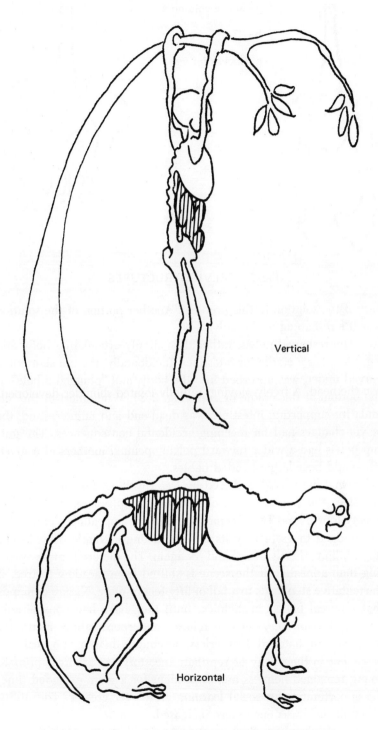

Vertical

Horizontal

Fig. 2-1   POSTURE, BACKBONES, AND INTESTINES

25

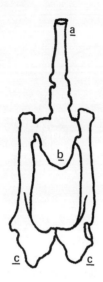
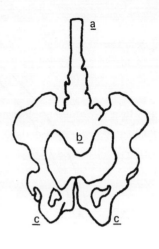

a - Spinal column

b - "Tail" structure

c - Socket for leg

Fig. 2-2 PELVIC STRUCTURES

part of the solution to this problem. Another portion of the solution was the reshaping of the pelvis.

The reshaped pelvis, rather than simply articulating body and leg, served as a cradle for intestines. Incidentally, the tail shortened, curved under, was absorbed into the body, and "plugged a hole" at the bottom of this cradle or cup (Fig. 2–2). While most of the formula for supporting intestines was dead-end and uninteresting, the pelvic changes had far-reaching accidental consequences. The gut-cup pelvis had a wider forward pelvic opening; mothers of a given size could bear larger-headed babies.

Social life was also altered by tree dwelling. For most animals our size, the period of absolute infant helplessness is less than twenty-four hours. There comes to mind the appealing picture of a colt nudged to its feet by its mother, taking a couple of awkward steps, falling, shortly to rise and try again. The picture is more appalling than appealing if the scene is shifted from meadow to tree, if the tentative step leads to a fall of fifty feet or more. Nature demands that arboreal babies be helpless until they have had considerable time to develop very reliable reflexes and coordination. Birds, for instance, are hatched featherless, although there is no scaleless precedent in their fishy or reptilian ancestory. As arboreal primate young remained helpless and dependent for a more extended time, the opportunities for social learning grew ever greater. The utility of intelligence was once more increased.

One further biological accident occurred at about this time. Its relation to the chain of causality here set forth is less clear than that of most of the other features. It may well have been a by-product of the internal bodily adaptations to vertical posture. One would suspect that the redesign of supportive structures and attendant relocation of organs might have had an effect on the functioning of some of those organs. Whether this is the case or not, the estrous pattern of sexuality in females was specialized into a menstrual pattern.

The form of estrous cycle that characterizes most animals leads to a flow of hormones and ovum production in the mature female that is so regulated as to produce a relatively short period during each cycle when, simultaneously, she is sexually attractive, sexually receptive, and fertile. The remainder of the cycle is devoted to pregnancy, birth, and child rearing, or, should pregnancy fail to occur, to solitide and sexual latency. When pregnancy and birth occur, given the relatively short period of infant dependency, the offspring achieves sufficient maturity to function alone and the mother returns to independence by the onset of the next sexual period in the cycle. Such animals are, then, characterized by two "family structures": the male–female family of the mating season and the mother–child family of the maturation period. The two alternate throughout the cycle with no overlap in time. The length of the cycle is different for different species but is roughly proportional to the size of the animal. For animals of the body size of man, a cycle of about a year would be expected.

Frequency of ovulation and consequently of fertility is higher in the menstrual cycle and sexuality is relatively independent of this cycle. Man, apes, and some monkeys have a relatively high level of constant sexual interest and activity through the cycle and year-round. In early primates, the consistent recurrence of sexual drives and sparse population led to a pattern of long-term cohabitation. Simply, such animals found it easier to live in heterosexual groups than to jump yelling through the woods everytime they got the urge, now that the urge came so often. Menstrual sexuality formed a biosocial bond between male and female analogous in consequence, if not in form, to the dependence bond between mother and child. The long-term character of these two attachments created a full-blown human-type family of adult male, adult female, and their immature offspring. The sociability and intelligence components in the evolutionary pattern received another boost.

At this point, interest in arboreal evolution subsides. The details of adaptation to tree dwelling have been set forth. It was a well-formed and successful set of adaptations. Simian types within this basic pattern grew highly variable and they grew larger, both indices of evolutionary success. And, as the ultimate mark, they survived. Any further adaptations to tree dwelling were highly specialized for the conditions of arboreal life and represented evolutionary "blind alleys," in that they had no further structural consequences and limited the future adaptability of the carrier. What characterized most of the changes described was the opposite—they were conservative and flexible adaptations. They did not, for instance, prevent a readaptation to ground life. Some of these apes came down out of the trees.

OUT WALKS MAN

Much anthropological speculation has been concerned with why this return occurred. That is not really a sensible or relevant question. What is important is that it could occur. The onetime rat-or-hedgehog-like creature whose greatest recommendation was his insignificance was by then a relatively large and powerful and agile animal with the finest sensory apparatus and mechanical tools known. He had the capacity to learn, and perhaps even invent, a variety of problem-solving and survival-enhancing behaviors. Because humans are now so used to depending on each other and their technology, they tend to underestimate their relatively high toughness rating "in a state of nature." They are not the largest or the most fearsome of beasts. But large enough, powerful enough, and unorthodox enough to get by. This unorthodoxy rests in the peculiarity of their anatomy and fighting techniques. The attack techniques of most predators, developed in pursuit of more standard animals, are relatively ineffective against man, whose backbone, for instance, is in the wrong place to be broken by a large cat's "death blow." This is not to say that men will ordinarily be victors over tigers or the like, but should they be killer rather than killed in one of ten trials, the deterrent is sufficient. This is little consolation to the other nine men, but neither can tigers afford the practice of seeking their meals among species where every tenth attempt for a meal is a lethal one.

Some further speculation on the question of man's terrestrial survival ability is less ego inflating. It has been suggested that the habits of garbage and sewage disposal developed during millions of years of tree dwelling, where wastes generally simply drop out of sight without special care, have left the advanced primates as filthy animals. The insensitivity of their sense of smell makes them oblivious of this condition. When they reinitiated ground dwelling, then, they did so in the unappetizing stench of their own feces and decayed food particles, which were no longer automatically removed. Nothing wanted to eat them.

In any case, they could come down from the trees, and some did. They were not perfectly suited to terrestrial life but were too far committed in several directions to make a return to the pre-tree body design. A return to quadrupedal posture and locomotion, for instance, would have required several monumental adjustments. The internal organs and supportive structures would have had to be altered once more for a horizontal position. The manipulative hand would have been lost, if used as a foot. The acute stereoscopic eyes would have focused on the ground a foot ahead of the animals progress. The nearly useless nose would have been in a position to smell things.

At least three points of weight support are required for stability of structure, according to Euclidean geometry. Bird dogs at point, camera stands, kangaroos, and milking stools confirm this principle. Protoman had only two legs to spare. A tail, like that of the kangaroo and some lizards, would have been an engineering possibility, had it not already been turned in and under. The solution appeared in structural changes in the foot: elongation of the tarsus and development of a pair of arches. The major arch extended laterally and was based in the heel (a new development) and the fore part of the foot. The second arch, less well defined but as important, ran across the front of the foot and was based in the outside edge and the ball (also a new development). Three weight-supporting points in each foot were the result. Not one, but two tripods resulted. This allowed men to stand on one foot, provided that the center of gravity of the body were directly above the triangle the three points formed on the ground (Fig. 2–3).

A change in the form of the spine was essential to this accomplishment. The spines of most mammals, as was mentioned earlier, are arches. The back as an arch, butted at each end near the legs and supporting weight in a horizontal dimension, is sound architecture. With tree dwelling, this aspect of architecture mattered very little. For hanging vertically from a top support, with weight draped down, an arch will do. So will a stick or rope. But a vertically arranged structure with the weight resting on the bottom is another thing entirely. Here an arch simply will not do. Its own weight will tend to crumple or fold the top half down into the bottom. The middle (keystone area) will tend to "fall out" backwards. A compromise

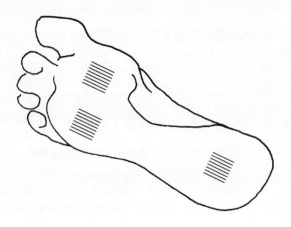

Fig. 2-3 HUMAN FOOT WITH TRIPOD SUPPORTS

solution somewhere between the vertical and horizontal alternatives that sets the lower end of the arch to its foundation nearly vertically, allowing the upper part to bow forward, may be sound from the point of maintaining the structural integrity of the arch itself but creates radical problems of weight distribution. The structure will tend to topple forward. Stable structures have their center of gravity between their foundation points. Men who would walk on two legs must, therefore, offer some structural substitute for the arch as a backbone and center their body weight forward of the heels, behind the ball of the foot and between the left and right outside edges.

These requirements were met by the evolution of the recurved spine: two arches joined by a reflexive third. This form resembles a spring or a spiral staircase more than an arch. It is good design for weight support in a vertical plane and "stacks" the weight very true within that plane. Further changes in the shape of the hip bones assisted the adaptation to vertical posture and opened the birth canal still further, permitting another increase in head and brain size.

To be sure, this bit of evolution was somewhat imperfect. Most humans today have some modest form of back trouble—usually in the lumbar, or recurved, region—to remind them of their humble origins. But the alternative is far less attractive. Some other apes came out of the trees at about the same time as did man, and, in part because they failed to do anything about the spine, they are still apes. They have the compromise forward-leaning bow. To avoid falling flat on their faces they rest their hands on the ground and, therefore, lose part of the advantage of those hands. They have remained semi-upright by the evolutionary lengthening of the arm in proportion to the body, and the shortening and bending of the leg. Alternatively, they can rear back and perform a balancing act for a few steps of bipedal locomotion or (and this is really an ordinary performance of some kinds of apes) run like crazy to keep their legs under the place onto which they would otherwise be falling. This is an ungainly adaptation. Man's closest relatives are not doing very well, evolutionarily speaking.

The lower end of an ape's spine, nearly vertical, bends upward and forward till the upper end is nearly horizontal. At the end the head must be held on and up. This may not sound like much of a problem, but that is because you have not tried it. Let your head drop forward until your chin is on your chest and then raise your head some, but not all the way to its normal position. If you then walk around with it that way for a couple of hours, you will have sore muscles where you didn't know you even had muscles.

The powerful muscle structure that allows apes to support their heads in this fashion, and which incidentally causes them to appear as if they had no necks, is anchored at its upper end in heavy corrugated bone at the base of the skull, the top of the head, and temple region.

Man, in contrast, evolved a balanced head squarely atop the upright spine. The constant but unconscious balancing act in which man engaged allowed him to support his head with lighter muscle attached to thinner bone, further reduced head space devoted to other purposes, and consequently increased the portion dedicated to brain. This new head position also set the face directly forward, thus permitting full utilization of the visual apparatus (Fig. 2-4).

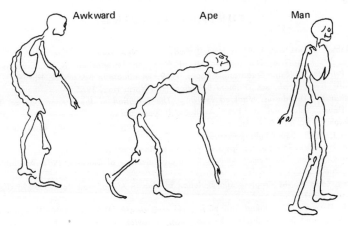

Fig. 2-4 POSTURE VARIATIONS

31

The miracle of this balancing job is lost on all of us until we have the experience of dozing off in a public place, only to be rudely awakened when the head is forgotten and allowed to "fall off."

The developments outlined in the preceding paragraphs had produced, by a million years ago, an animal that was biologically very manlike. Some of the more recent among those developments were trends still then and now in operation, some of the interacting effects continued to escalate, some small refinements have been added. To today's eyes that creature of a million years ago would look funny, primitive, repulsive, apelike—but functionally he was a man. He could do the man-thing. His biological potential allows and almost causes the development of human society. The central features of this biological potential are a high quality brain, sophisticated sensory apparatus (especially eyes), manipulable hands, constant sexuality, and extensive infantile dependence. No species without these features could sustain a social organization such as ours; a creature with these features does so as almost nothing more than an inevitable unfolding of this biological potential. There are many solar systems other than our own and many planets. Surely some of these sustain life. Surely some of this life is intelligent and social. But the science-fiction image of Super-Ant, Super-Octopus, or Super-Tree rests more on literary license than on scientific fact. The social forms of other beings will be no more like ours than the biological premises upon which they rest. Man's social condition is inextricably involved with, formed and limited by but not to, his biological condition. This statement at once justifies this chapter and leads to the next.

FURTHER READING

Campbell, Robert, and F. Clark Howell, *Early Man.* New York: Time-Life, 1965.

Clark, W. E. LeGros, *The Antecedents of Man: An Introduction to the Evolution of Primates.* Chicago: Quadrangle Books, 1959.* Available in paperback, Harper.

DeVore, Irven, et al., eds., *Primate Behavior.* New York: Holt, 1965.

Dobzhansky, Theodosius, *Mankind Evolving: The Evolution of the Human Species.* New Haven: Yale University, 1962. Available in paperback.

Hodgson, R. D., and E. A. Stoneman, *The Changing Map of Africa.* New York: Van Nostrand, 1968. Searchlight paperback.

Hulse, Frederick, *The Human Species.* New York: Random House, 1963.

LaBarre, Weston, *The Human Animal.* Chicago: University of Chicago, 1954. Available in paperback.

Leakey, Louis S., *The Progress and Evolution of Man in Africa.* New York: Oxford University, 1961*

Morris, Desmond, *The Naked Ape.* New York: McGraw-Hill, 1967. Available in paperback.

Roe, Anne, and George Gaylord Simpson, eds., *Behavior and Evolution.* New Haven: Yale University, 1958.

*Difficult, specialized, or technical.

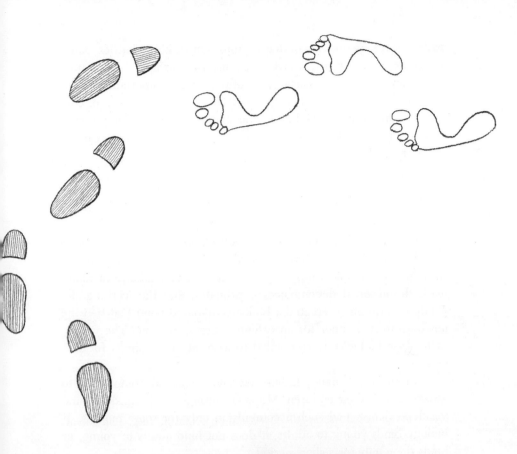

3 MACROHISTORY

In the preceding chapter, we compressed the events of 100 million years into only a few pages. In this chapter, we shall proceed at a much more leisurely pace, devoting approximately twice as many pages to only the past million years. While this represents a considerable deceleration, the rate is still higher than that of most history books, some of which have been known to squander all their pages on a few hundred years or less. My swifter coverage does mean that we must ignore kings, battles, dates, and other such matters toward which historians exhibit an unhealthy attraction, but I can assure you nothing really important will be omitted. *Importance* from our perspective is defined in terms of contribution to an understanding of the shape of human society generally and its specific form today. This overview of history can be called macrohistory.

FAMILIES

We shall begin, then, where we last left off. One million years or so ago there were manlike creatures who had big brains, year-round sexuality, and helpless offspring. The nursing dependence of mammals, the arboreal dependence of primates, and the learning dependence of humans created a biologically-based bond that tied the newborn to its mother for an extended period of time. The young, then, were biologically compelled to associate with adults for several years.

On the other hand, fathers had no biological compulsion to associate with their children. Mothers, through the reciprocal nursing dependence, had such a compulsion only for some months. If biology binds young to adults, it does not bind adults to young, or binds them only for a short period.

Adult mates, however, were mutually bound to each other by the sex drive. This attachment lasted throughout virtually the entire adult life.

The sum of these biological bonds provides no source of attachment of father to offspring, or of mother to offspring past the nursing period. A family based only on the biological bonds that were in operation would be curiously deficient in interpersonal attachments compared to a standard human family model. Other attachments did develop to overcome these deficiencies. These supplemental attachments were not directly biological, but developed socially out of biological potential and conditions.

The large and sophisticated brain carried not only an enhanced intellectual capacity, but a greater emotional capacity as well. Animals bearing such capacity, who were bound into close association by biological needs, came to like, even love, each other. Habitual mating with the same partner produced not simply sexual satiation, but affection. An emotional bond grew to supplement the biological one. The case for mother and child was similar. Moreover, the emotional attachments did not depend on prior biological ones, but simply on physical proximity, which filled some second-order biological need. The emotional attachment of mother to child, then, became a factor independent of the biological context in which it rose and continued after that biological condition was ended. Similarly, father and child, who were physically proximate to each other through their independent proximities to the mother–mate, developed an emotional attachment in the absence of a direct biological one.

At this point, and as a direct consequence of the biological conditions with which we started, we see "one or more adult male and one or more adult female and their immature offspring, living together over an extended period of time and with deep emotional involvement." This is approximately the sort of definition of the family that one finds in textbooks in the field, although it is unlikely to have been developed in this fashion. The family was then the first social institution, preceded the development of society itself, and in some senses even predated the development of man as man. The conditions of family living caused a manlike animal to become man and led as well to the development of extrafamilial social relations.

LANGUAGE

The basic social reality of the family is that of a small number of animals living together for a long period of time with deep and intimate emotional attachments. Emotions are communicable. An animal in the throes of any emotion undergoes certain physiological changes. Glandular secretions, heartbeat, respiration, muscle flex, and other conditions become in some sense abnormal. This is not to say that the animal thinks to itself "I am frightened. I must up my heartbeat by a factor of ten percent." Rather these are automatic reflex-like events that occur with, and in ways are, the emotion. Some of these conditions can only be measured with medical instruments; some are external and can be readily observed with the unassisted senses. The bristling fur of a cat's back, the bared fangs of a dog, and the blond's blush are examples of this latter class. These do not differ in physiological genesis from the interior and unobservable changes, but only in observability. They may be perceived by, and serve as stimuli for, other animals. In particular and for our purposes, such signs of emotion, when perceived by another animal of the same species, have the effect of reproducing themselves in the receiver animal. The receiver comes to have the same emotion, perhaps in attenuated but no less real form, as did the sender. It appears that this emotional communication process occurs for all mammals and, like the internal emotion-sign process, is a reflex-like condition, or behavior that does not have to be learned. Because it will assist understanding at this point and be of service later as well, let us take a quick look at learning and related matters.

One of the most famous experiments concerning the learning process was conducted by Ivan Pavlov, a Russian physiologist. Over a long period of time, he rang a bell at every feeding of a group of dogs. At the end of this learning period, the dogs would salivate whenever the bell was rung, even in the absence of food. They had come to associate the bell with food. In addition to salivation, we may assume that there were other signs that signalled a state of "pleasurable anticipation." These responses to the bell as stimulus were learned. A collection of untrained dogs might ignore a bell or offer a variety of different responses. On the other hand, Pavlov did not have to train the dogs to salivate, and so on, in the presence of food. This is a biologically built-in response, a reflex or, despite its sometimes mischievous connotations, an instinct. To bring this discussion to our point, let us introduce a "naïve", untrained dog into a pen with Pavlov's trained ones and then ring the bell. The new dog will salivate and otherwise exhibit the symptoms of, and presumably feel, pleasurable anticipation. He will do so not in response to the bell, but in biologically built-in response to the emotional signs of the trained dogs in his company. The same kind of communication process may start a fight, with escalating feedback of anger, or create panic in a crowd. It is utilized by gifted actors in causing their audience not simply to understand the play but to feel within themselves the love, anxiety, and other emotions of the play's characters.

Emotional communication, then, was biologically inherent in animals long before the appearance of man. What was new was the deep interpersonal emotional involvement of the communicators and the experience of sustaining this communication with the same individuals over most of a lifetime. Deeper interpersonal empathy, a higher-level brain and greater mental capacity, and practice effect led in the long run to more perfect communication, stylization, and extension.

The following example may be oversimplified and somewhat

distorted, but it will hopefully illustrate the points that we have been discussing for the past few paragraphs. Suppose that for a presocietal human family the main dangers were attack by wild boars and leopards. The father-husband has had a variety of experiences leading to special and distinguishable emotional orientations toward trees, ponds, fields, hills, and so on. Perhaps he is disgusted by ponds but finds trees delightful. Some of these experiences were shared by the other family members, but in any case the rest of the family has been exposed to the father–husband's emotional responses to these differing environs. One day, the father-husband, after a short absence, comes running toward the wife and offspring, presenting the signs of fear, plus the sign of either disgust or pleasure. We may expect the other family members to feel sympathetic fear—to feel "fear-and-we-must-jump-into-the-pond" (for a leopard is coming and he hates water and that is the way to escape), or "fear-and-we-must-climb-a-tree" (a boar is coming and cannot climb and that is the way to escape). That such alterations in communication would occur is, given the mental capacity of the family and the social situation, plausible. Such finer communication would be adaptive; families that acted on the basis of such communication would escape the pursuing danger more often than those families that had to operate on the basis of simple and generalized fear. Moreover, the hypothetical relationship between pond-emotion-sign and leopard is in the same class as that between bell and saliva for Pavlov's dogs. This is so because the male's emotional orientation toward ponds is intrinsically unrelated to leopards; it is arbitrary, learned (for the other family members), and free of biological imperatives. Given enough practice in this kind of usage, such signs can be called forth even in the absence of the emotion-generating stimulus.

When signs became highly stylized, divorced from emotional underpinning, communicative without necessarily developing the same emotional state in the receiver as in the sender, and arbitrarily related to that for which they stood and hence separable from it, they were no longer merely signs. Something so radically different deserves a new name: symbols. Verbal behavior came to predominate over other forms because it offered so many discriminable variations and did not require body or sensory investment that would radically interfere with other functioning; most symbols are verbal.

Once such communication developed it was unlikely to be lost and was transmitted to future generations in the family line. Symbolic communication, developing in the family, brought an escalated potential in a variety of ways. Within the family, communication took on a richness, an ease, a precision it never had before.

Beyond the communication function are other more important implications, which rest in the nature of thought and symbols. Other animals, non-symboling animals, live in the world of the here and the now. Their behaviors are responses to present and external stimuli; the connections between stimulus and response are biologically inherent or experientially learned. In either case, the tie between the two is fixed and exists only when the stimulus is present; only then is the behavioral responses called forth. Animals show the signs of fear only when they perceive something that makes them afraid. Men can speak of fear whenever they so desire, because the relationship between the symbol and the referent is in the mind, not in the environment or the physiology. This symbolic capacity is what makes an animal a man, what more than anything else differentiates him from the other animals, and what allowed me earlier to say that the family precedes man. A manlike animal had to live in families and create symbols before he became man.

Such symbolic qualifications allowed incipient man to anticipate needs, to think through problems and come up with solutions in advance. He then invented and made tools and saved them for occasions of need. The tools became extensions of the body, substitute claws, teeth, fur, legs, and so forth. An organism equipped with a rich variety of these pseudo biological characteristics was better able to meet the challenges of the environment, to survive and reproduce. The man-ape with a better brain could solve more problems, anticipate more needs, make better tools, and hence survive more easily. Selection for superior mental capacity was given another boost. Man grew brainier.

These symbols allowed him to deal with what was outside his immediate perceptual field: with the past, the distant, the future, the unreal, the general. These capacities cast him far apart from his animal cousins. He remembered. This was not simply a learned residual capacity for responding to a stimulus that might occur again, but a memory that was with him and could be possessed in ways similar to the way he possessed the perceptual present. He could project this past beyond the present by depending on regularities and amplifying trends. Prediction, planning, and even future-awareness developed for the first time. Man could abstract, dream, combine known but improbable elements, generalize, and discriminate. He came to an awareness of self that no other animal could have.

This is so because the "knowledge" of animals that do not use symbols is limited to the perceptual present; they can never separate themselves from their surroundings. Man, on the other hand, can contemplate the forest he left yesterday as a world without his presence. This separate recognition of "world" is prerequisite to a separate recognition of self.

All this learned material could be transmitted from one co-symboler to another (from one family member to another). The central implication of this fact came when that communication was from old to young, when the accumulated knowledge, experience, and learning of a lifetime did not die with that individual but was passed on and furnished a base from which the next generation started. The accumulation of wisdom began the human social journey and is still central to it.

The symbolic venture was not all rosy. Man inherited a number of problems as well as enriched capacities. Only he who predicts can fail. Only he who is aware of self must worry over the nature of self and the universe. Only he who is aware of self and world and predicts can predict his own death and that of the family members in whom he has high emotional investment. Only he is faced with issues of the meaning of life. These and related questions and problems placed an enormous psychic burden on emergent man, a burden of terror, confusion, and unease. Without some form of resolution capable of sustaining psychological security for the individual, his survival was in doubt. Mankind's biological and social evolution surely narrowly escaped a dead-end in this period, when his symboling led toward the raving insanity of each individual member of the species.

In addition to this psychological problem, a social one of similar genesis arose at the same time and nearly destroyed the family in which symbols developed. Although a particular male and female might at first form a more or less permanent relationship for the satiation of biological sex drives, they soon developed strong emotional ties for each other as well. All this, of necessity, occurred before the arrival of offspring. In the presymbolic situation the newcomer may have been viewed with some surprise, but, apart from the mutual lactation symbiosis with the mother, with neutrality, until a period of togetherness bred liking. If, some years later, the sex drives of the matured offspring cancelled its liking for the parent of the same sex, this too came as a surprise. The greater strength, virility, and attractiveness of the young may have allowed sons to kill or drive off their fathers and monopolize sexual access to their mothers. The disruptive danger of daughters was symmetrical. For animals which could be surprised by this development, the disruption came in the form of a mating contest between mature adults who happened to be parent and offspring. Although the consequences may have been drastic for some individuals, the effect on the species was probably one of selection for fitness and strengthening of the genetic strain.

A symboling parent, however, could predict this situation long in advance of its occurrence and act to forestall it. He could recognize the adult potential in the newborn and anticipate sexual development. The rational course for fathers was to kill their newborn sons (a) while the child was still young and helpless, before he became an able contestant in a battle that the father might lose, and (b) while the child was still a stranger, before he was around long enough for the father to become attached to him. Mother's action toward their daughters should have been similar. If each parent killed all offspring of their own sex, there would have been no survivors. The species would have died out in a generation. The knowledge that symbols bring was, then, nearly fatal at an early age.

RELIGION AND MORALITY

Happily, symbols carried the seeds of their own salvation as well as of potential destruction. The solution to the psychological and social problem was through the symbolic potential. Although man generated in language both mental anguish and social chaos, he also generated a capacity to symbol, to think of worlds beyond the sensory, and to find or create there remedies for these problems. Gods and religious faiths offered answers for man's otherwise unanswerable questions, ease to his otherwise tortured psyche. Solutions came from outside the empirical world for issues that were insolvable within it: life and death, ultimate meaning, failure, futility, self and universe. Religion may come in a number of guises, but there will always be these common traits: a deeply held belief-set with nonempirical content, which serves to answer life's otherwise unanswerable questions. Its effect on early man was to forestall debilitating psychological confusion and terror.

While the core of religion is in the nonempirical, or at best the mind-life, world, religion will have implications for this world as well. For a symbol bearer, mental content is related to behavior. A metaphysic implies an ethic; morals accompany theology. Appropriately loaded theologies can then shape family behavior to avoid the social chaos mentioned earlier. The moral component needed at the outset of the family-language-religion era was, specifically, an incest taboo. Social-ideological restraints against parent-child sexual relations could prohibit the usurpation contingency that parents feared; children were therefore allowed to survive. The force of the taboo rested in the religion and, hence, in the old, dark fears which that religion laid to rest. As the family was the first social institution, it now became the first cultural structure. Its first symbolically regulated behavior concerned sexual avoidance between parent and offspring.

A few pages earlier I said that this chapter deals with "social evolution." This was neither sloppy usage nor a catch phrase, but was intended to indicate some real points of analogy between social and biological development. The particular reference point here is the relationship between variation, cause, and survival of a characteristic. With regard to biological evolution, I earlier insisted that potential utility of a biological trait did not cause its rise, but those which happened to arise would be tested in utilitarian survival terms.[1] The biological-social analogy is not perfect, because symboling, predicting, contemplative men sometimes perceive social necessities and create social traits that meet those necessities. For example, at the point under discussion here, it is possible that anticipation and social design entered in. Some calculating new mother, wishing to preserve her lactation release, may have invented the incest taboo, foisting it first on her mate to prevent him from killing their son, and only later on the son. Symboling man was, even then, rational enough to create and accept nonrational solutions to irrational fears and problems. It is just as possible that religion, the incest taboo, and other moral rules developed by accident. Striking but coincidental natural events, chance juxtapositions, and so forth, might give rise to a wide variety of religious and moral precepts. As in the case of biological traits, only those with survival advantage were assured of conveyance to the next generation. It may be that some men sometimes perceived the beliefs and rules under which they could survive, but it is certainly true that only those who somehow hit upon such rules did survive. Families that did not happen to develop incest

[1] See page 22 for the extended version of this argument

taboos led themselves to extinction; those with the taboo flourished and left a heritage of maturing individuals to carry the belief to the next generation.

At first, therefore, religion provided only psychological security for the individual, but it very quickly supplied the basis for social stability of the family as well. Further social implications came as the incest taboo forced more matings outside the family group. Brother-sister matings may have been common, for the incest taboo we have uncovered prohibited only parent-offspring mating. However, not all families included male and female children. Given the prohibition against sexual access to parents, maturing offspring would regularly have been seeking mates among strangers. In consequence, the religions and morals and even languages that evolved exclusively within a family line tended to spread, and, over several generations of breeding back and forth, we can expect a single set of these to have come to be shared by all the people within a particular territory. This provided the basis for the formation of social groups larger than the family.

Many older texts offer a touching myth concerning the origins of human society. In its generalized form, it pictures a collection of separate families of early man living in a valley. Things go along well until a food shortage occurs. There is food in the mountains, but no male can go hunting there and leave his family unprotected. The men, therefore, get together and decide that some will go hunting while the others stay to protect the women and children. Here their cooperation is born, and they live happily ever after.

This is a lovely myth, but can be no more than that. Its plausibility fades when we note that pre-man and early man were cannibals. "O.K., Charley, we're all starving, so you go across the mountain while I stay here with your tender wife and children." "No, Sam, *you* go, I'll stay, I'm sure your kids will be good for me." Only rational predicting men could have planned cooperative activity involving such a division of labor. Rational and predicting men would not have dared. Society could only start when humans had a shared basis of trust, one based in a shared religion and the sense of oneness that that sharing provided. The first morality was the incest taboo, and the stability of the family followed from that. The first social morality must have been "thou shalt not eat thy neighbor." Society

42

was built on this foundation. Social life began from that point. Other regulations of behavior followed.

Biologically, man began about a million years ago. The social trends just described had run their course in a little more than another half a million years. Human society, with government, language, religion, tools, families, and so on, has been in operation for some three hundred thousand years. Although there has been variation and elaboration, the substance is the same now as then. We will go on to discuss further developments, but the categories of analysis will not change. When in later chapters we take a look at the form of society, the analysis will fit Soviet, Brazilian, Eskimo, and Japanese society, as well as our own. It will also fit the earliest society as well as the most recent.

THE BIG DARK AGES: TRIBALISM

Historically, once society and its major institutions emerged, most of the remaining three hundred thousand years were very dull. Tools grew increasingly varied and more sophisticated. So did social rules. Man spread his population more widely across the globe. The number and kind of societies increased, as groups moved into new territories and developed new cultural responses to new environmental problems. The simple fact of isolation through time permitted the growth of unique patterns.[2] But the changes were minor and the variations merely elaborations on the same basic theme. Nothing very important happened. Nothing much did until the last ten thousand years. This later period brought explosions of change, but before we move to it, let us see why it was preceded by a long and ubiquitous dark age.

Man in early society was a wondrous biological creature. Additionally, his social life meant that the basic unit of survival was the group rather than the individual. The tools he created gave him an edge beyond his biological equipment. But his relationship with his environment was much the same as that of any other animal. Man lived within the environment and survived on terms set by the environment; he utilized the resources of that environment as much as he was able; he competed with other species on the same grounds.

Any environment offers a variety of differentiated resources.

[2]For those of you who are familiar with the principles of biological evolution there is another analogy to social evolution here. The factors of the two preceding sentences correspond, respectively, to adaptation and genetic drift.

Each resource is directly utilitarian to some species, but not to others. From the perspective of some particular species, other species may be part of the resource. Man, for instance, uses water and oxygen, rabbits and berries—but not carbon dioxide or sunlight, grass or plankton. Other organisms with different needs and designs can coexist with man, using the resources he does not exploit. All species tend to overreproduce. The number and kind of organisms that survive in a particular territory is limited by their abilities to get resources. The excess and the unsuccessful die. A "balance of nature" is established for any particular territory.

For man specifically, the tribal group survived by gathering roots, vegetables, berries, and nuts, by hunting game, insects, and fish. Typically, this group migrated through a relatively large territory, following the food supply with the shifting seasons. The population increased until it reached the ceiling set by availability foodstuffs. If this ceiling was exceeded, the checks of famine and disease quickly reduced the band to appropriate size. If the population fell much below the limit, excessive births and a lowered mortality rate soon brought the number back up. In most environments, this ceiling was between twenty-five and one hundred persons.

The main effect of living in bands that contained the maximum population for the available resource was that the resource had to be exploited to its fullest.[3] Every person had to spend all his time wresting sustenance from the environment. As the major meaning of sustenance is food, everyone was a full-time food producer. If there was a division of labor at all, it was a rudimentary one within the family and was based on age and sex. The tools, education, art, social forms, religion, government, and philosophy of the tribe were produced by jacks-of-all-trades in their spare time, of which they had little. Of leisure they had virtually none. Everyone spent all day every day in the routine activities that sustain life. This scramble for existence describes most of the lives of most of the world's people for those hundreds of thousands of years.

Many factors inhibited the advance of society. The following few paragraphs will be devoted to a discussion of some of these factors.

The population is small. Not all human beings have equal capacity to invent. A popular recognition of these differing capacities appears in the recognition of "genius." Although granting that intellec-

---

[3]Economists recognize this as a condition of decreasing marginal productivity and inelastic unit demand or propensity to consume. Each person added to the population made life harder for all.

tual ability is continuous, rather than an either-or factor, surely there are some threshold levels below which an individual would be unable to contribute a major cultural development. Whatever the level, only one person out of a very large number is above it. A small band would have to wait many generations before the odds favored the appearance of such a person. Even then, if his mother dropped him on his head or if his family experience molded him into rigid and unimaginative lines, his potential would be lost. A large population simply contains more creative potential and offers more chances for fortuitous circumstances to foster genius.

The band is isolated. It is not in sustained and open contact with its immediate neighbors and surely lives in total ignorance of groups more than a few day's journey away. When inventions do occur, then, their benefit is likely to be restricted to the local group in which they rise. The same invention may be invented over and over again by different isolated groups, rather than all having the chance to develop further on the base of one another's advances. Bands do not get full benefit of each other's geniuses. The impact of smallness is enhanced.

The social relations are personalized. Partly because the population is small and isolated, everyone will know everyone else on a personal basis. A chance for privacy, for anonymity, does not exist. The pressures for conformity under such conditions are maximized. The inventor needs an opportunity to go his eccentric way, to deviate. The intimacy of tribal life denies him this and stultifies innovation.

There is no leisure time. The population-resource dilemma insures that each person is overemployed. There will be periods of rest, but these must be seen as recuperative and preparatory relative to the work—viewed, in a sense, as "occupied time." The opportunity to relax, to contemplate, to plan wildly, must wait an improved work-to-food-produced ratio.

The division of labor is minimal. There is at least a kernel of truth in the old saw, "Jack of all trades, master of none." A person who makes arrows once a year, on a cold winter's night after a hard day's hunt, will scarcely become skilled in the traditional craft in a lifetime. He will surely not spend his leisure time contemplating improved products or more efficient productive techniques. It is not that important to him; he is not that familiar with the work. His situation is the same for the many other tasks, tools, and materials in which he occasionally dabbles. A specialist would be in a much stronger position, but here there are none.

The band is homogeneous. Because it is small, isolated, and made up of persons who all do the same work, the band is homogeneous. Everyone does the same things, knows the same things, believes the same things, and acts the same way. These conditions are self-perpetuating. A person who is exposed to only one way of life—that lived by himself and all those known to him—is in an unlikely position to alter it. Indeed, even the possibility of alteration is unlikely to occur to him. In most folk languages, the word for "mankind" is the same as the tribal name. Similarly, the tribe's lifeway is seen as the inevitable human way.

Trade is insignificant. Trade increases efficiency of a group by allowing each individual to concentrate on that task at which he is most efficient. The total productivity of a group so occupied, who then exchange products with one another, is greater than for a group without such concentration and exchange. Moreover, once the principle of trade is established, it tends to spread across group boundaries. In this way it effects an increase in exposure to various cultures, lessening the impact of homogeneity and the small population. In the absence of a division of labor, trade never develops.

The little exchange that exists is traditionalized. Because there is so little trade, special cultural rationales concerning it are not developed. The patterns of trade lean on other institutional systems. The strongest influences are those of personalized social relations and suffocating homogeneity. If a person exchanges goods at all, he does so more as a ritualized gift than as a sale—for an established "price" and to a restricted clientele. He has no market for an increased productivity, no spur toward improved quality, no reward for innovation. Incentive is lacking.

The band is illiterate. Symbols are almost exclusively verbal, and hence ephemeral. They are born and die with sound mechanics. If they can be recommunicated, it is only with distortion, loss of detail, and reshaping by the secondary speaker. Materials can endure over time in this fashion, even over generations and centuries, but the only materials that will are those that are salient to each generation of speakers. An invention or discovery that is "useless" in its own time, then, will die with its inventor. If a use should arise some generations later it would represent a need that would be just as unfilled as if the invention had never occurred. Literacy allows direct communication of all accumulated knowledge across time. No discovery, whatever its relevance at some point in time, need be lost to later times.

The band is migratory. One way of describing the life of a people is to speak of their "cultural inventory." By this I mean the total list of their knowledges and material tools. Increase in number and variety of the cultural inventory is one index of progress. The material inventory of a migrant people is necessarily sparse. One crude but all-purpose tool has considerable advantage over many sophisticated and specialized tools for a person who must carry them long distances several times a year. The incentive to innovate is again stifled. Further, closets serve as cultural repositories in much the same fashion as do writings. Migrants have no such storage.

The cultural inventory is limited. Most inventions are not really new, but are combinations of already existing articles. He who would invent the automobile must have available wheels, gears, fossil fuels, metals, and many other items. New inventions produced by combinations of old ones are in some ways analogous to children produced by matings of adults. Likewise, the rate of knowledge growth resembles that of population expansion; both follow geometric curves. In the early stages of inventiveness, one is in the level part of the curve; knowledge advances slowly. As the knowledge base increases, the rate of new discovery builds; a "knowledge explosion" occurs.

Life is unchanging. This item serves as a summary of all the others, is a consequence of all the others, and serves further to cause its own realization. Simply, people who live in a traditional and unchanging world are traditional and unchanging people. The logic here is much the same as that offered above in connection with homogeneity. In fact, lack of change implies homogeneity over time.

These factors are not a list of separate items, each of which inhibits change, but rather an interlocking set. In many ways, some of which are more or less explicit in the argument above, they reinforce one another toward achieving the same ends. Together they explain three hundred thousand years of relatively slow change in the human condition. This phenomenon demands explanation, for man then was substantially the same, in intellectual capacity and biological feature, as man now. The differences in performance must be accounted for by the social conditions outlined above.

Because the inhibiting factors are so tightly interlocked, a breakthrough in any one of them would serve to unlock the hold of all. We must look to the past for a set of conditions permitting such a breakthrough. Throughout the period and without any breakthrough, two of the inhibiting conditions were subject to steady erosion. First, although the size of bands did not increase, the number of bands did. The human population spread over most of the world's surface, and the total human population grew. Second, the cultural inventory grew. Not rapidly, given its small base, but with the slow and steady increment that characterizes the flat portion of the knowledge-growth curve. These small trends did not make a breakthrough, but did assure, if continued long enough, that man was ready for one when the opportunity arose.

BREAKTHROUGH, PART ONE: AGRICULTURE

If you reexamine the inhibiting factors, I believe one condition will emerge as directly or indirectly causative to the rest. It is implicit in the discussion of environment-organism relations that preceded the list. A major breakthrough to progress would follow most surely from a change in food production. As long as each man worked all the time on his own food supply, the entire set of prohibitive factors remained in force. As long as population reproduction overreached available resources, each person was occupied full-time by food production. Small population, isolation, and migration, lack of trade, leisure, and a division of labor: all were directly consequent of this condition. The other factors followed from these.

A marked population decline or a sudden increase in the bounty of resources would allow the population to feed itself with less than total effort. In such a circumstance, the people could "skim the top" of the resource, utilizing only the portion most easily exploited. The amount of work required to furnish sustenance would decrease, leisure would appear, and an opportunity would arise for some members of a group to specialize in work other than food production. To have this effect, the population decline or resource increase must be great; a small surplus will not effect change of the magnitude we seek. The trend must be sudden. A gradual resource increase would find population increase keeping pace, with no resulting surplus. Population decline, though resulting in surplus, would also leave a group too small and with too limited social resources to be able to exploit the environmental resource. A sudden and drastic increase in the bounty of nature must occur for a relatively large and culturally sophisticated group. This is the sort of breakthrough condition we have been seeking.

Such a fortuitous combination of circumstances occurred with the end of the last ice age. With the most recent glacial recession, much of Europe, and similar latitudes around the world, gained improved climates. Lands that had been cold, wind-swept, partly ice-covered, and barren became temperate forest. This recession, like the advance before it, proceeded at approximately twenty feet per year. The climate change was similarly slow. Obviously, we have here a change of the magnitude required but not the speed. Areas close to the equator were never reached by glaciers, experienced much more modest temperature fluctuations, but also went through an accompanying moisture cycle. During the ice age, a great portion of the earth's water was committed to ice. In the absence of this water, the equatorial regions were arid. With the melting of the glaciers, the water was returned to the atmosphere and the equatorial regions received their share. These events occurred in such a fashion that the return of rains and rivers to the desert was much more sudden than any temperature change; arid regions almost instantaneously became verdant plains. The resulting surplus and leisure, for reasons which we shall soon see, permitted the establishment of agriculture where social and environmental factors were otherwise suitable. Favorable changes in food production ratio and drastic acceleration of social change in turn resulted.

The sacrifice required to initiate agriculture cannot be overstated. The seed that must be planted is the edible part of the plant —hence the need for surplus. To put such seed in the ground represents the sacrifice of food and, hence, the work time spent in its gathering. The many man-days spent in cultivation are not immediately productive. The would-be farmer must be supported by others who hunt and gather. For the band to stay together and protect the crop from depredation, the entire group must give up its migratory habits and remain by the farm plot through the entire growing season. In this fashion they sacrifice the most easily obtainable portion of their food supply, which is in other areas of their customary territory. These considerations echo our insistence on a radically and unusually greater natural resource as a precondition for the development of agriculture.

The conditions finally occurred and agriculture was first initiated about ten thousand years ago. This development appeared once or several times in the area between the eastern end of the Mediterranean Sea and central India. The domestication of animals accompanied that of plants.

The effect of domestication was to put man's relation to the environment on a different plane. Previously, he, like any other animal, lived in the environment on terms set by that environment. Afterward he fit the environment to his own ends. If he found only two palatable plant forms out of ten different forms growing in a field, he scraped off the other eight and planted the entire field in those two. He redesigned the environment so that a larger portion of its resource was in forms he could use. Under hunting and gathering, one day's work produced, on the average, one day's food. Even the most primitive agricultural systems produced one and a half to two day's food for one day's work. Some leisure was then available, and some members of the group could turn to activities other than food production. The group settled in at least a semipermanent location. The average size of the group increased somewhat to perhaps two hundred people. To prevent the group from becoming even larger in the face of expanding population, excess members formed new settlements in the abandoned portion of the original group's territory. The area that had once supported a band of fifty members later supported four or five villages. The total population growth was then much greater than the growth of unit size.

The first full-time specialists were priests, chiefs, artists, and magicians. Governance and religion became more elaborate and rationalized. Other specialties began to develop in crafts and handiwork: stoneworkers, toolmakers, basket weavers, clothmakers, and potters.

Pottery was invented at about this time. Though off the point, the circumstances surrounding this invention will be retold, because they illustrate so well the effect of permissive and prohibitive factors and interlocking causation. Pottery, or some similar container, was needed by agriculturalists to store the food supply, particularly grain crops, from one harvest season to the next. Small grains are not easily digested without some processing, for example, grinding and mixing with water to form a paste. Baking may have improved the palatability of some such pastes. The firing of clay and the discovery of pottery may have been incidental to baking. Storage of pastes may have been implicated in the discovery of the properties of yeast. At any rate, yeast, raised bread, and beer were discovered in this period, and this tentative explanation is logically persuasive. The storage of beer and similar intoxicants provided another use for pottery. Some time later metal smelting was invented, probably as a result of firing pots made of earth that included metallic ores. Finally, and obliquely, even if early tribal man had invented pottery, it is unlikely that the usage would have survived. Brittle, heavy, and cumbersome vessels would have been poorly adapted to his migratory way of life. Other invention-clusters followed similar patterns.

Despite this explosion of techniques and specialties, the number and variety of specialists at this stage must not be exaggerated. The number of such specialists was limited by the local market that they could serve, the village population, and by the ability of that population to support them. The population, in turn, was limited to the number that could be fed from the village land.

The typical village plan, through most of the world then and now, is a cluster of homes surrounded by farmland. Individual farms are pie-shaped wedges radiating out from the settlement. The outside boundary of the farmland is roughly circular. The radius of the circle is approximately a half day's walk. These uniformities can be understood from a quick analysis of the economic and social considerations involved. A cluster settlement naturally follows from the tribal band pattern. Mutual protection, companionship, and equal access to the nonfarming specialists also recommend this pattern. Any arrangement of farming rights other than one based on wedges would leave some villagers at a disadvantage. This system assures that each individual will have some land close to his home, some further away. Each farmer can, in effect, start working at his back door, cultivate his way from there to the extreme boundary of his plot, then back. Such procedure implies that the farmer must turn around at noon, so that he will get home by dark. If he turns short of the plot boundary, the remaining portion must be worked on some other day, and on that day he must spend several hours walking across the already-worked portion of the land. Hence, the half day's walk boundary is fixed. The village population in turn is limited to the number of persons who can be fed by food produced on the land within such a circle.

Even with these limitations, the acceleration of change was underway. The population was larger, more heterogeneous. There was more of a division of labor, more trade, and more leisure. Permanent residence was established. With the rise of new specialties, traditional restraints on exchange were weakened. The cultural base expanded and the seeds of ongoing change regenerated and multiplied.

Imagine a collection of more or less identical and typical villages of eight thousand years ago, scattered through a particular territory. With full population expansion, the farm boundaries of adjacent villages were ocntiguous. Each was about the same size, was supported by similar farm enterprises, and entertained identical sets of specialists. The craftsmen among these specialists can be expected over time to have developed new and improved products, again, precisely because they were specialists. Not all of them would have been innovative, but sooner or later, in the territory as a whole, someone was going to produce a superior good. Let us, for illustration, assume that it was a basket weaver in village X. Trading his baskets to his fellow villagers for food, he supplied them all with better baskets. They may have used these baskets to carry their newly harvested grain from the fields.

If a farmer from village Y happened to be at the outer boundary of his farm while an X villager was at the adjoining edge of his, they may have conversed. Should the Y villager happen to have complained about the leaky basket that caused him to lose grain, the X villager could have responded by showing his new basket, which avoided that problem. Remembering the loosened traditional ties that have already resulted from trade, is it not logical to assume that the next time the Y farmer needed a new basket, he would have purchased it from village X?

You can deduce the fact that the two villages were only a day's walk apart (a half day's walk for the farm area of each village). Our hypothetical Y farmer would carry food to village X to exchange for a basket. He was a farmer; food was the only good he had to trade. He was already accustomed to trading food for baskets with his local craftsman. The basket maker in village X was accustomed to selling his baskets for food. Nothing changed except the location of the exchange and the addition of a transportation factor.

Yet, as this action was duplicated by other Y farmers, and those of villages Z, Q, and so on, it carried large implications. One individual would not have been able to make all the baskets for all the people of the larger territory. He would have specialized even more narrowly in one particular kind of basket and left a market niche for other basket weavers, who devoted themselves to other narrow specialties. Alternatively, he would have established a factory-like basket production center, with many narrowly specialized assistants. Craftsmen in other trades would have been stimulated in, or attracted to, village X when it became a trade center and therefore something more than a village. If a stoneworker in village Q developed a superior technique, he would move his operation to village X, so that his wares could be displayed to the people of all the territories. These people came to village X for baskets, but might have been persuaded to go home with a sickle instead, leaving their food-exchange profit with the stoneworker. Over time, one village among many built from this sort of beginning. It developed or attracted superior craftsmen and narrow specialists in all the crafts. Still other nonagricultural occupations grew to cater to the needs of market-goers: the age's equivalents of motel and restaurant owners.

The bustling market center attracted immigrants and needed a large population to man the ranks of a burgeoning occupational table. It was able to support, to feed, this increasing population by its trade. The commodity brought to the market by outlying villagers was, most basically, food. These outlying communities became more impoverished. As some of their food was traded to the city, they could only support a smaller population than in a condition of independence. Local craftsmen disappeared as the customers all went to the larger community. But while the outlying communities grew poorer and more simple, the central one was so radically changed that we can label it a city. Cities are, essentially, communities that have grown so large that they cannot feed themselves. This dependence on a hinterland is not only a definitional mark, but also a key to the city's nature. Much of the character and the fate of cities follows from the single problem of seeking and sustaining outside support.

This support first came through the trade process suggested above. There have been well-developed cities for at least the last five thousand years. The earliest and most sizeable of these were located in the region where agriculture began, east Mediterranean to west India.[4]

The city was a crucible of social change. The trends of population increase, leisure, division of labor, trade, expanding cultural base, depersonalization, and heterogeneity continued. With the elaboration of the division of labor and increasing specialization they accelerated. They accelerated further with the stream of foreigners who came to the city as resident businessmen or transient traders. The trends rose still further on the expanded population

[4]Cities certainly developed in east Asia—China and related lands—at about the same time. Similarly, agriculture may have appeared early and independently in this region. This development will be ignored here because the parts of the story that are identical need not be repeated and because the points of difference between the Western and Far Eastern patterns show a faster rate of social change in the West. Specifically, Eastern agricultural patterns were more successful than their Western counterparts and resulted in population increase that was so great that it oppressed and stultified changes of some other sorts. Eastern urbanism, then, is analogous to some of the blind alleys of biological evolution. In its overelaboration of one form of adaptation it loses the capacity to adjust in other respects. By this note I do not intend to denigrate the content of Oriental culture, but simply to indicate that it is relatively more fixed than that of the West. Those countries of that region that are now changing most rapidly are doing so because they have adopted significant elements of the Western pattern.

that the outside food supplies supported. The act of trading with strangers and foreigners removed the remaining restraints of traditionalism concerning prices and markets. The movement of people and commodities through larger territories increased again the significant population and cultural base. Cities received the benefits of inventions by remote peoples and the stimulus of diverse and changing surroundings.

Although the impetus for this change was economic (basically trade and the concomitant specialization in crafts), rebounding effects occurred in noneconomic areas. The new city turned some of its superior sophistication to the realms of politics, religion, and the arts. The leisure-specialization cycle did as much for these kinds of practitioners as it did for craftsmen.

The city had a larger, denser, more polyglot population than ever before. It naturally required more complex administration and governance. The specialized role of chief or king, itself only recently developed, was soon supplemented with specialized administrative assistants, perhaps further with specialized judiciary, police, and welfare structures.

As the population grew more diverse in origins and practices, the unquestioned adherence to a monolithic religion became more difficult. People who were exposed to a variety of beliefs found their own beliefs more open to question. A specialized set of religious functionaries grew, who developed rationalizations and systematizations of the beliefs.

As the new cities grew, then, their central problem was that of feeding themselves, of gaining sustenance from their hinterlands. The tools they brought to this operation included those just mentioned: superior technology and craft products, large population organized under a single and advanced government, and sophisticated religion. Some cities leaned heavily or almost exclusively on one of these, others used a combination, but any one of them served.

The craft city leaned on its inventive and productive technology, traded produced goods to the rural dwellers for food and raw materials. The farmer became habituated to loading his excess food on his back and carrying it to the city to exchange for craft items, which he then carried home. The size of such a city, however, was severely limited. The reasons for this limitation follow a logic similar to that which limited the village. The village, you will remember, was limited to the population that could be supported on the land within a half day's walk of the center. Although later boundaries were much more extensive, the walking man was still the heart of the system.

Suppose, for the moment, that a man could carry twenty day's worth of food on his back. If he lived and farmed ten day's walk from the city and ate every day on his journey to and from the city, he ate twenty day's worth of food. From his personal point of view, his trip was in vain. If his own food requirements consumed all the food he could carry, he would have none left to trade in the city. Moreover, the trip was of no benefit to the city; the net amount of food in the city was unchanged by his trip.

The city's major problem is feeding itself. When the transportation costs (translated into food consumed) begin to equal food transported, the city can no longer grow. A ton of food in the city represents a ton of nutrition for the city dwellers, but each mile that ton is from the city reduces the urban value as increasing portions are consumed in moving. This limitation operates with equal force whether the transportation is effected by the farmer or by a transportation specialist. In either case, there is a mouth that must be filled during transport of food. In either case, someone who could be on the land producing more food is spending his time instead in moving it. Likewise, the limitation holds whether the transporter consumes part of his load or keeps it intact and obtains his meals from other sources. In either case, the food consumed is at the same distance from the city and has the same relative value.

If transportation was improved, as for example with a horse and cart, the boundary was stretched slightly but not broken. The horse and driver had to be fed during the trip. Though the horse ate different food than would a man, the horse's food took up space on the cart or on the land at the point of feeding, space or land that could have been used for human food. The cart-building time, likewise translated into food, had to be amortized over the number of trips a cart lasted. Cities of this sort could never grow larger than perhaps five thousand persons.

Water transport eased somewhat this limitation, but imposed a new one. Larger quantities of goods can be transported in ships or barges with relatively little labor (eating) cost. In the days of early cities, however, this transport moved effectively in only one direction: down-river or across seas with the wind. Food is bulky, and the largest craft cities grew in locations that were downstream or downwind from fertile hinterlands. The return offered for the food was necessarily restricted to very light, small objects that were easily transportable overland.

We can offer a concrete picture of how trade might have been pursued. Merchants or their agents, using land transportation, left the city carrying craft goods upstream: beads, mirrors, hand implements, and similar trinkets. At each of several villages along the route, the trader would exchange some trinkets for foodstuffs to be delivered to the city. He would also contract for raft builders and deckhands for shipment of the food, using trinkets as payment. Moving upstream in this fashion, the trader left in his wake tons of foodstuffs bound for the city in exchange for pounds of trinkets. When he reached the source of the river or exhausted his supply of trinkets, the trader rode the last raft back to the city and began the circuit again. The exchange had to take this form because of the transportation circumstances.

One further difficulty of the craft city arose with the success of its system. As the city exported goods, it could not help, in the long run, exporting technology. The city's act of exploiting its superior sophistication lessened that superiority. Hinterland people learned to produce imitations of the city goods. If these were not perfect imitations, they were at least close. The transportation cost of city goods required that they command a prohibitively higher price. The farmers turned more and more to local production, recreating, for those furthest from the city, something like the old self-sufficient village. The city had lost its market, and hence its food supply and its basis of existence.

This problem was most intense and developed most rapidly for the largest craft cities, those depending on one-way transportation. Here the limitation to small trinket crafts brought rural surfeit with these goods soonest. There were, after all, a limited number and kind of commodities that were unperishable, small, light, and relatively unbreakable. The city's inventiveness became exhausted and the farmer's home overflowed. The farmer had no incentive to put out the extra effort on food production and transportation assistance; he rewarded himself with leisure rather than trade; the city starved.

The situation of the city as religious center was similar to that of the craft city. The commodities exported were magic, salvation, security, and so forth. These were in demand in the rural area because those produced by the city grew out of greater sophistication. This sophistication in turn followed from specialization, cultural heterogeneity, and the other attributes of cities already discussed. The farmer brought his food to the priests in tribute or sacrifice as readily as to the craftsmen in trade. One-way trade was also possible, dogma and ritual were more easily transported than blankets and knives. The sophistication-gap served as a halter to continued city development just as surely here as in the economic realm.

If religious beliefs were assimilable by the hinterlanders, they soon produced their own home-based versions. If the city priests continued theological escalation in an attempt to stay more sophisticated than the local competition, they placed themselves out of the farmer's intellectual market. A religion that was only comprehensible to learned priests would not have served to part farmers from their produce or to provender a city.

Although the craft and religious forms of city development offered a limited future, they furnished the stage for the final eliminations from our list of factors curtailing change. Among the discoveries of this period were the techniques for smelting, forging, alloying, and casting metals. The utility of the new materials was immediately recognized; they were in great demand. Some of the ores were scarce or found in places remote from the early cities. More than any other factor, this consideration extended trade far beyond the boundaries of the food-supplying hinterland. At least 4,000 years ago regular trade was conducted across the length of Europe, from the tin mines of Spain to the cities of Asia Minor. The effective population base for invention and the breadth of cultural heterogeneity underwent this one more explosion.

The human voice, perfected as a mode of communication hundreds of thousands of years earlier, is ineffective over such distances. In the early years specialists in message-carrying, usually slaves, were selected and trained for memory. A businessman in the Tigris River valley could dictate a letter to his messenger, who would walk to Spain and recite the contents to the businessman's partner, a mine manager. This was not efficient communication. Moreover, without records and bookkeeping, either partner could have stolen the other blind. They couldn't even know when they were making a profit! These business needs were consequent to the expansion of trade and the detraditionalization of exchange. They accompanied the religious trend toward rationalization and a specialized life of contemplation. Both occurred in conjunction with the beginnings of bureaucratization in government. The net effect of these three thrusts was the development of written language. Writing is simply speech in another medium, but the medium endures through time and distance without loss or distortion. With this development recorded, we have chronicled all the major features of the city and hence of the drive toward accelerating social change.

Although governmental specialization in cities did not add anything so strikingly new to the story already covered, it held some developments worth attention. We have seen the use of economics and religion as mechanisms for feeding the city, let us now look at politics as a means to the same end. The political peculiarity of the city was the large population under coordinated leadership. The hinterland population of any city of that time radically outnumbered the people of the city itself, but the outlying regions included a variety of isolated, autonomous, culturally divergent village peoples. Even within any one of these villages, the people were more likely to be guided by tradition than by administration. New challenges were met by serial acts of individual improvisation. The city could bring to bear on any one of these villages a relatively large and well-coordinated army. This army was well equipped, thanks to the city's craftsmen and could operate under centrally planned strategy. It was only at that time and with the development of those characteristics that any social unit could lay claim to the name "army."

The governmental city became a military city and supplied itself by conquest. It overpowered the farmers and forced them to send food to the city. The rationalizations used by cities to justify such action are as old as the process. Their echoes ring in today's headlines. "We must bring them the benefits of civilization." "The common people must be freed from their oppressive rulers." "Their souls must be saved with the light of our gods." "The neighboring tribes have been warring; this is a peace-keeping expedition." "We must help their government put down rebellion." Loot, tribute, taxes, trade agreements—by whatever name and whatever the rationalization—military conquest supported the city.

This was altogether a successful adaptation. City empires rose and flourished for thousands of years. The transportation mechanics of one-way trade were as effective in this context as they were with trinkets. The "exported" armies provided their own locomotion; bulk-goods food followed the natural flow of wind or water. The greater the population of the central city, the larger armies it raised, the more territory it controlled, the greater the population supported. The famous city empires of the period—Roman, Grecian, Persian, Byzantine, and others—were all developed and sustained on this basis. Art, philosophy, engineering, social organization, law, science, and other cultural endeavors blossomed in such cities. The military city was not free of the same flaws that had hamstrung the craft or religious city, but it took longer for the flaws to "catch up" to this form. The military city had a longer period of success as a city than did the other varieties. This meant, simply, the development of larger cities and fuller realization of all the characteristics in city life that supported invention and change. Specific empires rose and fell for a variety of reasons, but the species survived. There were military cities somewhere in the area between eastern Europe and western Asia from 3000 B.C. to A.D. 1800.

Among the maladies that caused the downfall of certain military cities was conquest by another such city. As cities expanded, it was natural that they should find themselves in border conflict concerning the right to exploit boundary hinterlands. Such conflicts were likely to escalate into total war. The victor emerged with a satellite city far reduced in importance and with a radically expanded hinterland. The rapid but uneven technological and organizational advances of the period gave the advantage to one and then another region; relatively rapid shifts of preeminence and decline were the rule. The key consideration here, therefore, is simply that death by conquest implies a conquerer. The demise of one military city in this fashion guaranteed the survival of another. The players changed but the game went on.

THE LITTLE DARK AGES: FEUDALISM

Other problems of the military city resulted in more portentous fates. When city armies conquered and occupied a rustic hinterland, they did so on the basis of superior organizational techniques and superior weapons. The fact of conquest and occupation exposed the vanquished to the victors, and so the defeated people were not long in adopting the tools and tactics of their conquerors. In the longer run, their common fate as the vanquished, as the subjects of a distant city, as food-supplying vassals, caused a certain solidarity among previously disparate and autonomous tribal groups. The city's organizational and technological advantages were cancelled; the weight of numbers began to favor the rurals. Rebellion and resistance began to characterize the outlying areas of the empire. The principle of failure here was similar to the rural surfeit and sophistication that had caused the downfall of the exporters of trinkets or dogma.

Compounding these external difficulties was a political-economic problem of an internal nature. If an empire continued to expand, it continually conquered and occupied the next adjacent territory. As boundaries crept further from the city, communication with, and supply to, the army grew more difficult. The land area required to support one city dweller increased rapidly with the distance of that land from the city. That is, transportation costs, seen as food expended, grew larger with distance and demanded larger conquered hinterlands for a population increase of any magnitude in the city. Additionally, we must add the cost of feeding the soldier who monitored the farmer's behavior and who exacted the city's tax. As more area further from the city meant less support, a larger occupying force was necessary to yield a given amount of sustenance to the city. Armies, then, formed a larger proportion of the city's population, drew off manpower that might have been profitably employed in the city, and lowered the city's vitality. The scattering of these armies ever more thinly over continually increasing territory weakened the fabric of conquest, made the empire more vulnerable to provincial uprisings. An empire that continued to expand was likely, then, to collapse under its own weight in the long run.

If expansion were halted at some tenable point, these dangers could be avoided, but others were raised. Armies that were not kept busy on the frontiers became a domestic danger. The nonexpansion of empire allowed armies to become political tools; factionalism, intrigue, civil war, and ultimate self-destruction were probable outcomes. This probability was enhanced by the fact that these armies had been stationed at the ends of the empire, far removed from the city and from each other. Their central loyalties, then, were unlikely to lie with the central government or with the army as an entity, but rather with their own district governor or local unit general.

One final, and perhaps more obscure, point is this: stability was an anti-urban condition and an anchor against change of other sorts. The only prime mover of cultural innovation for a military city was continued expansion. The city that stood still was subject to decay.

By and large, all the military cities of Europe suffered from all these difficulties, except the one discussed last, and disappeared entirely. The fall of Rome, the last and grandest military city in the West, marked an end of creative urbanism in this region for hundreds of years. Further east, in Asia Minor and beyond, cities decayed rather than disappeared, falling victim to the debilitating stability mentioned in the preceding paragraph. Urbanism hung on, but it was not a creative urbanism. The only sociological interest in these cities is as repositories for the creativity of the earlier age; they added nothing new.

The five centuries following the fall of Rome are called the Dark Ages by historians. The sociological meaning of this period is that military urbanism had run its course and no viable urban successor form was to be found. To be sure, it was not so long or so dark an age as the tribal era that preceded agriculture, but it was a time during which nothing much happened. A new basis for city life was required to get things moving again.

BREAKTHROUGH, PART TWO: ANOTHER KIND OF CITY

The invention of the tacking sailing ship was the first step in developing a truly dynamic replacement for the dead or decayed military urbanism. This principle of sailing involved adjustable sails and a zigzag course, by means of which a ship could sail almost as well against the wind as with it. Such ships were developed around 1400. This development was important because it made two-way, equal trade possible. The city could import materials from the hinterland and return an equal volume. Goods offered to the rural areas were determined by market demand, rather than by the constraints of transportation.

The first consequence was a reduced likelihood of rural surfeit. Even when ship-borne trade was with distant lands and did not directly involve food, the bulk movement of goods in both directions at relatively low costs meant high volume and stable, continuous trade systems. This large and steady influx of "exotic" goods into the city gave it more materials for resale, with or without further processing. These goods could be offered to the hinterland farmers, and again reduced the likelihood of surfeit. In these respects the new form of city operation raised no new potential for success, but it lacked the potentials for failure that had marked its predecessors.

Much of the tacking-ship tonnage, particularly coastal traffic, was food traded for city goods. The focus of the urban contribution to this system was on what the farmer wanted. Among the farmer's chief desires were improved tools and techniques of production, and so, for the first time, the inventive power of the city turned upon agricultural processes. Improved farm implements and food-processing equipment began to make up a significant portion of the trade from city to countryside. Agricultural productivity increased; a given land area produced more food with less labor; the net support any area could provide the city increased. Larger cities, therefore, could be sustained on smaller hinterlands.

Incidentally, the tacking ship also ushered in the age of exploration. The developing urban world extended its boundaries over larger portions of the earth's surface and exploited the portion it did not actually absorb. All of the propensities for change inherent in urbanism became more active and effective. Later developments in transportation—perhaps railroads were the most important—simply extended inland the equal-trade possibility of tacking ships.

Another important development of this period was the utilization of different energy sources. Until this time, most of the energy that had been turned to human uses had been that of man himself and his domesticated animals. The sail and the barge, using wind and water current, had been the principal exceptions. Wind and water currents were also converted to mechanical energy, as with the water wheel or windmill used to drive a grinding stone, but these uses were minor and insignificant. With the new urban push, much more systematic use was made of these sources. Shortly, and again out of the inventiveness of the city, engines were developed using the energy of fossil fuels and converting it to mechanical energy, which replaced a large portion of the human energy previously used in craft production. The productivity of the city increased, then, without a corresponding increase in required food supplies. The per capita wealth of mankind likewise increased.

The source of this new wealth was crafts—now fast becoming manufacturing—and trade. These resources were basic in the classical city, but fell into disuse in the Dark Ages. During the relatively city-less Dark Ages, land was the primary source of wealth. However, renascent crafts and trade were not under the control of the landowner class; the new wealth was accumulated by a newly rising class, which found its wealth threatened and its aspirations forestalled by the feudal landowners who held legal and military power. Craftsmen and traders played one noble off against another, pledging their wealth and manpower to the one among the nobility who offered them the best deal. The long-run effect of this series of manipulations was the development of centralized national governments, often kingdoms, always autocratic, always in symbiotic, cooperative relations with the commercial and industrial elite.

During this period, a commercial and industrial elite had been developed just as surely as had political centralism. Ships, the backbone of commerce, became large and expensive items. The funds required to own and lade one were prohibitive. Banking, always closely allied with trade and now with the added involvement of a large central government, grew similarly. The small operator found it impossible to compete. Insurance, as a concept and a business, developed at this time, in response to the high costs and high risks of shipping.

Small producers were not in a position to contend with such powerful interests interposed between themselves and their suppliers or markets. Large-scale production began, then, simply as a marketing consortium to contend with the giants of distribution and resources. The earliest producing organizations were little more than bureaucracies monitoring the individual efforts of a number of small-scale, hand-craft producers and buffering their relations with other economic units. The imminent increase in the use of secondary energy sources changed this. A large water wheel and a pully system will run ten machines more efficiently than ten small water wheels will run ten machines. The already operating centralized production system was drawn into a centralized location. The factory emerged.

The crude economic theories offered above explain why, if a developed economy were to emerge from that period, it would be a concentrated one. They show how an era could begin with many independent traders and craftsmen and end with a few merchants and manufacturers. They do not explain why development occurred. They do not show which among the journeymen would become the capitalists. Such explanation depends on ideological as well as economic understanding.

The immediately preceding Feudal era was one of rigid class distinction, small principalities, and land-based wealth. This structure was sanctioned and supported by the dogma and practices of the Roman Catholic church of the times. Among the socially significant doctrines of this faith was the notion of *station*: that individuals were born to a place in this world as part of God's plan. Each individual served God's purposes by serving contentedly in that station. Such an idea served to perpetuate the system. Similarly, the hierarchical structure of the church mirrored the hierarchical structure of the secular society. Authority flowed from the top. Usury (at the time defined as any interest taking) was considered a sin. This religion hindered the rise of any new class and was detrimental to successful behavior of would-be members of a commercial or industrial class.

The Protestant schismatics offered a faith more in keeping with the demands of rising urbanism. I do not mean to imply that the Protestant reformers were opportunists who saw in the bourgeoisie a potential following, which they sought to attract. Nor do I intend to picture the reformers as wise social prophets setting out to design a religion for the wave of the future. Rather, they were honest theologians who had differences of opinion with the prevailing dogma and power structure. Such schisms may be found at any time, relative to any establishment, urging reform in any direction: The names and the faiths of most such divine exotics may be discovered only in the moldy pages of history. The Protestant Reformation took life and lived on because it came at a time of incipient social change, was compatible with that change, and gave added force and definition to the change. Twisting an aphorism to increase its validity, we can say that "A prophet is without honor unless he appears in his own times." Similar religions have appeared under other social circumstances, but unless the times were propitious, they were stillborn.

Unless an appropriate faith appears propitious times may also be stillborn. Some religion like Protestantism was essential to the rise of urban-industrial society. The logic here follows that noted earlier for biological evolution, technological change, and social innovations such as the incest taboo. The rise of new features, as variation, is almost random. If an adaptive innovation happens to be available it will survive and come to typify the unit in question. If unavailable, the change will fail to occur and the unit may fail to survive. The rise of Protestantism, in some senses fortuitous, permitted and stimulated the economic and technological revolution and was in turn fostered by those trends. Two caveats must be offered here. *First*, the requirement is for a religion that carries a similar social thrust to that of Protestantism, not for Protestantism as such. Contemporary Catholicism (for example that of Northern Italy, the Netherlands, Germany, or the United States), dialectical materialism, and Shinto-Buddhism are among the social equivalents. *Second*, as we seek social implications, our concern is with the popular faith or understanding, not with the scholarly-priestly doctrines as such. In our look at Protestantism, then, Luther's and Calvin's theology will be less central than will the behavioral imperatives of the day-to-day faith of those, who, generations later, considered themselves Lutherans and Calvinists.

Luther's disillusionment with the priesthood led him to enunciate the doctrine of *every man his own priest*. The relationship between man and God was to be a direct one, rather than through the intermediary of the church or its personnel. Each man became his own theologian. Each man discovered his own path to salvation. He could do so by interpreting the Bible for himself, if he could read and had a Bible. The printing press was developed at about this time. Although this point is subsidiary to the main argument here, it serves to illustrate more microcosmically the point of the main argument: the complex interdependency and mutual causality of ideology, technology, and social condition. Appearing earlier, a printing press would have found no market for books wide enough to pay its way. Appearing earlier, a populist theology would have had no vehicle for dissemination. Appearing together, the two provided motive and opportunity for widespread literacy. Printing, literacy, and Protestantism flourished together.

Moving back to the main thesis, we may note that a religion that permitted each man to establish his own doctrine allowed that man to justify, to himself and to others, a wide variety of lifeways. Further, the doctrine of "each man his own priest" led to the application of traditional thought concerning the priesthood to other occupations. Luther's conception of *calling*, was simply this. Each man was called by God to a particular occupation. God's message to the individual was personal, not something followed automatically from birth. The person glorified and worshiped God by actively striving for perfection in the performance of the tasks to which he was called.

Another tenet of Protestantism was Calvin's doctrine of *predestination*. By this he meant that God, being omnipotent and omniscient, must know the fate of every man. From the beginning of time, some had been doomed, some saved. Those predestined for heaven, the elect, could not sin enough to alter their status. The damned likewise could not escape their fate. God arranged the lives of each so that all fulfilled and deserved their destinies. The person was ignorant of his own condition, and of that of others around him. He simply lived out the pattern that had been constructed for him. The world was a testing ground where God constantly re-proved his own mastery and replayed the perfection of his own design. The individual strove to play his ordained part with good grace.

Both the Calvinist and Lutheran doctrines demanded a peculiar orientation toward this world. The world was regarded as a place of critical action, not to be ignored, important. Yet, the world was seen as the house of sin. The doctrine of *worldly asceticism* evolved to fit these premises. This doctrine placed upon each person an obligation to be actively involved in this world, but to avoid being captured by its pleasures. Men were encouraged to be in this world but not of it, commanded by a rigid self-discipline at all times.

In the popular mind, these doctrines did not long retain their original form. A person who accepted the notion of predestination, for instance, might wonder whether he was among the elect or the

damned. Lacking direct access to God's mind, he used such evidence as he had at hand. He evaluated his own actions, whether they seemed the sort of action that God would cause for one of his elect or visit on one of his damned. By actions and outcomes, then, one could guess the metaphysical salvation state of himself and his neighbors. Charity, careful husbandry of God's resources, and avoidance of sinful "pleasures of the flesh," were seen as symptoms of salvation. No believer wanted to consider himself in any category other than the elect, and so everyone strove to follow the path that would allow him to persuade himself that he was indeed among the saved. One small step further in popular corruption and the formula became: "Do well in this world and you will achieve salvation." If this was not what Calvin intended, so be it—it was what the people accepted and acted upon.

Luther's doctrine of calling was similarly popularized and redefined. The boundaries between occupations were sometimes unclear. "Success in an occupation" was ambiguously understood as "success in business" or "success in reaching an occupation that is at the top of a hierarchy." Finally, none of the early Protestant doctrines retained doctrinal integrity. Luther's ideas were confounded with Calvin's. Appropriate elements of traditional Catholicism were retained and intermingled. Protestant groups with other intellectual ancestries added variant features. In total combination, the Protestant doctrines gave to those who embraced them a push toward behavior quite unlike the prevailing Catholic mode. Individualism, hard work, striving toward success, savings and investment, self-discipline, opportunism: these were the kind of behaviors that followed from early Protestantism.

Not all of these behaviors were commanded by the Protestant morality. Nor did behavior necessarily follow belief. But there were some correspondences and some unintended consequences. All of these behaviors were generated. For example, Protestantism did not, doctrinally speaking, make a virtue of the accumulation of wealth. It did, however, insist that people act in ways that increase income (hard work, attention to tasks, and so on). It did prohibit catering to the pleasures of the flesh. In acting out his faith, then, the Protestant acquired money and was prohibited from spending it in nonproductive ways. Capital accumulation necessarily occurred; capital accumulation was essential at this time for economic development.

Many of the features of early Protestantism carried this kind of thrust. Early Protestants became members of the rising mercantile class. Early traders and fabricators were attracted to the rising Protestant faiths.

TRENDS TO YESTERDAY

The industrialization, reurbanization, and economic concentration that grew to characterize the modern world began from the intellectual considerations here and the economic ones of a few pages earlier. The trends continued virtually unbroken to the present. New energy sources were added. Specialization became more narrow. Bureaucratic organization blanketed more and more areas of life. Interchangeability of parts, the "line" production process, advertising and rationalized marketing, and similar refinements may have furthered the developments but did not alter them. Improvements in public sanitation and health made larger, denser cities more livable. Continued improvements in agriculture meant that fewer people were tied to the rural hinterland. But no change in the direction of change is remarked. The economic history of man is completed.

The social, political, and psychological histories have a few more courses to run. Man's psychological security and his social stability were originally assured, you will remember, by his religion. Society became possible on the basis of shared religion. Adhering to a religious faith was in turn made easier by the fact that all those with whom a man came in contact shared the same faith. Urbanism, as it brought together heterogeneous peoples, laid a foundation for doubt. A person who saw others around him dressing differently, speaking different languages, engaging in different social practices, and worshiping different gods could not be so sure that his ways and his faiths were right. This doubt, as we have already argued, was useful in exciting invention. However, it also reopened psychological unease and social disruption. These could be settled, to some extent, when a person understood his own position in the urban society. Unlike his position in tribal society, this was a position of mutual dependence. Whatever his specialized role in the division of labor, he was dependent on others who were in turn dependent on him. This mutual need provided social stability, buttressed mutual trust, maintained interpersonal relations, and served in part to replace the emotional bond of shared religion. Similarly, self-recognition of one's place in the social network helped maintain psychological security. But as society grew more complicated, as dependency relations grew more difficult to fathom, as one's place in the social system grew smaller, this sort of support became more tenuous. The renascent urbanism, the greater urbanism, of the modern world resulted in such a condition.

Moreover, the spread of literacy and the value of individualism came at this same time. These several forces created a man who could not accept the old-style religions. He was—in some degree—critical, knowledgeable, and rational. He could accept a faith, indeed he needed one, but only one that possessed certain characteristics not heretofore demanded of religions. Logical consistency was one such characteristic. With the printed word, it became easy to check one page against another, the force of the completed statement was not drowned in the rhetoric of the next statement. Only relatively tight and coherent and complete belief-systems, then, were able to meet the test of the age.

Religions deal with the realm of the nonempirical, but the new man began to demand that they have one leg in this world. Man did not suddenly become a radical empiricist, but he did seek and accept only those beliefs that were anchored in reality. The connection with reality could be tenuous or utopian, but it had to be there.

The condition of man at the time of the onset of the urban-industrial world, then, required faiths that were logically coherent and empirically relevant. We will call religious-like belief-systems with these characteristics *ideologies*. The urban-industrial age is, just as accurately, the age of ideology. Some traditional religions managed to rationalize themselves, and survived to have relevance then and now. Some new ones appeared. Much of the psychological and political history of the years from 1500 to the present is concerned with conflict between ideologies and with the rise and fall of ideologies.

Protestantism, Counter-reformation Catholicism, kingdom-nationalism, and conservative feudalism were among the first of these to emerge. Generally, revolutionary ideologies emerged before their conservative counterparts. Feudal aristocracy and feudal Catholicism were ways of life with accompanying belief-sets long before the rise of the alternatives. But they only took on the attributes of ideology in response to the threat posed by new beliefs and in reaction to the conditions developed in the new society.

Another old belief, then becoming an ideology, was democracy. The world had known a crude egalitarianism in the tribal epoch. If one man, through strength, cunning, or charisma, gained control, it was an individual superiority or one lasting but a few generations.

It brought him only a modest superiority over his fellows in access to life's desirables. The early city, with scarce metal weapons in the hands of the few, changed this. Political specialization and bureaucratization of the governmental system enforced the trend. Egalitarian impulses popped up regularly among some segment of the ruled, but had no long-term effect. Impulse does not provide the sustained motivation necessary to mount a revolution. The weapons of suppression, technological and organizational, were monopolized by the rulers.

The rise of new ideologies, or of old ideas with a new ideological cast, became easier after the invention of printing and with the spread of literacy. The rise of democratic ideology, specifically, was spurred by the individualistic and egalitarian strains in Protestanism. Further, in their quest for political access for themselves, the entrepreneurial class sowed unintended seeds of governmental reform and broadened participation. They evolved an ideology to suit their own political ends, but it proved adaptable to the classes below them as well; political ambitions and egalitarian wishes were more widespread and more persistent than ever before.

Wishes alone make poor politics. Power is a precious commodity, providing as it does enhanced likelihood of realizing cherished goals and leading a valued existence. It is zealously guarded by those who have it. Power is unlikely to be given, it must be taken. For centuries, the ruling classes had oppressed the masses with or without the latter's consent. The military and organizational superiority of the few insured their political superiority. Only when this circumstance changed could the rising tide of democratic ideals achieve societal realization. Ideological explanations only *have* force when joined to those *of* force. The introduction of gunpowder to Europe initiated such a trend.

Surely Billy the Kid or Gary Cooper or another of our folk heroes has noted that "all men are the same size with guns in their hands." Even if this is not perfectly true, gunpowder gave some impetus to democratization. Anyone can pull a trigger. Practice may increase the probability of hitting the target, but, given the low accuracy of early weapons, "sure things" would never occur even in a onc-on-one situation. The probability statistics of small-arms combat give little comfort to the numerically smaller side. Given this single condition, you can see how the rulers might have listened more carefully to the demands of the masses. The elite need not have become ardent democrats, but they surely became less militant obstructionists. If they did not, they became more easily surmounted obstructions. Democracy becomes possible when the populace has guns.

This is not to say that democracy will necessarily follow the introduction of guns, because ideological and social factors are also implicated. Nonetheless, the chronological correspondence is impressive. Popular revolutions brought democratic governmental forms relatively early to such developed nations as the United States and France; if such revolutions arrived in less developed nations, they arrived later and along with the widespread distribution of guns in the country.

The earlier so-called democracies, as in Classical Greece, were of course not democracies at all, but closely held oligarchies of the privileged few, supported by a token fringe of semifranchised commoners, an excluded mass, and slaves. The only nation that made real movements toward democracy prior to the advent of guns was England. England was also the only European nation with widespread use of the longbow. The longbow—in killing power, cost, and simplicity—is a near equivalent of the gun. Later but to the same point, America's founding fathers were speaking practical politics, not rhetoric, when they affirmed the people's right to overthrow a government that had become oppressive and nonegalitarian.

Governments established by the masses after successful revolutions generally had a broader political base than those they replaced and constantly followed policies designed to forestall further revolutions. Governments in societies where successful revolution might be possible strove to distribute privilege widely enough to head off discontent that might spark such a revolution.

Democratization in politics was as important as industrialization in the economic realm, urbanization of the community, or the rise of ideologies. All grew during the period following the end of feudalism and continued as trends to the present or recent past.

For most of this period, they reinforced each other. They began together and grew together. Democratization, however, reached a climax and began a decline while the others were still advancing. The others, past a certain point, destroyed democracy rather than fostered it. Continued development of military and organizational technology shifted the balance of power from the individual or the mass and toward the system. The individual may have been able to wield a gun and hence control his government; he could not wield a tank.

The latest weapons were tanks, machine guns, mechanized armor, airplanes, and, ultimately atomic weapons. The latest supporting systems were modern surveillance and security measures, mass media indoctrination, and programmed bureaucratic administration. The state alone created these devices and controlled them. The state became an impersonal monolith, one insensitive to the human desires of its subjects. This was a more impersonal system of subjugation than any that had gone before. We will call it *statism*. The governmental shifts in developed nations since 1920 have been away from liberty and equality and toward statism. I choose this date because it seems to me to match the historical facts, and because World War I saw the development of the instruments of statist control. This timing, like that mentioned earlier, varies with the state of development of the society in question. The shift to statism was gradual and unpunctuated by violence, compared to preceding shifts in the other direction; this shift was a gradual encroachment of state on individual and a slow withering away of the individual's power to resist. No change in the locus of superior force was involved, but simply an increase in force inequity. Statism is the trend of the most recent past.

Statist, bureaucratic, industrial, ideological, urban—this is the character of modern society. This is our present. The mission of the past two chapters was to arrive at the present; that has been accomplished. The hope of these chapters was to assist in your understanding of the present; perhaps that has been accomplished as well. The remaining chapters of this book will deal with the present in more specific detail and with some persistent truths about human society generally. Urbanization, industrialization, and bureaucratization— the basic themes of the metamorphosis of society—carry other implications not yet fully unfolded, implications that herald the end of statism, for instance. These incipient developments are intrinsic to, and inseparable from, modern society. They are incremental and irreversible. They lead us to the future, where we must live in any case.

FURTHER READING

Adams, Robert M., *The Evolution of Urban Society*. Chicago: Aldine, 1966.

Bendix, Reinhard, *Work and Authority in Industry*. New York: Harper, 1963. Torch paperback.

Childe, V. Gordon, *What Happened in History*. Baltimore: Penguin, 1946. Pelican paperback.

Clark, J. Grahame, *World Pre-history: An Outline*. London: Cambridge University, 1961.*

Gilmore, Harlan, *Transportation and the Growth of Cities*. New York: Free Press, 1953.

Goode, William, *World Revolution and Family Patterns*. New York: Free Press, 1963. Available in paperback.

Mumford, Lewis, *The City in History*. New York: Harcourt, 1961.

Sjoberg, Gideon, *The Preindustrial City: Past and Present*. New York: Free Press, 1961. Available in paperback.

White, Leslie, *The Evolution of Culture*. New York: McGraw-Hill, 1959. Paperback.

Wolf, Eric, *Peasants*. Englewood Cliffs, N.J.: Prentice-Hall, 1966. Available in paperback.

*Difficult, specialized, or technical.

ELEMENTS OF SOCIAL ORGANIZATION: ORDER AND DISORDER

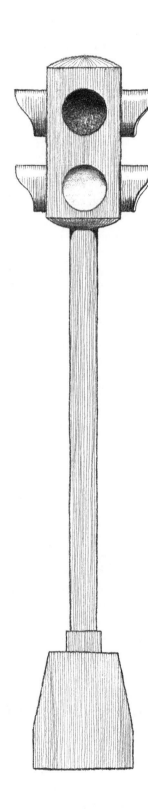

4 VALUES AND NORMS, PERSISTENCE AND CHANGE

In the past few chapters we tried to understand human society by reviewing how it came about. We took a very general look at society and the problems that go along with it, the bio-social development of man as man and the history of man from about a million years ago to the present. Now we will take an analytic approach. We will try to explore the units and relationships that make up social systems. This chapter will deal with the most general issues of social order and disorder, and with the phenomenon of change.

THE MIRACLE OF ORDER

One of the most striking characteristics of human society is that it "works." Any society consists of a large number of individuals. Each has his own personal goals, beliefs, and motives. Each will have had experiences that differ somewhat from those of any other person. Each is, in some senses, a free agent; he can do what he wants. There may be a wide variety of different actions by different actors, but the result is order rather than chaos. You may be so accustomed to it that this miracle is not surprising, but I insist that it is miraculous nonetheless.

In Chapter 1, highway driving was offered as an example of the problematic aspects of social life. One can never be absolutely sure that the guy in the other car will stay in his lane. Still, isn't it nice that he does stay in his lane most of the time? Traffic patterns are a very simple sort of social order. Whether everyone drives on his own right, as in the United States and continental Europe, or on his left, as in England, is purely arbitrary. For order to prevail and for driving to be possible, *some* regular rules must be observed by most of the participants most of the time.

Breakdowns of this order may, as in the case of highway driving, be fatal to the participating individuals. Sometimes they will be merely embarrassing or confusing. Have you ever been introduced to a person and offered your hand for a handshake, only to find that the other person didn't put his hand out? What do you do? There you are with your hand hanging out. You can mumble and let it fall back down to your side, feeling the flush of embarrassment. You can turn the gesture into a feeble wave or a spastic adjustment of your clothing. In any case, the social system has momentarily broken down and for you the moment is ruined. Handshaking seems a very simple and routine action. Even so, it involves the combined acts of two people and is extremely sensitive to misbehavior on the part of either actor. For the event to go smoothly, each party must extend the right hand, and then there must be a mutual squeezing with nearly equal pressure and a modest pumping motion. This must be timed to coordinate the actions of the two.

Both highway driving and handshaking are simple social orders involving relatively few actors and relatively few behavioral rules. In both cases the actions hang together and order results because the actors all follow the same rules. A properly executed handshake requires identical acts from both actors. Many other examples of social order depend on different actions from the different actors, on varying rules for the various participants. Such action systems may involve actors in very complicated relationships.

Isn't it remarkable that a shoe store has never tried to sell you two different shoes for the same foot or a pair that does not match? Every box on the shelf, even the ones they don't show you, contains two shoes: one right, one left, same size, same style. This is not the result of a conspiracy of hundreds of people who are dedicated to this specific outcome, yet hundreds of people's actions have contributed to this result. Most of them are no more consciously concerned with this problem than you are. They do whatever they do for a variety of reasons and with a variety of results, but the final outcome is as if they had conspired. Each box contains two shoes: one right, one left, same size, same style.

If you don't want a pair of shoes right now, how about sampling some other result of the organizational miracle? Get a meal in a restaurant. Turn on the TV set. Tell a juicy bit of gossip to a friend and wait to hear it again from someone else. Travel by commercial airliner. Get married or divorced, as applicable. Go to a party. Any of these actions will be connected with hundreds of other actions of hundreds of other people. Some of these acts will have taken place months or years before your moment; some will occur at the same time; some will follow. They will involve persons widely scattered in space, strangers to one another and to you. Still, they all fit together and combine to make your moment something it could not otherwise have been, yet something that is pretty much what you expected it to be. And all of these combinations of actions in turn fit together in the larger society of which they and many more are a part.

I have not gone through all of this simply to leave you gaping in wonder at the fact that human social behavior results in an orderly system. Rather, I did want you to see that it is wondrous, so that we could go about discovering how this remarkable thing happens. In this sense, my earlier reference to this condition as "miraculous" was inaccurate. Miracles are more properly those happenings that cannot be understood. The flowering of social order from a jumble of human happenings can be understood and explained through reference to the nature of social behavior.

Human actions are based in part on what the actors know and believe. If actions are to be understood, knowledge must first be understood. A brief list of bits of knowledge follows:

1. One plus one equals two.
2. Grass is green.
3. Negroes have a natural sense of rhythm.
4. Three times zero equals three.
5. A Sazarac is made with rye, Pernod, and Peychaud's Bitters.
6. The American Broadcasting Company prohibits the picturing of toilets on its television shows before 8:30 P.M.
7. Red China has forty-seven operational nuclear devices.
8. At the time you read this, you have _____ cents change in your (purse, pocket). [Fill in the blank and cross out the appropriate word to make this statement true.]

These statements all represent knowledge, but differ among themselves in several respects.

They differ in how widely they are known. Within the United States and discounting any effect of their appearing in this book, they are listed approximately in descending order. Virtually everyone knows Statement 1, almost as many know 2. Relatively fewer know Statements 3 and 4; fewest know 8, which is known only to you.

These statements also differ in their truth value. By the criteria of science and scholarship, Statements 1, 2, 5, 6, and 8 are conditionally true. The others are conditionally false. The concept of knowledge does not require truth, only acceptance. Each individual's knowledge, patently, consists only of things that he believes to be true. In the context of his beliefs, it makes little difference that by other standards some of his beliefs may be correct, some incorrect. Note also that truth and falsity are not perfectly correlated with the number of believers. More people, in ignorance, "know" that three times zero equals three, than "know," in truth, ABC's toilet policy.

Truth values have still another dimension. Statements 1 and 2 were both labeled conditionally true, but the nature of the conditions in the two are different. "One plus one equals two" is true as long as we are dealing with the standard English language and the standard arithmetic. This is a matter of definition. No new data could change the truth of this statement. "Grass is green," on the other hand, makes a substantive assertion about the real world. It is therefore subject to scientific disproof or to evidence that strengthens the basis for acceptance. It may be hedged with modifiers for season or genetic strain. Statements 1, 4, and 5 are definitional (5 only partly so); the remainder are substantive. Again, notice that this dimension is not perfectly related to either true-false or believed-not believed.

One final feature in which these bits of knowledge vary is their social significance. Knowledge is related to behavior; behaviors mesh to form the social system. Some bits of knowledge are more likely to influence behavior than others; some behaviors have more impact on social order. On these grounds, Statements 4, 7, and 8 rate very low. Variation in this respect is to some extent independent of all the others. Statement 3, although false, is believed and acted upon by far more people than 5, which is true. The behaviors implied by 3 have more direct social consequences. Truth or falsity do not predict social significance. Some substantive knowledge has high social impact, some low. The same can be said for definitional knowledge. Finally, the spread of the knowledge is not a sure indicator of social significance.

Try telling some of your friends "I have _____ cents in change with me." Tell an equal number that China has forty-seven operational nuclear devices. The former will elicit minimal significant social response; the latter may encourage much more. Some people whom you inform may write their Congressman, change their voting behavior, or build a bomb shelter. This could lead to repercussions through a considerable range of the social system. Actually, you probably shouldn't tell your friends that China has forty-seven operational nuclear devices, because, you will remember, I labeled that statement conditionally false. I picked the figure out of thin air. It *could* be correct, but I doubt it. I have no evidence for preferring forty-seven to forty-six or forty-eight or even four or four hundred. As this is a substantive statement, it is always subject to the evidence, and I have none. Somewhere, there is a small collection of people who have the best evidence available to any Americans. They probably include a few intelligence officers and the members of the National Security Council. Their knowledge, "China has _____ operational nuclear devices," may or may not be correct. Their statement is likely to be closer to true than ours, but there is no guarantee. Their knowledge is a tightly held secret, known at most to a few dozen. Ours, on the other hand, is known to the entire readership of this book, plus anybody you lie to. Theirs has greater social significance. They use it to decide national defense policy and from this springs behaviors influencing tax rates, employment in major industries, size and composition of military forces, and a wide range of other social operations.

This bit of knowledge induces behaviors that are bonded to other behaviors. This bit of knowledge is bonded to many other bits of knowledge. The system of related behavior is closely paralleled by the system of related bits of knowledge. The behavior system, we have already noted, is called society. The corresponding knowledge system we will call culture.

If we look at human behavior by itself, we see a number of people acting individually and are at a loss to explain why the result is not chaos. We can look at knowledge by itself with the same result. When the two are considered together, we can notice how they act on each other to produce order. Knowledge is derived from experience, experience flavored most highly by social behavior. Behavior that happens to be orderly (predictable, smooth, producing desired results) is, on a variety of psychological grounds, more likely to be repeated. The development of the salient knowledge encourages more behaviors that are compatible with it. Culture and society constantly influence each other and adjust their contents so that each becomes more systematized.

Society and culture can each be seen as an infinitely large jigsaw puzzle. Each person carries around with him a collection of pieces. Some of his pieces will resemble pieces carried by other people; some will be relatively unique. When the analogy is to culture, the pieces represent knowledge. You are carrying a "one plus one equals two" piece, just like almost everyone else in our society. You are carrying an "I have _____ cents" piece that is virtually unique. You are carrying thousands of other pieces. Your collection is not culture. The total collection of everyone's pieces is not culture. Culture is the name of the phenomenon in which everyone throws his pile of pieces on a big table and the puzzle falls into place.

Society puzzle parts are behaviors. When you interact with any individual, you extend one or more pieces, he does the same, and the pieces tend to fit together. If they do not fit neatly, you draw those back and offer others. Meanwhile, you may go to work, filing the edges of the ones that fit poorly. Small social interactions fit together because the actors "work" the puzzle. Still, for society as a whole, there are no supervisors who actively solve the puzzle. Society as a whole fits together on the same sort of grand table as did culture.

If we notice that behavior pieces and knowledge pieces correspond, we can explain the seemingly magical fitting. As behavior pieces are reshaped in interaction to make small social systems orderly, knowledge pieces are also reshaped. These reworked bits of knowledge will tend to mesh with each other, even beyond the confines of the interactions where their original interlocking grew. Culture forms a system because of interaction. When behaviors are derived from systematic knowledge, they tend to form an orderly pattern. Society, including noninteracting relationships, forms a system because of culture.

The two puzzles solve themselves because they do correspond. Everyone comes by and throws his pieces on the tables. When a part does not fit on one table, it and its corresponding part on the other table are thrown off. The actors pick up the leftovers, break, sort, and throw again. Sooner or later almost everything fits. The fit is never perfect and the process is never-ending. Disorder and change are constant characteristics of social and cultural systems. For the most part, however, an order is achieved, an order that is necessary for the psychological survival of the humans and the systematic survival of the society.

NORMS AND VALUES

Throughout the last section, the emphasis was on knowledge that had special relevance for behavior. The most explicit of these guides are called *norms*. Norms are *normal* in at least three senses. First, they are normal in the arithmetic sense. The behavior which occurs most frequently, for a given class of persons in a given kind of situation, is the average or normal behavior. An outside observer, knowing nothing about the individuals or their society or culture, could go around and make observations of behavior. When he had finished counting his observations, he would be able to describe the behavior in terms of the norms. This would be a much more economical description than if he had to list each behavior as a separate entry. Part of what we meant by social order is revealed in the fact that such economy of description is possible.

Second, norms describe the social expectations of others in the situation. The average expectation about how an individual will behave in a given situation defines the norm for that situation. Those who have these expectations are inside observers. They may be potentially affected by the behavior and have some cognizance of the actor and the situation. Suppose the outside observer, the stranger, wished to identify norms in this sense? The best way would be to look at the behavior of the others rather than at that of the actor. He would look for startled reactions. Most of the people on the social scene have the same expectations concerning how someone is going to behave. If he does not behave in that fashion, they will be surprised. Behavior that is greeted routinely will be behavior that was in conformity with the norm.

Third, norms are the knowledge-behavior combination with which the individual actor faces the situation. A norm is how an individual thinks he ought to act. The outside observer could only find this out by questioning the actor. "If you were in this particular situation, what do you think you should do?" This may or may not be the same as what he would like to do. The concern here is with *oughts*, with constraints on behavior rather than motives.

A term with three definitions might seem a bit much, but, happily, all three resolve into one and designate the same phenomenon. We have already pointed out the strong connection between behavior and knowledge. Nothing could be more natural than that many individuals will behave in the way they think they should behave. The personal aspect of norm definition tends to realize the statistical.

Knowledge is learned. An actor acts in a way that he considers appropriate. If others consider this behavior incorrect, they will be surprised. Due to this surprise, they may act awkwardly and inappropriately in the situation. This breakdown of the situation will be painful to all of the participants and reduce the chances that any of the participants will realize desired goals from the interaction. These penalties attach to the original actor as well as to the others. They will discourage repetition of the behavior and encourage redefinition of the personal norm from which it derived. The others—insulted, shocked, frustrated—may exact further penalties from the actor. They may punish him for failing to match their expectations. Similarly, the achievement of intended goals and perhaps other rewards will attend the offering of appropriate behavior, as the others severally define it. Penalties for inappropriate definition and rewards for proper definition provide a solid learning situation for the individual actor. Enough of these experiences will tend to make his conceptions of norms match the general normative anticipations of most other actors. *Sanctions*, as rewards and punishments relating to normative behavior are called, push the personal aspect of norm definition toward the social.

Sanctions may also be effective in controlling behavior even in the absence of change in personal norms. The individual, even when he thinks he should do one thing, is likely to avoid that behavior if he knows he will be punished for it. He may choose to act instead in a fashion that will be rewarded, even if he thinks it is wrong. Since sanctions are associated with the social definition of appropriateness, the social impact of norm definition has an independent influence on the statistical.

Interaction is a two-way street. While the others are influencing the actor, he may be influencing them as well. Should he persist in his unexpected behavior, they, unless they are slow learners, will no longer find it unexpected. The general expectation may change. The social aspect of norm definition may be affected by the personal.

If most of the actors in a situation behave in the same way, this sort of influence on social expectations is even more likely. It may be easy enough for the general population to define one person as a deviant, but if everyone in his position acts the same, the general conception of what is deviant is more likely to shift. The typical behavior tends to become the expected behavior; the statistical aspect of norm definition modifies the social.

Even stronger pressures fall on the individual actor when he sees that, for others like him, everyone is out of step except him. One way the actor learns the norm is by observing the normal. The statistical aspect of norm definition helps develop the personal.

When each aspect influences, and is influenced by, all the others, it is no wonder that they come to be virtually identical. When the mysterious stranger gets home and begins to analyze his data, he will surely notice that all three observational techniques discovered the same norms. The term must include all three meanings and point out their deep mutual involvement, which may border on conjunction.

There must be norms to define all the richly varied behaviors that combine to make up human society, otherwise the behaviors would not be defined at all. It follows that normative prescriptions will be a richly varied lot. Some variations and examples chosen from the extremes in American society follow.

Norms may be *universal* or *special*. They may be constraining on all the members of a society or may apply to only a few persons.

Universal Clothing will be worn on all public occasions.
Special Members of the Golden Dragon Gang will refer to boys who participate in the City Physical Fitness program as "Puke-Finks."

Norms may be *general* or *situational*. They may govern all of social life or only a special, even singular, situation.

General Children should respect adults.
Situational Nobody in the Jones family may make a noise while Mr. Jones is
watching the football game.

Norms may be *abstract* or *concrete*. Some offer specific and precise guides to action. Others are cast in more general terms and must be interpreted and applied by the actor.

Abstract A Scout is courteous, friendly, helpful, loyal, clean.
Concrete Applicants must complete three copies, hand printed in ink. All copies
must be identical. The first (white) copy will be forwarded to the vice-
president. The second (blue) copy will be turned in to the personnel
office. Both submissions must be completed within twenty-four hours of
receipt of this notice. The applicant will retain the third (pink) copy for
his own records and is advised to bring it with him if he should be
invited for a personal interview.

Norms may be *folkways* or *mores*. They may be regarded as merely customary, as matters of only small importance. Violators will be regarded as merely odd and will be subjected to only modest sanctions. Alternately, the norm may be considered to touch on the things most precious to the society. Upholding the norm may be a matter of grave import. Violators being sinful, even inhuman, may be subject to severe punishment.

Folkways Don't stare in public.
Mores Don't steal.

Norms may be *informal* or *formal*. Informal norms stem from tradition and depend on consensus and informal sanctioning. Formal, law or lawlike norms are apt to be written, to be very specifically detailed, and to have fixed and automatic sanctions for conformity or deviance.

Informal People here don't talk like that.

Formal Prisoners who leave pop bottles anywhere except in the container for empties get two days solitary confinement.

These are certainly not the only varieties of norms, but do present some of the important kinds of variation. If he is to be a normal social being, the individual must wade through this jungle and learn a bewildering large number of them.

He must also learn which ones are appropriate for him to follow, and when. In a sense, there is a set of norms for selecting norms. Further, the individual who has decided on a particular norm as the appropriate guide to action in his current situation must still be motivated to follow the norm—to act it out. The presence of sanctions alone will not suffice. A society could not operate successfully if all the people had to be seduced or coerced all the time. Actors must want to do the right thing.

This line of argument leads to people's conceptions of ultimate purposes, of goodness and truth, of ultimate reality and meaning. It moves into the area of religion, or, more broadly, of *values*. Values underlie norms and provide motivation for following norms and grounds for choosing among them. Following these hints leads to a simple but effective definition of values. Values are the ultimate "whys" of a society. Take any action of any individual. Ask him why he did that. If he answers that he expects his action to result in some desired goal, ask why he desires that goal. Continue the process until you get no more answers, until you have stumped the informant. When he can no longer provide reasons underlying the reasons, when he is driven to "just because," "its only natural," or "that's good," the last sensible preceding answer closely approximated one of his values.

This is purely an individual value. To discover societal values would require repeating the process for a wide variety of behaviors and a large number of persons, then looking for the common factors or recurrent themes. Alternately, because values are so intimately related to norms, values can be imputed from norms and behaviors. Still, because values, like knowledge, abound in marked variability and distribution through the population, these processes will not be easy. In deciding which knowledge should be considered part of culture, we used the test of social significance. Values can be more clearly understood with a similar test. We must be able to distinguish between values and other bits of belief that seem to resemble values.

A statement such as "I like beer" is not evaluative in form. It simply reports (we hope accurately) an individual's statement of his taste. The preference is found in the relationship between the individual and the object, or even in the mind of the individual. Contrast this with the statement "Beer is good." Here the goodness is imputed to the beer itself. It is phrased as an absolute, apart from any psychological or physiological considerations on the part of the person who makes the statement. Value is ascribed to the object. This is a value-type statement. A quick check will find a number of other persons subscribing to this statement and many others denying it. This particular example would appear to be a personal value, not a social one. Another statement in the same form, "Sobriety is good," offers better prospects. The society will not approach unanimity, but a nice majority will subscribe to this one.

Values, however, must be related to norms. They must provide motivation, grounds for choice, and buttressing strength. A norm following from this value statement would constrain people toward abstention or moderate drinking behavior. Checking up, we will find that most people most of the time do act in such a way as to remain sober. Still, not everyone, not all the time. Behavior tends to match values, but not perfectly. Some violations are accidents of people who intend to follow the norm but fail. There will be a few holdouts who refuse to accept the norm or its application to them. They will insist that they like to get drunk, that it is proper for them to get drunk. The norm reaches closer to the value than did the behavior, but not all the way.

Individuals will have feelings toward the behaviors. Most people will be repelled or scandalized by drunkenness. Some will be amused; some will be overjoyed. This region does not offer any more unanimity than some of the others explored.

Individuals will have feelings toward the norm—usually feelings of approval, respect, awe—which tend to instill respect for the rule and conformity with it. Still, the hold-outs will have contempt or hostility for the rule. Neither alcoholics nor bartenders will evidence universal support.

Unanimity of opinion arises in the realm of values. Everyone will approve of everyone else's approval of the norm. Even the confirmed alcoholic will not wish drunkenness on everyone. If nobody was sober, who would make the beer? Norms about feelings about norms are the core of values. "Sobriety is good" is a value statement. The value sense is, "It is good that people think sobriety is good." This sort of value can provide support for, and motivate behavior conforming with, norms such as "Never have more than two martinis before dinner." It can also lead to value judgments with direct implications for behavior, such as "Drunkenness is bad, but drug addiction is worse."

The linking of values to norms implies that values have some of the variability that norms have. Values may be shared by all the people in a society or by a particular segment, may apply to all situations or only a few, may be extremely important or relatively unimportant.

The most universal and important values of a society, the ultimate values, are an important factor in guaranteeing that the actions of the society's members will be concerted. They also provide a social-psychological basis for a feeling of oneness, for identification with the other members, and for mutual trust and involvement. Naturally, they support the behaviors and norms that are universal and general.

When norms are special or situational, when mothers, millionaires, migrants, millers, morticians, Motowners, militarists, and mathematicians must all act differently from each other, their norms must be supported by variant values. These will not replace the ultimate values, but will supplement them. Each occupation, each social class, each significant social category or group will possess some special variant values.

Individuals will have purely individual variations in beliefs, and these may often be phrased in the value form. Earlier, these were labeled individual values. They are important in accounting for individual, socially insignificant or idiosyncratic, behavior. Still, if they are purely individual in character, they lack normative ties and cannot be true values. If these purely individual tendencies were to become the prime motivating force behind the behavior of individuals, social systems would not operate; chaos would result. As it is, individuals are restrained by norms and values that are integrated in culture and tested in interaction. Order rather than chaos results. It is a shifting, changing, stressful order, but order nonetheless.

CHANGE: REVOLUTIONARY AND OTHERWISE

It might seem that change and order are contradictory, but this is far from the truth. A human being is a more orderly biological collection than a pile of protozoa containing the same number of cells. The human developed from the protozoan through the process called evolution. Evolution may well be described as a kind of change that tests for order and passes the most organized entities on to the future for more changes and more of the same testing. The fashion in which normative (behavior) and cultural (knowledge) systems influence each other with the net effect of greater organization for both can then be seen as a special case of evolution. The biological changes described in Chapter 2 and the societal ones in Chapter 3 may be considered two examples of the same process. The process is a series of changes—alterations, innovations, deletions—which produces greater order with each succeeding development.

There are kinds of change that maintain order without increasing it; other kinds, surely, imply disorder. The numerous complications here make it advisable to start with a very simple case in an attempt to develop some categories of analysis. I will use the family as a sample system in connection with a time-frame description. It will be as if we entered a house at designated intervals and took pictures of whatever we found there.

One very simple sort of change occurs when the same kinds of changes are repeated over and over again. The net effect is as if there had been no change.

CYCLIC CHANGE IN A FAMILY

FAMILY ROLE	TIME		
	Now	10 hours later	24 hours later
Father	Harry	—	Harry
Mother	Mary	Mary	Mary
Child	Larry	Larry	Larry

The chart shows regular periods of presence and absence for Harry, probably implying that he works. The family operation proceeds alternately with and without him. In this particular case, the family would undergo major change (they would all starve to death) if it were not for the minor and repetitive changes implicit in the work cycle. Other cycles, such as those we might find with a fifty-year frame on men's hair styles, do not have even this sort of impact. In either case, cyclical change within the system means no change of the system. Other examples would include: the circulation of blood in the body, the movement of pistons up and down with the cylinders of a running engine, and liberal and conservative swings of a government.

Another kind of change invariably contributes to the maintenance of the system. If the piston rings on an engine wear out, they may be replaced. The engine then continues to operate as before only because the rings have been changed.

MAINTENANCE CHANGE IN A FAMILY

FAMILY ROLE	TIME		
	Now	2 years later	10 years later
Father	Harry	Harry	Harry
Mother	Mary	Terry	Terry
Child	Larry	Larry & Gary	Gary

When Mary dies, the family system is less changed by introducing a new wife-mother, Terry, than it would have been by trying to operate without her. Replacement may even anticipate the need, as when a second child, Gary, is added before the first, Larry, grows up and goes away. Even more radical forms of maintenance change may maintain the system as a type at the cost of some specific examples of the type, or maintain the larger system of which the subject system is a part, as the following example illustrates.

MAINTENANCE CHANGE IN THE FAMILY STRUCTURE

FAMILY ROLE	TIME		
	Now	30 years later	50 years later
Father	Harry	Larry	Barry
Mother	Mary	Sherry	Jerrie
Child	Larry	Barry (& Harry)	Perry

In this case, the family of Harry is long gone by the end of the time span. The starting family is not preserved. Individuals who fill one slot at one time shift to a different slot for the next. Poor Harry, in his senility, is relegated to a child's position in the family of his son. These changes will be hard on the participants; at times the burdens of the adjustments will make for considerable disorder within any one of the series of families. Still, the family system survives longer than human life will allow one particular family to survive, and because the family continues to furnish new members and to train them, the society survives.

Change that is less static than this shows time frames which resemble each other less.

TREND CHANGE IN A FAMILY

FAMILY ROLE	TIME		
	Now	2 years later	4 years later
Father	Harry	Harry	Harry
Mother	Mary	Mary	Mary
Child	Larry	Larry & Gary	Larry, Gary, & Kerry

In this form, there is no repetitive pattern, but still we are able to anticipate what the next frame might look like. The parts on a running engine consistently exhibit more wear. It may be said that a society is becoming more authoritarian each generation. Exotic atomic isotopes deteriorate at a constant rate. There is a predictable trend to this kind of change. Evolution is a type of trend in which the change is consistently toward greater order. Other trends might be toward greater disorder, or might be totally irrelevant to order. An evolving family would be one in which the relationships between Harry, Mary, and Larry were becoming more regularized and clearly defined with the passage of time. A growing family would be one in which the number of participants consistently and predictably increased. Both would be subject to trend changes. In effect, the notion of trends introduces another dimension of order: Order through time. Trend changes are those in which the relationship between the various *times* is orderly.

Cyclic and maintaining changes are moderately orderly and finally result in little real change. Trend change is very orderly and implies significant change; the system becomes increasingly different from the original through time. Some change is significant and disorderly, involving a major and unpredictable break from the past.

SCHISMATIC CHANGE IN A FAMILY

FAMILY ROLE	TIME		
	Now	1 year later	2 years later
Father	Harry	Harry	Harry
Mother	Mary	Mary	Fairy
Child	Larry	Larry	Larry

That Harry should throw out the faithful Mary and replace her with a boy friend may not surprise those who really know Harry, but it is relatively rare for a homosexual to take over as mother of a child as well. In any case, all we have to work from is the previous time frames; we must see this development as a startling break with the past. I do not mean to imply that schismatic change necessarily involves socially disapproved or disruptive developments. Just as schismatic a change would be noted were a confirmed homosexual to suddenly marry and father a child. If a society with a long history of conflict and internal dissension should suddenly settle down to domestic tranquility, the change would be schismatic. The explosion of a previously smoothly running engine would be similarly classified, as would the appearance and disappearance of molecules in one small part of a large gas-filled space.

Schismatic societal changes, particularly those involving violence, are often labeled revolutions. I suspect that this sort of label serves more to confuse than clarify the situation. Consider the following two societies.

CHANGE IN TWO SOCIETIES: POLITICS

SOCIETY	TIME				
	20 years ago	15 years ago	10 years ago	5 years ago	Now
Zoomia	Totalitarian	Repressive elitist	Permissive elitist	Partial liberalism	Libertarian
Moozia	Totalitarian	Totalitarian	Chaotic revolution	Libertarian	Libertarian

On the face, Zoomia has experienced trend change and Moozia schismatic. Yet both societies started in the same place and ended up in the same place. If we had only the first and last time frames for each case we would have classed them identically as schismatic change. The provision of additional information permits us to recognize the trend in Zoomia. Instead of additional frames, we might have been able to see the trend in Zoomia with more detailed information concerning the first time period. If we saw, for instance, a young intellectual elite with liberal ideas, we might have been able to predict the occurrence and direction of change. The same sort of argument applies with equal force to Moozia. Much schismatic change is not truly a break with the past, but only an apparent break with the past. If the conditions of the past are fully understood, the future will be seen to follow from it—as trend, cycle, or what have you.

To be sure, there are radical breaks with the past, but the scope and frequency of these is seriously overrated. Marxian theory suggests that every system carries the seeds of its own destruction. While this may not be perfectly true, it is surely true that every system carries the seeds of its own future: perpetuation, alteration, destruction, or whatever else that future may be. The seed may be small and difficult to discern, but that gives us no excuse for writing off the attempt at understanding. A very noncommunist British anthropologist agreed that every society's present leads to its future, but warned of the difficulties in making interpretation.[1] He likened society to an animal and suggested that societies could grow, develop, age, and die. However, he held that societies are unlike animals in one respect: no sick pig ever recovers as a hippopotamus, whereas a society can become ill in one form and recover by becoming an entirely new society. This sort of change is the kind we have been labeling schismatic and happens regularly for societies. Radcliffe-Brown insisted that if we knew enough about the pig and the kind of sickness it had, we could see an orderly trend in its becoming a well hippo. What appears to be schism is usually an uncomprehended trend.

Some events may occur without causes, or with such an obscure and complex set of causes that their explanation must be written off. Such occurrences are called random. Random change plays a significant part in social life. But sincere analysts must never relegate a change to this category until exhaustive attempt has been made to uncover trends, cycles, and other causal interpretations. Most change will be found to be orderly, and consequently understandable and predictable.

Whether the change itself is orderly has little to do with whether the changing system is orderly. The orderliness of change is ascertained by finding out how closely Time 1 is related to Time 2, and so on. The orderliness of the system is determined by measuring the neatness of relationship among the several social units of one

[1] Alfred Reginald Radcliffe-Brown, A Natural Science of Society (New York: Free Press, 1957).

society at one time. For Zoomia and Moozia, one kind of question is whether the progression from totalitarianism to libertarianism was an orderly one. The last few paragraphs have expressed a preference for the affirmative. Another question entirely is how orderly were the societies at any one point in time or during the total period.

Moozia ten years ago, in the throes of chaotic revolution, was probably a very disorderly society. Conflicts of values, contradictory norms that failed to bind the actors, unorganized behavior, disjunctive cultural elements, and jumbled interaction situations are likely to have been the mark of the period. The old order was overthrown; the new was not yet clearly established. Revolutions need not be of this sort. Some revolutions are quite orderly and stylized struggles between old and new factions of the society, with each faction retaining an organizational integrity and with relations between the warring factions clearly developed. Violence and similar phenomena are just as capable of organization as are any other human relations. Revolutions may be orderly, but the time frame in question for Moozia describes a chaotic revolution.

Any social change of the system implies some disorder within the system. A totalitarian society differs from a libertarian society in norms, values, organizational arrangements, and culture. If the one is to become the other, these societal components must change. They do not change all at once and in a piece, but with a change in one area having repercussions for other areas, with jerks and starts and constant readjustments. As the mutual corrections of culture and society operate, the two will be out of phase with each other—not totally, for if this were the case there would be no society—but partially and in a thousand little ways. To whatever extent the two are unhinged from each other, neither is tightly organized within itself. Therefore, social change implies disorder. If Moozia and Zoomia started the same and ended up the same, each encountered the same amount of disorder on the journey.

While Moozians concentrated the entire disorder in one upheaval ten years ago, Zoomia endured small quantums of disorder all through the twenty-year history. A totalitarian society does not become a repressive elitist society without some strains: conflicts of values, contradictory norms that failed to bind all the actors, unorganized behavior, disjunctive cultural elements, and jumbled interaction situations. Time frames presenting conditions of order in the two societies for the time period in question might look like this:

CHANGE IN TWO SOCIETIES: ORDER

SOCIETY	TIME				
	20 years ago	15 years ago	10 years ago	5 years ago	Now
Zoomia	Modest disorder	Modest disorder	Modest disorder	Modest disorder	Little disorder
Moozia	Little disorder	Little disorder	Little order	Little disorder	Little disorder

The strains in reaching from one stage to the next are proportional to the difference between the two stages. No society is ever totally disordered; if it were it would be a collection of human beings but not a society. No society is ever totally ordered; if it were it would have to be manned by something other than human beings.

Change, revolution, and order will come up again in Chapters 5, 7, and 11. As a matter of fact, the contents of this chapter will be relevant to much of the rest of the book, for this chapter has been filled with the basic stuff of social organization. The remaining three chapters in this section deal with specific subsystems of society that are also basic in cementing the whole together. Each of these three chapters focuses on one particular kind of mechanism of order. Because their content is a little more specific, they are probably easier than this chapter has been, and more fun.

FURTHER READING

Aron, Raymond, *Progress and Disillusion: The Dialectics of Modern Society*. New York: Praeger, 1968.*

Berger, Peter, *The Sacred Canopy*. Garden City, N.Y.: Doubleday, 1967. Available in paperback.

Caplow, Theodore, *Two Against One*. Englewood Cliffs, N.J.: Prentice-Hall, 1968. Available in paperback.

Coser, Lewis, *Continuities in the Study of Social Conflict*. New York: Free Press, 1967.*

Eisenstadt, Shmuel N., *Modernization: Protest and Change*. Englewood Cliffs, N.J.: Prentice-Hall, 1966.* Available in paperback.

Malinowski, Bronislaw, *Crime and Custom in Savage Society*. Paterson, N.J.: Littlefield, 1959. Paperback.

Mauss, Marcel, *The Gift: Forms and Functions of Exchange in Archaic Societies*. New York: Norton, 1967. Paperback.

Moore, Wilbert, *Order and Change*. New York: Wiley, 1967.

Seeley, John R., et al., *Crestwood Heights: A Study of the Culture of Suburban Life*. New York: Wiley, 1963. Science Editions paperback.

Shibutani, Tamotsu, *Improvised News: A Sociological Study of Rumor*. Indianapolis: Bobbs-Merrill, 1966. Available in paperback.

*Difficult, specialized, or technical.

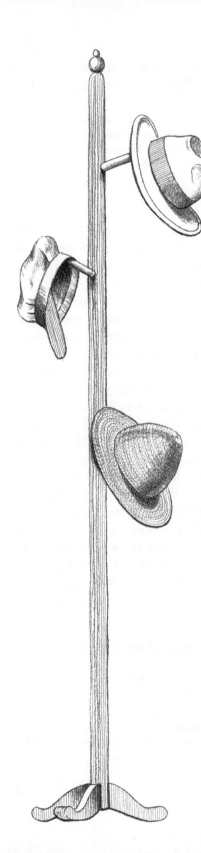

5 INEQUALITY

If we place any faith in the Declaration of Independence, we know that all men are created equal. They may be created equal, but something apparently happens to this equality as men begin to take up various roles in society. Some actors begin to acquire certain advantages over others, an inequality arises. A survey of the causes and effects of inequality is the purpose of this chapter.

A research team from the

National Opinion Research Center selected a representative sample of United States citizens and asked them the following question:

I am going to read to you a list of names of occupations. Judge each occupation as having *excellent, good, average, somewhat below average,* or *poor* standing [a "don't know" option was also offered]. For each job mentioned, please pick out the statement that best gives *your own personal opinion* of the *general standing* that such a job has.

In executing this survey it became fairly clear that there was something "out there" that people felt they were able to rate. The number of potential respondents who refused to participate in the study because they couldn't understand what was being asked, or because all occupations were the same or so different that they couldn't be compared was infinitesimal. Some people refuse to participate in studies generally because they are too busy or do not want others prying into their affairs. Some refused to rate certain occupations saying that they were unfamiliar with the occupation. Both of these are quite different refusals from the ones given by those who did not understand the survey or who thought all jobs were equal.

The words "general standing" in the question do not give a clue concerning the basis for judgment. There are many qualities, possessions, and attributes, in terms of which it could be said that some people have excellent, poor, or intermediate standing. Some of these, such as amount of hair or capacity for love, would appear to be unrelated to occupation. Many other characteristics—income, education, table manners, place and type of residence, working hours, habits of dress, family relationship patterns, degree of on-the-job supervision, opportunity for public service—are related to one's employment. Probably no one of these is the standard criterion used by all the people responding to the survey, yet somehow they were able to make positive judgments. The results of this survey are summarized in the table that follows.

HOW PEOPLE RATE OCCUPATIONS*

OPINIONS OF THOSE RESPONDING,
IN PERCENTS

OCCUPATION	Excellent	Good	Average	Below average	Poor	Don't know	NORC SCORE	RANK
U.S. Supreme Court Justice	77	18	4	1	1	1	94	1.0
Physician	71	25	4	—	—	1	93	2.0
Nuclear physicist	70	23	5	1	1	10	92	3.5

OCCUPATION	Excel-lent	Good	Aver-age	Below aver-age	Poor	Don't know	NORC SCORE	RANK
Scientist	68	27	5	—	—	2	92	3.5
Government scientist	64	30	5	—	1	2	91	5.5
State governor	64	30	5	—	1	1	91	5.5
Cabinet member in the Federal government	61	32	6	1	1	2	90	8.0
College professor	59	35	5	—	—	1	90	8.0
U.S. Representative in Congress	58	33	6	2	—	2	90	8.0
Chemist	54	38	8	—	—	3	89	11.0
Lawyer	53	38	8	—	—	—	89	11.0
Diplomat in the U.S. Foreign Service	57	34	7	1	1	3	89	11.0
Dentist	47	47	6	—	—	—	88	14.0
Architect	47	45	6	—	—	2	88	14.0
County judge	50	40	8	1	—	1	88	14.0
Psychologist	49	41	8	1	—	6	87	17.5
Minister	53	33	13	1	1	1	87	17.5
Member of the board of directors of a large corporation	42	51	6	1	—	1	87	17.5
Mayor of a large city	46	44	9	1	1	—	87	17.5
Priest	52	33	12	2	1	6	86	21.5
Head of a department in a state government	44	48	6	1	1	1	86	21.5
Civil engineer	40	52	8	—	—	2	86	21.5
Airline pilot	41	48	11	1	—	1	86	21.5
Banker	39	51	10	1	—	—	85	24.5
Biologist	38	50	11	—	—	6	85	24.5
Sociologist	35	48	15	1	1	10	83	26.0
Instructor in public schools	30	53	16	1	—	—	82	27.5
Captain in the regular army	28	55	16	2	—	1	82	27.5
Accountant for a large business	27	55	17	1	—	—	81	29.5
Public school teacher	31	46	22	1	—	—	81	29.5
Owner of a factory that employs about 100 people	28	49	19	2	1	1	80	31.5
Building contractor	22	56	20	1	—	—	80	31.5
Artist who paints pictures that are exhibited in galleries	28	45	20	5	2	4	78	34.5
Musician in a symphony orchestra	25	45	25	3	1	3	78	34.5
Author of novels	26	46	22	4	2	5	78	34.5
Economist	20	53	24	2	1	12	78	34.5
Official of an international labor union	21	53	18	5	3	5	77	37.0
Railroad engineer	19	47	30	3	1	1	76	39.0
Electrician	18	45	34	2	—	—	76	39.0
County agricultural agent	13	54	30	2	1	4	76	39.0
Owner-operator of a printing shop	13	51	34	2	—	2	75	41.5

OCCUPATION	Excellent	Good	Average	Below average	Poor	Don't know	NORC SCORE	RANK
Trained machinist	15	50	32	4	—	—	75	41.5
Farm owner and operator	16	45	33	5	—	1	74	44.0
Undertaker	16	46	33	3	2	3	74	44.0
Welfare worker for a city government	17	44	32	5	2	2	74	44.0
Newspaper columnist	10	49	38	3	1	1	73	46.0
Policeman	16	38	37	6	2	—	72	47.0
Reporter on a daily newspaper	7	45	44	3	1	1	71	48.0
Radio announcer	9	42	44	5	1	1	70	49.5
Bookkeeper	9	40	45	5	1	—	70	49.5
Tenant farmer—one who owns livestock and machinery and manages the farm	11	37	42	8	3	1	69	51.5
Insurance agent	6	40	47	5	2	—	69	51.5
Carpenter	7	36	49	8	1	—	68	53.0
Manager of a small store in a city	3	40	48	7	2	—	67	54.5
A local official of a labor union	8	36	42	9	5	4	67	54.5
Mail carrier	7	29	53	10	1	—	66	57.0
Railroad conductor	6	33	48	10	3	—	66	57.0
Traveling salesman for a wholesale concern	4	33	54	7	3	2	66	57.0
Plumber	6	29	54	9	2	—	65	59.0
Automobile repairman	5	25	56	12	2	—	64	60.0
Playground director	6	29	46	15	4	3	63	62.5
Barber	4	25	56	13	2	1	63	62.5
Machine operator in a factory	6	24	51	15	4	1	63	62.5
Owner-operator of a lunch stand	4	25	57	11	3	1	63	62.5
Corporal in the regular army	6	25	47	15	6	2	62	65.5
Garage mechanic	4	22	56	15	3	—	62	65.5
Truck driver	3	18	54	19	5	—	59	67.0
Fisherman who owns his own boat	3	19	51	19	8	4	58	68.0
Clerk in a store	1	14	56	22	6	—	56	70.0
Milk route man	3	12	55	23	7	1	56	70.0
Streetcar motorman	3	16	46	27	8	2	56	70.0
Lumberjack	2	16	46	29	7	3	55	72.5
Restaurant cook	4	15	44	26	11	—	55	72.5
Singer in a nightclub	3	16	43	24	14	3	54	74.0
Filling station attendant	2	11	41	34	11	—	51	75.0
Dockworker	2	9	43	33	14	3	50	77.5
Railroad section hand	3	10	39	29	18	2	50	77.5
Night watchman	3	10	39	32	17	1	50	77.5
Coal miner	3	13	34	31	19	2	50	77.5
Restaurant waiter	2	8	42	32	16	—	49	80.5
Taxi driver	2	8	39	31	18	1	49	80.5

OCCUPATION	Excel-lent	Good	Aver-age	Below aver-age	Poor	Don't know	NORC SCORE	RANK
Farm hand	3	12	31	32	22	—	48	83.0
Janitor	1	9	35	35	19	1	48	83.0
Bartender	1	7	42	28	21	2	48	83.0
Clothes presser in a laundry	2	7	31	38	22	1	45	85.0
Soda fountain clerk	—	5	30	44	20	1	44	86.0
Share-cropper—one who owns no livestock or equipment and does not manage farm	1	8	26	28	37	2	42	87.0
Garbage collector	2	5	21	32	41	1	39	88.0
Street sweeper	1	4	17	31	46	1	36	89.0
Shoe shiner	—	3	15	30	51	2	34	90.0
AVERAGES	22	31	30	11	7	2	71	

*Adapted from Robert Hodge, Paul Siegel, and Peter Rossi, "Occupational Prestige in the United States: 1925–1963," *American Journal of Sociology,* 70 (1964) 290–92. Dashes within the table indicate less than one half of one percent. NORC scores indicate the average judgment of all (651) respondents as follows: 100=excellent; 80=good; 60=average; 40=below average; 20=poor.

As evidence that no single criterion underlay all the judgments, note that insurance agents (NORC score, 69) by and large have higher incomes than county judges (88). Welfare workers (74) generally have more schooling than army captains (82). Bartenders (48) possess more special skills than store clerks (56). Similar contradictions can be found using any other single standard; yet each one seems somehow related to the general judgment.

The table contains some fascinating data and generates some interesting questions. Why does college professor rate so much higher than economist, when a great many economists are college professors? Why do ministers and corporation board members, who would seem to have so little in common, arrive at identical scores? (But also note that they arrived at identical averages on the basis of rather differently distributed judgments.) Do the occupations of people in your neighborhood represent a narrow or broad range on the scale? How does your occupation or anticipated occupation compare with your father's occupation or past occupation? What was in the mind of 1 percent of the raters when they said that street sweeping had an excellent standing? For that matter, what was in the mind of the 46 percent who gave it a poor rating? What is in your mind as you look through the list, agreeing, disagreeing, or feeling surprise concerning the position of some of these occupations? I suggest that you pause, examine the table carefully, and consider these and other data and questions before you proceed with the text.

There is nothing intrinsic to the occupations themselves that could lead to their ranking; typical or necessary accompanying features of persons engaged in the occupation must be considered. Which has better standing, prince or pauper, cabbage or king? The only sensible answer is another question: "What for and in what way?" No single standard will produce the general ranking; evaluations must be based on a complex mix of features. One could try to imitate the rating process by juggling attributes in different combinations and assigning different weights to each attribute, but to do so is unnecessary, and probably even perverse. First, it would be embarrassing for the sociologist to spend months feeding complex formulas through his computer in an effort to arrive at judgments that every man in the street could do in his head when the survey people asked their question. Second, analysis is easier if the myriad factors are lumped together under some radically smaller set of headings. Third, there is a feed-through feature to the judgments that cannot be built into any judgment program formula except redundantly.

Let us look at the first and third of these roadblocks. The man in the street continually makes judgments of social standing on his own, not just for the survey researcher. He passes judgments in casual conversation: "Smith has come a long way, his father was a night watchman (50) but now he owns the company (80)." He passes judgment in child-rearing: "Son, wouldn't you rather be a respected physician (93) than a dirty old railroad engineer (76)?" He passes judgment in arranging his social conduct and intercourse: "We got invited to the Joneses' (truck driver, 59) party, but I wouldn't be caught dead there; let's invite the Wilsons (bookkeeper, 70) over for a quiet evening instead." The numerical scores are not really there, but the ranking and sorting for equality, superiority, and inferiority is a constant thread in the social fabric. The feed-through comes after the individual has made these judgments often enough that he no longer needs to refer to the associated criteria upon which his judgments may have at one time rested. It comes with the social learning of rankings unaccompanied by justification or explanation based on external criteria. In this manner, "social standing" becomes an independent social reality. In examining the first and third factors we have uncovered a start on the second. One of the major dimensions of social differentiation is judgment of standing, of community respectability, of prestige, of status. NORC, then, did not create but simply discovered these judgments, through an approximation based on occupation. It is neither simplistic nor tautological to say that one of the factors in the standing of an individual in a group is the collective judgment of that group's members concerning his standing. This topic will be pursued more fully in the following section on prestige inequality but must be deferred until the other general features of differentiation have been uncovered.

Wealth and the things wealth can purchase are fairly constant themes in the criteria mentioned over the last few pages; wealth is related to occupation and to social standing. This factor is easier for Americans to see than it is for people in less money-oriented societies than our own, but access to economic goods is always an important differentiating factor in any society. Certainly it serves as an overarching factor, subsuming many smaller criteria and simplifying our analysis.

With wealth and respect now listed as two basic criteria of differentiation, it should be clear that our list of criteria is also a list of human desires. This is not strange and might have been offered deductively as the start of this chapter:

In human societies, some things are desired or valued (see pp. 85–87).
In human society, individual's "standings" are judged (see p. 96).
Individual's "standings" are judged in terms of their relative access to the valued goods.

One other major desire, and the last that is general and social in character, is the desire for power. Power implies an interpersonal relationship, as does respect—there must be a granter of respect and a respected, a controller and a controlled. A degree of differentiation is built into the power concept. Respect may be mutual, but power is a one-way street that establishes differing standings by its presence or absence.

These three general features, prestige, wealth, and power, are together virtually sufficient to explain the judgments of standing with which this chapter began. Each of the three will now be dissected.

WEALTH

The uneven distribution of several forms of goods builds a stratification system. Wealth's tangibility makes it the easiest of these forms with which to deal. Still, it has many natures and measurements, and care must be taken to avoid oversimplification. Income, accumulated goods and wealth, marketable skills and possessions, future economic prospects: each poses problems within itself and relation to the others. These problems can perhaps be resolved without resort to complicated economic accounting measures if we note that no measurement at any single point in time, however accurate it might be for that time, will substantially substitute for the whole system.

Let us imagine a pair of twins, employed by the same business organization and performing identical calculations on adding machines in the billing department. Their incomes are identical. Their "net worths" are identical; their savings accounts, value of personal property owned, and debts are the same. It might seem that the economic standing of these twins is identical. Suppose one of them is a high-school dropout whose experience in the organization has allowed him to work up to assignment to this job. Suppose the other is a college graduate who was employed by the organization as a management trainee and drew this assignment as one of the jobs he is to rotate his way through before stepping into an executive job. What then? The stratification judgment of the reader will surely now assign them to unequal levels. So will the stratification judgments of those who know them. Their department supervisor, for instance, will be much more likely to lunch with the executive trainee than with one who is among his more ordinary subordinates. Calculating secretaries will prefer to date the former. The bank will lend the trainee more money on less security. The bank action, more than the others, reveals the source of these variabilities. The bank loans money after judging prospects for repayment, and, despite their present equality, the two individuals have differing prospects.

The economic aspect of stratification is based not only on the present, but also the past and the probable future. It is not simply how much money a person has, but how much he is likely to have or how much he could get if he wanted to. The standard sociological term for these economic prospects is "life chance." This is what differentiates the prince from the pauper.

Much of the rest of the analysis of the distribution of wealth rests in the hands of the economist. He has the techniques for such analysis; they will not be covered here. For instance, wages, for any individual or for any service, are established in the labor market. The labor market operates in terms of supply and demand much like commodity markets. There are some small peculiarities. Labor cannot be "stocked" for later sale. There is some traditional restraint against "odd figure" pricing. This restraint stems from the notions of human dignity that intrude on market rationality and generally prevents an individual from working for $2.99 an hour. Three dollars, $2.75, even $2.90 may all right. Such additional factors can be taken into account by the economist before he runs his usual analysis. What has been illustrated here for wages holds as well for such things as inheritance and accumulations. The allocation of wealth remains mechanistic. These mechanisms need not concern us. The effect of this allocation, understood as life chances, is basic to social differentiation.

Life chances determine an individual's opportunities to acquire and dispose of wealth. They affect his chances of having a dishwasher, two cars, a yacht, college education, children, tuberculosis, his name in the newspaper, Rotary Club membership, prison experience, a happy marriage, friendships, premature death, and many other things as well. Not all of this list is directly economic; not all of it is directly a part of life chance. Surely this shows that "life chance" as a technical term is related to "life chance" as defined in everyday English: economic differentiation spills over into the rest of life.

POWER

One aspect of life, affected by wealth, but surely not part of economics, is that of control. Suppose a survey team had gone around the United States asking about power: "Would you rate this occupation as being *very powerful, moderately powerful,* . . . ?" Would they have found as much agreement? Could they have received meaningful answers from as many people? I suspect not. People can give meaningful answers regarding social respectability, because the respect is in their heads, which is where the answers are coming from. It is not necessary even to ask about wealth; we can measure it extrinsically. Power analysis offers neither of these points of clarity. It provides instead a maze of obscurities.

Starting with a very small case, let's look at power relations between my wife and me. At noon, my wife suggests a menu for dinner that will include steak and peas. I say that I don't want peas, but would prefer broccoli. She says that she has planned the dinner to include peas and is reluctant to change. I say that if we don't have broccoli, I will hit her right smack in the mouth. We have broccoli.

Here is a straightforward power situation. There is disagreement on an issue between two parties; the decision, the action carried out, follows the wishes of one party at the expense of the other. As elements of this power process we can identify the *decision-issue* (what vegetable will be served), the action *units* involved (my wife and I), a conflict of *interests* (desired actions or goals), the *resources* available to the units (I am stronger than my wife), and the *outcome* (I won). We can look deeper into this example, vary the conditions a bit, and find more obscure and confusing material beneath the power label.

In this example, the threat of the force is utilized, but not the force itself: I did not actually hit my wife. The outcome is the same. Even if the situation were considerably less open than it is, we can note the same elements in play. My wife may know I don't like peas, and so she never purchases them. This could go on for years without any open confrontation or any high level of consciousness concerning the issue on either of our parts. The outcome is no less real and no less a result of power. To be inclusive, power analysis must deal with potentialities as well as with concrete historical cases, with probable rather than actuated power. The logic of this extension is similar to the emphasis on life chances rather than wealth in economic differentiation.

Suppose we expand the time focus. Some days later, I may feel guilty about having threatened my wife and agree that she should buy a new dress. For this larger situation, her total interests (peas and dress) may be nearer total satisfaction than mine (broccoli and money saved). Resources favoring her position, which brought into play my guilt feelings, were greater than my physical strength. These are added content for the old elements of power, but a new element has been added as well, the one that ties the two decisions together. Power can be spent, saved, borrowed. The accounting position of an individual with regard to power at any particular moment of decision will influence the outcome. We will call this aspect *exchange context*. As another example of exchange context's effect, the above decision-issue might have been characterized by gracious yielding without threat. If our meals recently had featured several dishes that my wife knew I disliked, she may have felt she "owed" me a decision. Exchanges with parties other than the contesting units may be involved in the power process as well; we will look at this possibility later. The point here is simply that the outcome of a particular power struggle may not reflect the absolute relative power of the contesting parties. Analysis must be extended through time to see how the power exerted in a particular contest is affected by borrowings or payments against the past or future.

Another outcome, which may not reflect power, occurs when one action unit does not exert all the power available to it. This is likely if the interest of that unit is not of particularly high *salience* to it. My wife may not really care whether we have peas or broccoli; what appears to be yielding on her part may be a matter of total indifference. Salience is a critical element. It must be taken into account on its own and must also be seen as interacting with other elements. For instance, a strong exchange position on interests that an individual considers important may be arrived at by yielding on a number of interests of low salience.

Reminding you again that power need not involve open confrontation or even consciousness, let's return to my dinner table in search of more elements of power. The fact is that I usually have very little to say about the menu. My wife does the grocery shopping, the cooking, the planning. I routinely leave for work in the morning before the day's evening meal is planned, and by the time I return preparations have already committed us. The variable here, which gives my wife greater power, is her *access* to decisions. Automatically, as a matter of routine, she is in a position where she can, even must, make these decisions. The effect is an outcome that favors her interest; but unless some other party goes "out of the way" to participate in the decision, the exercise of power will never become apparent. It is in operation nonetheless.

Whether other action units make such an effort to enter into the decision process will depend on their *awareness*. They must be aware that an opportunity for decision exists. They must be aware of opportunities for participation. They must be aware that the decision will affect their interests. Opportunities for awareness are variable in much the same way as in access. If I know when my wife plans to go to the grocery, a request for a particular food registered at that time will be more effective than at any other time. If my son is in the room when my wife and I argue peas vs. broccoli, he may wish to throw his weight on the side of broccoli. My daughter has no preference regarding the two vegetables, but other decisions may be contingent on this one. Suppose my wife has planned not simply vegetables, but whole meals. Suppose peas are to go with steak and if we switch to broccoli we also get fish in place of steak. My daughter hates fish. If she is aware of all the implications of the vegetable controversy, she will want to enter in on the side of peas.

Having now introduced my children into the scene, we can examine the implications of adding their power in one way or another to the situation. The original units (my wife and I) may form coalitions with other units that increase their ability to achieve outcomes favorable to their interests, hence increasing their power. Units may differ in their opportunities for coalition. Exchange position relative to such other units will, as you were forewarned, be a factor to consider here. So will access to other units and awareness of other units, although the restricted referent of these terms here places them beyond the analysis above. If my children like mother best, her opportunities for coalition will exceed mine; her general power position in the family will be the stronger for it. *Unit context* is one more element of power.

The simplest general statement about power which follows from the above is: *if the interest of units on an issue differ, if the interest is of equal salience to the units, and if the exchange positions of the units are equitable, the outcome will favor the more powerful unit.* Although the concluding phrase of this statement is commonplace, the qualifying phrases are not. We have already shown how identical interests prevent power from appearing, how differing saliences may lead to a decision favoring the intrinisically less powerful unit, and how exchange position can result in distorted power outcomes. Power can only be directly measured on the relatively few occasions when all these preconditions obtain. Even then, it will be a crude measure—X is more powerful than Y when the outcome favors X— but with no indication of how much more powerful, or of the power of these units with regard to anything except each other. Another more general, more useful, but less direct measure of power may be obtained by analyzing the units in question with regard to the other aspects of power. Analytically and generally, then, *the power of any unit is the sum of its awareness, access, unit contexts, and resources.* Exchange context will modify this power; the amount available for exertion on any particular occasion may deviate from the general sum.

These terms can be used to analyze either any power situation or society in terms of power differentiation. In the United States, producers' lobbies are more powerful than those of consumers. Consumers, taken together, have more resources, but their unit contexts are not opportune for getting together to exert power. Lobbyists also have awareness and access; it is their business to know when influence should be used, upon whom, and how leverage can be obtained.

Bureaucratic administrators have considerable power because they possess resources not available to persons in other positions within the system. For instance, they often have the authority to discharge employees, to recommend promotions and wage rates. They also have access; papers that put them in a position to make decisions regularly cross their desks. Secretaries in bureaucracies have virtually no resources but have the same sort of access that executives possess, and secretaries are relatively powerful.

The strategic committee positions of Congress can be understood in these same terms. I will not go on to list further applications; you may want to try a couple molded to suit your own inclinations. More to the point, you might want to return to the NORC ratings at the beginning of this chapter and assign weighted values to the power elements in the hands of different occupations, noticing how this helps account for some of the variation.

Of course, power, like wealth, is not perfectly related to occupation. Different persons with the same occupation may have different amounts of power. Some forms of power are available entirely outside the occupational structure, but there are some close ties. Such elements as access vary principally with position. Certain positions in communities, organizations, and group contexts carry built-in power potential. Individuals may "work around the edges" of the system and wield power other than that of design, but this sort of pirated, enterprise power will form a relatively small portion of the whole. Most power is legitimate. The allocation of power within the system is, then, basically a reflection of that system. The exercise of that power serves to fix the design of the system. Usually, the circularity of these two statements and of the two conditions they describe serves to perpetuate the system virtually unchanged. There is room, however, for power to become a prime mover of social change.

PRESTIGE

Although wealth and power contribute to social respectability, they do not equal it. There is a portion of prestige that is not reducible to these terms. It is analyzable, but only on its own grounds.

The first source of prestige is inheritance. Certainly, wealth and positions that contain power can be inherited. Little was made of this fact in the previous sections because it is so obvious. Somehow, it seems to surprise people more to find that honor can also be inherited, and when they do note this fact they consider it unjust or irrational. It may be both of these, but no more in this case than in the other forms of inheritance. Every community contains old families that are held in special social reverence. In reality, of course, all families are equally old. The designation "old family" has nothing to do with number of generations as such, but rather with number of honorable generations. Membership in broader kinlike categories, such as favored ethnic or racial groups, is a similar source of prestige.

A second source of prestige will be labeled "value-proximity." As was noted in Chapter 4, every society has a set of cherished beliefs or ideals. Individuals who exemplify or adhere to these or who work toward the fulfillment of the goals related to these ideals will be respected. Said another way, persons or actions in proximity to the values will also be valued. In a society that believed that "cleanliness is next to Godliness," several differentiations in social reputation would be possible. First, persons who assisted the entire group to achieve cleanliness, for example, street sweepers, would be respected. Second, persons whose positions allowed them to retain a personal cleanliness, for example, department store floorwalkers but not street sweepers, would be respected. Finally, persons who, apart from any occupational or situational condition, maintained personal cleanliness, for example, frequent bathers, would be respected. Of course, the achievement of one sense of the ideal may, as in the case of street sweepers, prohibit the achievement of the ideal in other senses. Similarly, no society operates with only one value premise; the conjunction of several values, as they may bear on an individual or a position, would serve to establish respectability.

Certain habits, customs, life-styles, although too minor to directly involve the values of the society, nonetheless call forth respect. This matter of life-style is the third source of prestige. It is better to play golf than to bowl; it is better for a man to wear a shirt and tie than a T-shirt, although this rule may be subject to some situational variation; it is better to eat pilaf than grits. There are thousands of such rules; persons who know and follow them are considered more worthy of respect than those who do not. These rules are all nonrational. The sense of "better than" is arbitrarily established by custom and the community. The definitions can shift from time to time, and the privilege of introducing changes in some rules is reserved to those who follow the other rules most assiduously.

We are not talking here about life-styles that high income makes possible, although some styles are more easily achieved by the wealthy. Obviously, most of us do not have the means to play polo, even though we recognize it as a socially desirable pastime. Still, there are equally acceptable, inexpensive pastimes, but we must know what they are. It is our ignorance that places us outside the social elect, not our poverty. It costs no more to serve a proper wine with dinner than an improper one. Life-style deals with consumption patterns, with niceties of style and etiquette. It would take years of concentrated study to learn the rules, but even that achievement would not bring prestige, because by the time a person learned one set of rules, a new set would have replaced the old. The more quickly the masses absorb the rules, the more rapidly are the rules changed or replaced. Those with high status are known to one another and to the general public by the mark of their exclusive life-style. If their social inferiors adopt this style, the style no longer serves as a sorting criterion. The special honor of the elite has disappeared, unless they invent a new basis for distinction. Of course, they always do.

Although this discussion has focused primarily on life-style differences between the elite and the rest of society, similar distinctions can be found marking off all the status levels.

The fourth, and final, source of prestige is association. This one again seems nearly tautological. The respectability of a given person is derived from the respectability of those with whom he associates. It is not perfectly circular, for judgments of respectability based on other criteria are confirmed by acceptance in a social group. Acceptance into such a circle lends an individual some of the status of that circle, even if he lacks the other standards appropriate to membership.

Prestige is the most obscure, irrational, and conservative of the keys to social stratification. Although it has a tight internal logic, it is the most difficult to isolate, but its impact is both considerable and unique.

PUTTING THE PIECES BACK TOGETHER

Surely you have noticed that the three forms of stratification—prestige, power, and wealth—are related to one another. They are not simply different species of a common genus, but are integrated parts of a mechanism; they have a working, as well as a classificatory, relationship. They intrude upon one another's realms. For instance, some life-styles are accessible only to those with great wealth; status associations may provide power access or advantageous unit contexts; wealth is a power resource; family inheritance helps set a level for all three forms of stratification. Further, one form can be exchanged for another.

In a very simple instance, a judge may be bribed. The person with wealth spends that wealth and gains control over other units—those whose case the judge is hearing. The briber has less wealth, but more power. The judge, on the other hand, has more money but has given up the power to decide the case himself. Exchanges of any stratification advantage for any other is possible. The process may become more complex, but the principles are the same.

Among such principles are the following. There is no fixed price; the explicit or implicit bargain between the exchanging parties sets the terms; these may or may not appear "fair" to an outside observer. The net amount of the separate forms never increases; what is gained by one party must be lost by another. There is often a "friction loss" in exchange, so that the total of all forms available to the exchanging parties may be less than the initial total; the remainder is either lost entirely or dissipates throughout the social system. Some exchanges are purely personal; others may be regularized or customary within a particular society.

One important exchange that took place frequently in recent European history was an exchange of wealth for status between old, impoverished nobility and *nouveau-riche* businessmen. Marriage into the noble family provided status to the bourgeois family and financial help to the blue-blooded in-laws. With modest variation, this system still operates, though less frequently. In the United States today, election to public office requires the expenditures of great sums of money, an exchange of wealth for power. The fact that such exchanges can take place does not mean that they always will, nor does it obliterate the intrinsic separateness of the three forms of stratification.

A given person's standings on all three forms will tend to be similar, but there are exceptions. Semimythical Americans represent a variety of extreme combinations.

The impoverished southern gentleman has a fine manner, a decaying mansion, and a grand old name. He is too much of a recluse (and perhaps too much of a gentleman) to compete for power with politicians, and all of his family's wealth was in slaves and Confederate War Bonds.

The Chicago ward heeler is incorruptible and tough and has a heart of gold. What small funds he may obtain go toward the aid of "his people," strengthening his political control over them. He lives in the same old neighborhood and affects the same old ethnic speech, dress, and life-style. He swings the vote of the city and is a major force in politics.

The eccentric miser is occasionally arrested for vagrancy but is released when he displays the hundred thousand dollars sewed in the lining of his ragged coat. He has the life-style and related social standing of a hobo and no effective power, but in his younger days he made a few million dollars in the trash business.

The mafioso is both wealthy and powerful. Dope and numbers are doing very well. A decline in prostitution and protection is offset by diversification into legitimate businesses. But men who have nicknames like "Fingers" or "Little Leo," who display the remnants of rural Italian cultural ancestry, and who, above all, are involved in affairs so widely contrary to some of the basic values of society are not likely to be accorded high social respect.

The fighting senator, who worked his way up from the traditional, nostalgic log cabin, is prestigious and powerful but barely breaks even economically.

The best-selling novelist is acclaimed and respected. With Book-of-the-Month Club and movie rights, his economic rewards are great. However, he operates no bureaucracy that he can control and, unless he is able to establish credentials independently, he has no real political lever.

If this gallery is overdrawn, it is only because we were reaching for extremes. Smaller discrepancies abound in everyday life. To speak personally, university professors have more status than power, more power than income. Skilled factory machinists generally have little power and prestige but fairly high incomes. Surely, enough examples have been provided to make the point. Beyond this, a similar argument could show that there are discrepancies within each of the forms of stratification. Some people may have relatively great incomes but low reservoirs of capital goods. Some may have higher life-styles than their inherited status would indicate. Others may have power access but not power awareness. The complexities and variations multiply.

Societies vary in the degree to which they display such discrepancies. The above examples are all from the contemporary United States. In other societies, such examples might be easier to find or more difficult. There have been societies that approached perfect symmetry, in which any person's position on any two scales would be perfectly predictable from his position on the third. The traditional caste system of India and the traditional status system of feudal Europe approached such a model. The social implications of relative "neatness" in stratification demand two comments.

First, it is no accident that the two prime examples of orderly, congruent stratification were labeled traditional societies. The segmentalization of forms of social superiority and differentiated access to them create a society that is in flux. The specialization of superiority is in effect a division of labor in superiority and carries the same propensity for change as does any other division of labor. Exchanges of one stratification commodity for another, which is encouraged by individuals holding disparate amounts of the several forms, serve as a bar to the entrenchment of custom. Where the avenues to superiority are varied, higher motivation to a greater variety of behaviors will result. While high activity levels and varied behavior may not sound like a perfect description of progress, it surely is one definition of change. Finally, the phrase "vested interest" connotes at the same time individuals with more than their share of something (including wealth, power, or prestige) and individuals desirous of preserving that something. Basically, people who are getting more than their share of the pie will be against cutting the pie in any other fashion. If that larger slice includes a major segment of the power, they will have the means to successfully pursue the policy of changlessness. The most stultifying combination here is power and prestige. The inherited, irrational, and traditional nature of prestige may be combined with the power to perpetuate these characteristics, thus resulting in a very conservative system. Diversification of superiority means exchange and its accompanying dissipation and a contest between elites, which tends to cancel out the power of all elites and leaves operating room for the discontented to initiate change.[1]

Second, only in traditional societies with orderly and symmetrical inequality does the *strata* sense of *stratification* apply; only with regard to such societies does a discussion of social class make sense. To this point, this chapter has assiduously avoided referring to social classes. The simple fact is that relatively few societies have classes, although all have superiority-inferiority differentiation—what I have called stratification or inequality.

One standard referent of the term *class* is some kind of social group or organization. Although it is true that most Americans are willing to label themselves middle class, it is clear that this is quite a different sort of labeling than when they call themselves Methodists or Rotarians or New Yorkers or General Motors employees. If we investigate any one of the latter type of designations, we will find that the individual labels himself and some other persons. If we check those others, their labelings will correspond nicely. If one

---

[1] Materials bearing on social change which touch on these points may be found in Chapters 3, 4, 6, and 11.

Rotarian names a group of people as fellow Rotarians, almost all of those who were named will admit that they are Rotarians and will also agree that the first is a Rotarian as well. Nothing like this occurs for social classes in the United States. Your middle class may not be mine, nor is your definition necessarily the same as that of your middle-class brother. Moreover, there are regularized social involvements—a relational system—that bind Rotarians or General Motors employees together. These may be emotional and personal; they may consist of direct interaction, as in the case of Rotary. They may be bureaucratic and symbolic, consisting of tight interdependencies, as in the case of General Motors. Nothing like either of these is true for any middle class you could find or imagine.

The other sense of *class* is as a collection of objects that share certain qualities. In this sense one could speak of the class of heavy objects, or of the class of heavy, hard, rough, inorganic objects. Similarly, in societies where differentiation forms are regular, one could speak of, perhaps, a middle class—those who have middle amounts of wealth, power, and prestige, and of the several components of each. Surely such a class exists in the United States. But it contains very few members. If a class were created and labeled for each of the combinations of characteristics, it would take almost as many classes as there are people. The only advantage of classification is simplification; this avenue does not offer that prospect for complex societies. It did for traditional societies precisely because the several attributes of superiority are coincidental. Elsewhere in this book the term "class" is used, and it springs up regularly in the literary gardens of sociologists and social commentators. We grow that sort of weed, I suppose, because it is easier to cultivate than some more productive plants might be.

Conflict between different power units is real. The occurrence of such conflicts and their outcomes strongly influence the character of a society and the fate of individuals within that society. The uneven distribution of economic goods and the system that perpetuates that inequity have similar effect. The prestige hierarchy, in the minds of the society's actors and in its organizational manifestations, explains a substantial portion both of human behavior and of the social order. The sum of these factors and their meshing together yield a multifaceted complex of equality and inequality close to the core of social organization.

Appreciating the implications for an individual of his standing in several respects of inequality requires recognition of the respects in which he differs from his fellows as well as the respects in which he is the same. Analysis of the inequality system follows most surely when attention is focused on the conflicts, coalition, and other actions and interests of the real action units within the society.

FURTHER READING

Broderson, Arvid, *Soviet Worker: Labor and Government in Soviet Society.* New York: Random House, 1966. Available in paperback.

Dobriner, William M., *Class in Suburbia.* Englewood Cliffs, N.J.: Prentice-Hall, 1963. Paperback.

Domhoff, G. William, *Who Rules America?* Englewood Cliffs, N.J.: Prentice-Hall, 1967. Available in paperback.

Kahl, Joseph, ed., *Comparative Perspectives on Stratification: Mexico, Great Britain, Japan.* Boston: Little, Brown, 1968.* Paperback.

Lenski, Gerhard, *Power and Privilege: A Theory of Social Stratification.* New York: McGraw-Hill, 1966.*

Miller, Herman, *Rich Man, Poor Man.* New York: Crowell, 1964.

Presthus, Robert, *Men at the Top: A Study in Community Power.* New York: Oxford University, 1964. Available in paperback.

Reissman, Leonard, *Class in American Society.* New York: Free Press, 1959.*

Schorr, Alvin L., *Poor Kids: A Report on Children in Poverty.* New York: Basic Books, 1966.

Turner, Ralph, *The Social Context of Ambition.* San Francisco: Chandler, 1964.

*Difficult, specialized, or technical.

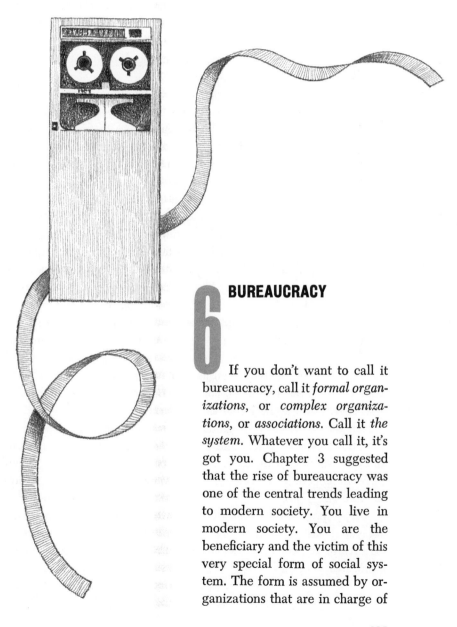

6 BUREAUCRACY

If you don't want to call it bureaucracy, call it *formal organizations*, or *complex organizations*, or *associations*. Call it *the system*. Whatever you call it, it's got you. Chapter 3 suggested that the rise of bureaucracy was one of the central trends leading to modern society. You live in modern society. You are the beneficiary and the victim of this very special form of social system. The form is assumed by organizations that are in charge of your health, education, entertainment, feeding, government, transportation, defense, information, charity, interests, communication, protection, money, morals, work, and leisure. When you die, your affairs will be concluded through the joint efforts of a bureaucratic funeral home, a bureaucratic church, a bureaucratic insurance company, and a bureaucratic government.

Because you are so deeply involved with these establishments, it would be well for you to understand them a little better. This is easier than it might seem, for they are all the same. Obviously, they are not the same in every respect—the insurance company doesn't want to bury you, but the funeral home does. Organizationally they are identical.

Look around you and you will see manufacturing executives becoming government officials, military officers becoming corporate executives, foundation heads becoming university presidents, and, yes, insurance men becoming funeral directors. All of these shifts are accomplished without major retraining of the person who shifts. After all, the only thing that really changes when he changes organizations are the goals. The system is the same; if he was able to operate with organizational success in one context, he will experience the same success in the next. Further evidence of interchangeability is provided by the trend toward what industry calls conglomerates. What is the goal of Ling-Temco-Vought? Is it the production of aircraft? Electronic components? Transportation services? Information? Commerce? Household cleansers? It is all of these; it is none of these. The organization adjusts itself to the achievement of several diverse goals. It remains true to itself, as an organization. Conglomerate governments, churches, and schools are just as widespread, but the phenomenon has not been as widely recognized as in industry. To note that these are indeed conglomerates, figure the proportion of total energy and activity that takes places under the auspices of the church that is actually religious in character. Do the same for the United States government and governing, and for a major university and education. If your accounting is accurate, the percentages will be small indeed. Much organizational energy is devoted to a variety of "foreign" goals.

If we have shown that all organizations are the same, we have not yet shown what they are. Let us look, then, at the universal features of bureaucracy. Let's see the kind of beast that so totally permeates your life.

Bureaucracies are social systems; they are made up of units held together by relationships. Social systems have already been discussed in Chapter 1. Because bureaucracies are a special sort of social system, we might begin looking for something special about their units and relationships.

There are a lot of units in a bureaucracy. Bureaucracies tend to involve *large numbers of people* in the nominal pursuit of *large-scale goals*. Size alone, however, is not a distinguishing characteristic. Societies or social classes may have even larger numbers.

The units in bureaucracy are highly *differentiated*. Here we may be getting someplace; these grounds will distinguish bureaucracies from social classes, if not from societies. Bureaucracies have a refined division of labor. The individuals involved exhibit a wide variety of behaviors and background characteristics. Each individual has a narrow action-repertoire. He does his little thing over and over again. He never trades off with anyone else. Each of the others sticks to his own equally circumscribed action.

If we have a whole lot of people doing a whole lot of different things, it seems that the result would be chaos, but it is not. Somehow, all the bits fit together. The overall impression is one of order rather than chaos. The consequence of all these actions together is the accomplishment of the large-scale goal mentioned a couple of paragraphs ago. This fitting together requires us now to look at relationships rather than units. Bureaucracies are *formally organized*.

The organizational relationships, or at least the parts of the system salient to their own actions, are clearly and unambiguously understood by all the actors in the system. It is likely that an overall plan of organization was consciously created, similar to the one shown in Fig. 6–1. Whether any specific organization has such a chart or not, one could be created. It would resemble the specimen. This formal organization is relatively permanent and serves as a court of last resort in determining the appropriateness of any behavior within the organization.

There are three keys to the formal articulation of units within a bureaucracy. These are *division of function, chain of command,* and *pyramid of authority*. Division of function is an organizational complement of the specialization or differentiation we have already noted. To the general notion that there are lots of different jobs, we

Fig. 6-1 ORGANIZATIONAL CHART
(expansion is shown for only a few departmants, because of space limitations)

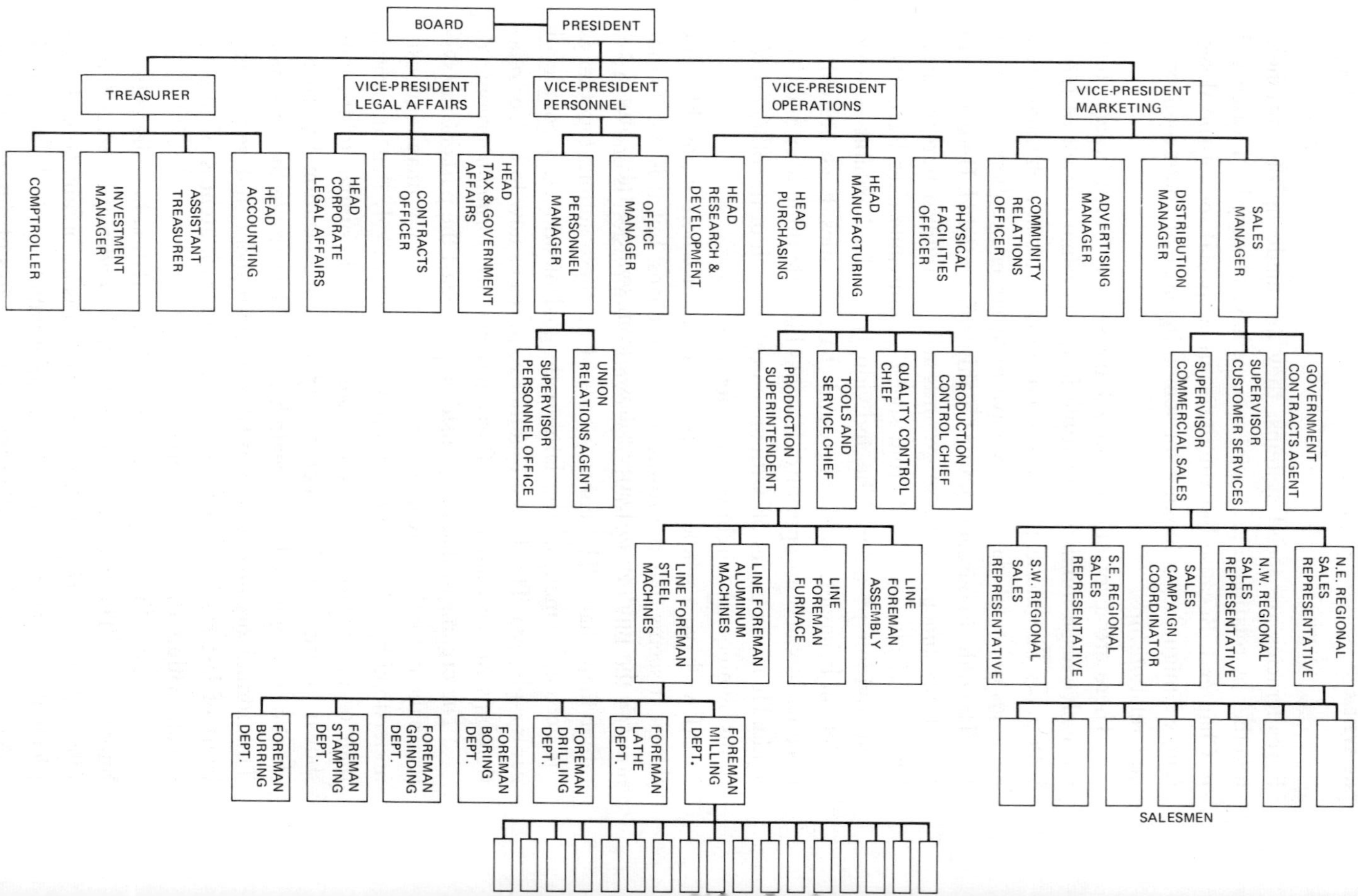

are now adding the provision that similar jobs tend to be grouped together. If you start from the top of the organizational chart, each branch you choose will embody a more restricted collection of tasks or functions. "Personnel" is not just a division, it is a subsystem. All of the jobs under the vice-president for personnel concern the personnel function; all are more involved with one another than they are with sales or operations. As we move further down the chart, the groupings grow tighter. At the very bottom levels we are likely to find all the members of a unit engaged in precisely the same actions, for example, the milling machine operators.

Chain of command implies unilinear paths of communication and hierarchy. Ideally, each person communicates only along the lines of the chart. An individual communicates with the one who is his immediate superior and with those who are his immediate subordinates. Orders are passed down, one step at a time. Deference is owed only to the person one step up on the chart. For his own performance, an individual is responsible only to the person immediately above him. This relationship is semitransitive, in that any individual is responsible to his immediate superior both for his own performance and for the performance of all those beneath him in the same chain. The various chains are linked only at their tops.

The pyramid of authority follows from some of the features already discussed. Superiority-subordination, responsibility-obedience, and their linkage to chain of command have been made clear. We might add the further notion that *authority* implies legitimate power. Within the organizational context, superior position means the right to give orders and the acknowledgment of this right by the subordinate.

One more characteristic of the organization is the pyramidal nature of these relationships. Every lower level tends to contain more individuals than the unit above; each superior has more than one subordinate. Persons in the lowest level have no subordinates. If we leave them out, the mean number of subordinates for all other positions in all organizations is seven. An organization with only two levels will then have, on the average, eight members (one supervisor and seven subordinates). If we add a third level at the bottom, seven subordinates for each of these subordinates, we will have an organization with forty-nine new members, or fifty-seven altogether. Continued expansion will show rapid increases in organizational size with additional levels, as the next few steps indicate.

NUMBER OF EMPLOYEES FOR VARIOUS LEVELS OF ORGANIZATION

Number of levels	Hypothetical number of members
4	400
5	2,801
6	19,608
7	137,257

Should you care to engage in such esoteric pursuits, the general formula for any number of levels is:

$$\sum_{n=1}^{L} 7^{(L-n)} = X$$

where L is the number of levels and X is the hypothetical number of employees.

For a variety of reasons, real organizations seldom reach the size this formula suggests. Some chains are truncated near the top. In a six-level organization, for instance, if *one* of the president's seven subordinates has no subordinates, the effect would subtract a fully complemented five-level organization from the total. An organization that has six levels may have that many only in a couple of branches; the others may include components with two, three, and four levels. Also, the "seven subordinates" with which we started was a crude average. Actually, the number of subordinates is highly variable. It may range from one to over one hundred.

The *span of authority*, as this factor is labeled, depends on several factors. One, obviously, is the amount of work to be done in a particular functional division. In our sample chart we might look at union relations. Because of space limitations, the person at the lowest level shown on the chart is the union relations agent. Suppose there is only enough work in this area to occupy the time of three people? The agent presumably has, then, three subordinates (who are not shown). It would be very silly of this company to hire an additional four employees in this area. If they did so, the supervisor would be fully occupied (with a full complement of seven subordinates) but the four extra workers would be underemployed. The result would be more waste than savings. Another alternative would be to find another small department and combine the two. Make the supervisor head of "union relations and investment management." You can see that to do so would violate the principle of division of function. Two sensible alternatives remain. One is to eliminate the position, agent of union relations. Let all three union relations people report directly to the personnel manager. This not only eliminates the underemployed agent of union relations, it also more fully utilizes the supervisory capacity of the personnel manager. The other alternative is for the company to recognize the shortage of work in union relations (for the scale of the whole organization) and find more work of this sort to do. Four extra workers in the union relations department would be added, and the company would "sell" union relations services to other companies. In some cases, none of these alternatives may be practicable; underutilization of management must be accepted. Many managers who could handle more subordinates will not have them.

How many subordinates can be handled is another variable. One sense of *span of authority* is how many subordinates a supervisor is *able* to supervise, rather than how many he *does* supervise. If all of the subordinates are engaged in an identical task, if the task itself is simple and repetitive, the supervisor can handle more subordinates than if the tasks involved are complex and varied. Supervision can be practiced in at least two styles. One possibility is that the work itself be monitored. If the supervisor is to check on his subordinates' work by peering over their shoulders regularly, he cannot be in charge of very many shoulders. The other form of supervision rests on accountability. Under a system of accountability, it is not necessary that work be checked in progress. Rather, the worker is held accountable for the end product. An occasional check of the outcomes of his labors, with rewards and punishments contingent on satisfaction, may induce appropriate performance as efficiently as monitoring, and with much less supervisory attention. When conditions permit, accountability is certainly the more efficient of the two forms. It is also the more truly bureaucratic. Some tasks, however, do not end with the kinds of products that can be readily checked, and some outcomes do not neatly reflect diligence or neglect in activity. Monitoring, then, may be the only form of supervision that will serve for some tasks. When this is the case, the span of authority will be smaller; a supervisor will be able to supervise fewer subordinates.

A final factor is the degree to which the subordinates are themselves devoted to standards of performance. The professions serve as a model of this kind of performance. Persons such as physicians, lawyers, professors, and architects do not need direct supervision. In the process of becoming professional, they have adopted standards of work and ideals involving both technical competence and a code of ethics. They adhere to these standards in private practice, if they are engaged in it. In a bureaucracy, they would continue to perform by the same standards. Supervision becomes little more than coordination. Some skilled trades and managerial skills have much the same character. In these cases, the number of subordinates handled by a supervisor will tend to increase.

Some of the principles governing span of authority are contradictory. More complex and diverse work-sets, for instance, are most likely to be governed by professional standards. The complexity and diversity suggest close attention of the supervisor and a narrow span of authority; professional standards imply absence of need for close supervision and a wide span of authority. Nonetheless, each factor has its effect; if all are examined, we ought to be able to understand the span of authority of any department.

We have spent a great deal of time on the question of the pyramid of authority because this is a critical feature in the formal relationships that bind the units of bureaucracies together. I hope you have not forgotten, however, that we started out inquiring into the features of bureaucracy itself. The pyramid of authority is one of these features and the formal organizational ties are derived from this pyramid. We have one additional basic feature to explore.

The units that are bound together in bureaucracy are not really persons or jobs, but *offices. Office* is the last, and perhaps most basic, feature of bureaucracy. By office I mean a rigidly prescribed set of rights and duties that fit logically together and attach to a position. Just as the organizational chart formally prescribes relations between positions, so there is likely to be an organizational rule book that prescribes appropriate behaviors for the holder of any office. Each of these descriptions is office specific; it applies only to that office and to the person occupying it. This is not just a lump of rights and duties, but a logically cohering cluster.

These rights and duties attach to the position, not to the person who holds the position. Persons may come and go; the office endures. The rights and duties of a new incumbent will be precisely the same as those of his predecessor. The predecessor, in turn, loses the rights and duties with his removal from the office. Subordinates owe allegiance and obedience to the office, not to the individual. This recognition of superiority, like all the other demands and privileges, is restricted to official matters covered by the rule book. Both superior and subordinate occupy offices; the conditions of office act on each of their behaviors and serve to define relationships between them, in the organizational context. The rights of a factory manager would include telling his foremen how to arrange the week's production schedule. Acceptance of these directives and following through with appropriate actions would be part of the duties of the foremen. Illegitimate and "unofficial" demands by the manager, such as ordering the foremen to vote for a particular candidate in a national election, would carry no such obligation for obedience.

Officeholders are selected on the basis of standardized criteria. The standards for appointment might include receiving a certain score on a test, the possession of some background experience or education, or a variety of other requirements. The point is that whatever the standards, they are uniform and at least in part germane. One single set of standards is used to measure all applicants. Additionally, at least some of the requirements have something to do with the ability to perform the tasks associated with the office. For any selection standard, we could sort the potential applicants into those who meet the standard and those who do not. Those who do should, on the average, be able to operate better the rights and duties of the office. There is a moldy old story about a basketball coach who had a six-foot four-inch door leading to his office. Over the door was a sign: "If you don't have to stoop, don't come in." Although we might not want to label the coach's athletic operation a formal organization, the story illustrates something of the nature of recruitment to offices. The door did not change sizes; its height tested all potential entrants by the same standard. Not all tall people are good basketball players, nor all short ones bad, but the odds favor the tall. The coach was using a standardized and germane criterion in the appointment of persons to the office of basketball player.

If only persons who meet a set of unchanging standards are selected to fill an office, we might expect that all the holders of an office would resemble each other. They do. This fact is recognized every day. A cartoonist needs only a few lines to suggest a sergeant. His caricature will never be mistaken for a second lieutenant. In art and in everyday life, you may find easily recognizable stereotypes of the politician, the professor, the cop, and the ad-man, along with similar stereotypes of the Jew, the black, and the Pole. The similarity between the two forms is only on the surface. Although it is certainly not true that "all Jews are alike," there is truth in the notion that "all sergeants are alike." Bureaucratic offices build and attract living stereotypes.

One gets to be a Marine sergeant only by remaining in the Marines for several years as an enlisted man and by building an acceptable service record during that tenure. Surely those who enter the Marines as enlisted men differ from those who enter as officers. Their educational backgrounds, temperaments, class backgrounds, and motivations are different. They are just as different, in age, physical condition, or motivation, from those who enter the Army, Navy, Air Force, or no service, or who are draftees rather than volunteers. Most of those newly enlisted Marines will leave at the expiration of their obligation. Only a very special sort will sign on for further hitches. Of these, some will eventually rebel against the authoritarian style of the military; only a few will revel in it and these are on their route toward becoming sergeants.

Some would-be sergeants will fail the tests of discipline that military life imposes. They will be insubordinate or derelict too often. They will have a record too spotted with trouble: superior officers, women, liquor, hours. Some will lack the technical aptitudes, will be unable to master the skills associated with the lower grades on the way up. Some will simply not *want* to be sergeants—and even the Marines does not ordinarily force a man into an unwanted promotion. Only a very special few, special because they have met this special set of uniform qualifications, will become sergeants. The uniformity of the qualifications has now become a uniformity of the men.

When each becomes a sergeant, he falls heir to the rights and duties of the office. He must begin *acting* like a Marine sergeant. These requirements are, again, identical for all individuals who inhabit the office. All sergeants act alike. The more alike they act, the more alike they seem, and become.

Although the stereotype is more striking in some cases than others, similar arguments could be advanced for any bureaucratic office. This equivalence or interchangeability of personnel makes bureaucracy the finely-tuned and enduring social system that it is. All the parts go on. Each part is replaceable without affecting the overall operation. Each part has its own sphere of action and specified and specialized rights and duties, which differ from those of all other parts. The parts are bound together in a formal organizational arrangement that allocates function and responsibility. The result is the coordination of many separate tasks in order to achieve a goal. The goal "belongs" to the organization, not to its members. The goal is achieved only through the blend, not through the actions of any of the members.

The essentials of this system are the same regardless of the particular organization or the special goal that it might be pursuing. In essence, church, government, industry, and the rest are identical. This essence is *the formal articulation of a large collection of differentiated offices.* That's what bureaucracy is.

A system of this character can accomplish many goals more efficiently than can any other kind of organization. It can even accomplish otherwise impossible goals. It permits the coordination of the activities of very large numbers of persons. This can be managed even when the commitment of the individuals to the goals or to the organization is low. The organization becomes virtually deathless and can continue its operation past the life span of any of its members, perhaps indefinitely. These special advantages explain why your life is now so totally caught up in the system. Never forget the power of formal organizations. Do not let this, however, blind you to their weaknesses.

SICKNESS IN THE SYSTEM

In the last section, I did not talk about the special features of schools or hospitals but tried to stick to the general features of bureaucratic systems whatever the organization in which they were manifest. Now, I would like to do the same thing for the illnesses to which such systems are prone. I will not discuss any single organization or type but will deal with problems that occur generally. Also, I might point out that the previous section did not describe organizations as they are, but rather as a "perfect" type. Some real ones match the type well, some poorly; some match better in some respects than in others.

Many of the failings of this section can be understood as failings to live up to the preceding models. For instance, when I said the selection of office holders was on the basis of standardized and germane criteria, you knew better. You can think of cases in which a company's vice-presidency went, not to the best man for the job, but to the president's son-in-law. Secretaries are often selected on the basis of looks or sexual acquiescence rather than typing ability. When this sort of thing occurs, it does not mean that the principles of the previous section are incorrect, merely that they are often violated. Organizations that behave in this fashion are less than fully bureaucratic.

A closely related violation of bureaucratic principles occurs when those who have official power use it for unofficial ends. Superiors attempt to gain personal as well as organizational goals. They attempt to influence the behavior of their subordinates outside the boundaries of office but use the power of office to enforce the demands. This results in an inefficient allocation of bureaucratic resources, and also weakens the organization. An executive may, for instance, have work done on his home by a company repairman. To whatever extent the work is done on company time and with company materials, there is cost to the company. More damaging is the cynicism and loss of respect for authority that will be engendered in the repairman. He may later even use his "guilty knowledge" to avoid meeting legitimate responsibilities.

Both of these bureaucratic problems occur because of conflict between organizational requirements and the personal motivations of individuals who make up the organization. The clash of these twin demands is the major source of deviations from bureaucratic principle. One of the strengths of bureaucracy, we noted earlier, was its ability to organize the behaviors of diverse persons who had low levels of commitment to the organization and its goals. That the resources are then marshaled less than perfectly, that members "cheat" on the system, is not surprising. Still, the organizational form keeps this sort of problem to a minimum; the efficiencies of the system work against this weakness. As bureaucracies are more fully developed, this sort of problem will diminish.

More numerous and more serious are the ills that grow, rather than diminish, with the development of bureaucracy. These are illnesses that follow from the characteristics of the system rather than from violations of the system. As a bureaucracy grows more elaborate, these problems will grow worse, not better. Physiologically, cancer is abnormal and unlimited cell growth and reproduction. Cell growth and reproduction are normal and necessary processes. Carrying these same tendencies too far gives disease. We want to turn our attention to several forms of organizational cancer.

Offices are circumscribed by certain rights and duties, and the holder of an office who fails to perform in accordance with these standards is subject to punishment. One of the great strengths of bureaucracy is this: it is not necessary for every individual in the system to understand the total-organization goal or the implications of his performance for that goal. He follows his rules; his behavior is appropriate. We can expect the individual in this circumstance to develop an attachment to his rules, to become almost hypnotized by them. He becomes so attached to the rules that he follows them *whether they fit the circumstances or not.* Such an individual is said to be suffering from *trained incapacity.* This does not mean that he is extraordinarily stupid or perverse. His whole position and experience push him to this condition. He is an ordinary man, trapped by routine. All of you have experienced the consequences of trained incapacity. You encounter it almost every time you place an unusual demand on a bureaucratic system. The official representatives whom you encounter refuse to deal with your problem. They deal instead with the rule book.

Whether you are mailing a package at the post office, registering at a university, seeking an accounting at a bank, or dealing in some other way with some other organization, the result is the same. It is frustrating. It is maddening. Any sensible person can see the commonsense solution. But the official is not a sensible person, he is an officeholder. He behaves on the grounds of rules, not commonsense. If his behavior were left to his own discretion and common sense, and if the same were true of every individual in the organization, the result would be chaos not bureaucracy. As it is, the result is a series of nagging petty frustrations and minor inefficiencies. Bureaucratic procedures are rigid; previous blind adherence to official procedures begets an inability to adjust to unanticipated circumstances.

Perhaps the finest hour of trained incapacity came at Pearl Harbor. The Japanese surprise attack found American bases virtually defenseless. Japanese planes strafed and bombed at treetop level and were vulnerable even to small-arms fire from the ground. Some enlisted men, panicky and determined, wished to fire on the enemy planes with rifles, but the rifles were locked and guarded. The petty officer on guard refused to issue the rifles. Regulations required that he issue the rifles only on written request from the base commander. The base commander, meanwhile, was dead, on leave, or otherwise unavailable. Picture a military official remaining calm, while all around was confusion. Calmly, steadily, he fulfilled the duties of his office. He kept the guns locked up. Meanwhile, for the first time in twenty years, there was an enemy to shoot at, and people willing to do the shooting. The picture is ludicrous, horrible, and predictably bureaucratic.

The rule makes sense. In peacetime, unless weapons are kept under strict control, they will be abused. They will be pawned for the price of an evening's entertainment. Ammunition will be expended shooting rabbits or civilians. The system of check-in and check-out, of requiring written permission, reduces such abuses. It helps assure the organization that weapons will be available when they are needed. In this emergency, the system also assured that weapons were not available. This incident really happened and later formed the basis for a scene in James Jones' *From Here to Eternity*. I recount it here because it so vividly illustrates trained incapacity. The world of formal organization is rife with other manifestations, although few of them are so vivid.

Another bureaucratic malady leading to ineptitude of performance in offices has been labeled the Peter Principle.[1] It arises from the intrinsically bureaucratic policy of merit promotion and tenure in office. An individual in a bureaucratic position who performs that position well can expect promotion to the next higher level. Here he will find a slightly more complicated set of tasks and slightly more exacting standards of performance. Should he perform well at this level also, he may expect, after a time, another promotion. Only if he does not perform well is he not promoted. In theory, every individual is promoted one step above his potential performance and spends the rest of his career at that level. Bureaucracies are filled, then, with individuals who are slightly incompetent for their assigned tasks. This notion can be seen to be related to trained incapacity, as it is precisely the slightly incompetent and slightly insecure person who will develop the heaviest dependence on the rules.

Another source of organizational illness is the communications net. Official communications follow one kind of channel: the chain of command. *Communications filters* in organizations give rise to systematic misdirection, suppression, and distortion of messages. Because of the formal organizational design, messages may simply fail to reach the portions of the organization where they would be useful. From the organizational chart on page 118, it can be seen that an incidental bit of information available in the milling department, would have to go through eleven sets of hands, six up and five down, before it reached a salesman. If he had the information, the salesman might be able to use it to sell the product. At this communication distance the salesman is unlikely even to know the information exists; the milling machine operator is unlikely to recognize its possible utility.

Bureaucratic messages generally travel up or down the line. They involve communication between immediate superior and subordinate. This fact creates additional conditions that limit communication. Any form of interaction between superior and subordinate

---

[1] Laurence Peter and Raymond Hull, *The Peter Principle* (New York: William Morrow, 1969).

tends to be awkward and uncomfortable to the participating parties. Consequently, they keep interaction to a minimum and rely on formal rules to set the norm. Many bits of information that would be useful remain unavailable. The person in possession of the information does not pass it on, because to initiate the message, which would spread the information, would involve entering into a painful relationship.

This is simply loss of information; how about distortion?

Many other kinds of messages are intentionally suppressed or distorted. A person may feel that he has no work to do, that the duties of his office are unnecessary. He will not convey this feeling to his superior. Were he to do so, his superior might abolish his job and fire him. We cannot expect him to act so contrary to his personal interests. He is similarly unlikely to tell his boss that he has botched his job, that he doesn't understand his assignment or orders, that the orders the boss gives are stupid, or that he refuses to carry out his responsibilities. In protecting his own position within the organization, the individual serves as a filter for possible messages.

Many messages are suppressed and distorted not only by the subordinate's predispositions, but by the superior's as well. The boss is not going to hear that he is stupid. Nobody wants to tell him—and he doesn't want to hear. John LeCarré, whose delicate and informed works include *The Spy Who Came in From the Cold*, makes this point. In several of his spy novels, one character or another comments on the nature of intelligence work. In every case, the substance of the remarks is the same. A good intelligence agent is one who can guess what his government wants to believe about the opposition and then provides it with information supporting that view. This information will be accepted; the provider will be rewarded. Contrary evidence will be rejected as unreliable and so will the spy who furnished it.

From your own experience with formal organizations you can add as many more examples of filtered communication as you wish.

One effect of filtering is a series of organizational ailments pointed to by Parkinson's laws.[2] Concerning organizational behavior, Parkinson, with tongue only partly in cheek, asserts that work will expand to fill the time allocated for its performance. The implications of this simple statement are profound. If you put one person to work on a job (in a bureaucracy), the job will keep him busy. Add another person to share the job, and there will be enough

[2]C. Northcote Parkinson, *Parkinson's Law and Other Studies in Administration* (Boston: Houghton-Mifflin, 1957).

work to keep them both busy. Give each of these men ten assistants, and all twenty-two people will be fully occupied.

Suppose the job were counting traffic on a highway. With twenty-two workers, the organization will establish northbound and southbound specialties and a rotating work schedule so that everyone works an eight-hour shift and has some weekends off; the traffic is counted twenty-four hours a day every day of the year.

If we add another hundred workers, will Parkinson's law find exception? No. Our counters will be able to absorb this manpower. Some of the addition will be absorbed in administrative effort. Crew foremen and shift supervisors will be inserted between workers and heads. This division is now large enough to need a personnel department—supervisor, assistant, secretaries, and filing clerks. A quality control department—checkers, statisticians, and more clerks—can monitor the accuracy of the counts. A liaison staff to the larger bureaucracy of which this is a part will be used to retain good relations with the higher administrative body and preserve the operation. A research and development group will be charged with finding new, important, and time-consuming aspects of counting, which are not now a part of the operation. We may find right side and left side counters for the same vehicles. Counts may be offered on the basis of vehicle class, license plate, number of occupants, condition of paint, and speed. A documents group can create, edit, print, and distribute a monthly pamphlet that displays the results. Add another thousand workers and the process will expand accordingly.

All of this, for counting traffic on one highway, seems silly. To my knowledge, it has not happened. But many thousands of actual cases reflect the same principle in some degree. Communications flaws in bureaucracy mean that no officeholder ever says his job is unnecessary. If he has no work, he will find or create some. The importance of a supervisor, his job, and his reward level in the organization depend on how many men he supervises and how many levels he controls. So he, in turn, doesn't want to hear that his subordinates are useless. If instead they can report that they are overloaded and need assistants, the supervisor will be happy to support this recommendation. Bureaucracies tend, then, not simply to absorb the time allocated them, but to ask for more time as well. If we had not "given" extra workers to the traffic counting crew, sooner or later they would have requested them. One implication of Parkinson's Law and the forces underlying it is that all bureaucratic units tend to expand.

Small units within organizations and whole organizations themselves develop a vested interest in their own survival and expansion. *Survival and expansion become the primary goal of all bureaucratic organizations,* far outweighing the nominal goal that they proclaim and with which they may have started.

We must not ignore the nominal goal; it is still useful in explaining some behaviors of some organizations. But the goals of growth and continuity explain far more. This is a central truth about bureaucracy and a special kind of malady in the system. Perhaps we need to do two things here: we need to prove that this hierarchy of goals actually characterizes organizations and that it induces elements of sickness. Both positions make analytic sense, as I believe I have already demonstrated, but what about evidence?

Tobacco companies are diversifying more widely and rapidly than any other American industry. As more and more people give up cigarettes, as new generations include larger percentages of nonsmokers, as government regulations grow more restrictive, the production of tobacco products will not support companies of their size. Their diversification is a hedge against these trends. It demonstrates that they must be understood as organizations devoted primarily to survival and only secondarily to tobacco production. The trend toward conglomerate companies, mentioned early in this chapter, is built on the same logic. If an organization has enough nominal goals, it can count on the continued viability of some of them.

A few decades ago, the National Foundation (March of Dimes) was a charitable foundation devoted to care for victims of polio and to research designed to find a control for the disease. It was also a bureaucratic organization composed in large part of promoters, advertising men, and their supporting staffs. Since then, the development of the Salk vaccine (through research partly supported by March of Dimes funds) and the more effective Sabin vaccine (developed independently of March of Dimes funds) has virtually eliminated polio in the United States.

Today, the National Foundation (March of Dimes) is a charitable foundataion devoted to care for victims of birth defects and other childhood cripplers and to research designed to eliminate these maladies. It is also a bureaucratic organization composed in large part of promoters, advertising men, and their supporting staffs. The possible conflict between nominal and organizational goals is not always apparent. When, as with the sudden and virtually complete realization of the nominal goal, the conflict appears, the organizational response to this crisis reveals which goals are most important.

This kind of commitment to survival may interfere with an organization's pursuit of its nominal goal. When the auto industry for instance, expended organizational effort in an attempt to discredit Ralph Nader, it was protecting itself and its procedures. The same expenditure toward producing safer cars might have pleased Mr. Nader and would surely have been more in the public interest. In another vein, the United States Army used mounted cavalry in a few battles in early 1942. Yes, I mean with real soldiers on real horses. (I love the military, it provides such splendid examples.) While we can understand the mounted cavalry's organizational drive for self-preservation, we can also note that in this case it runs counter to the physical survival of the soldiers who made up such units. From the point of view of overall military efficiency or overall societal requirements, the allocation of resources to mounted cavalry was perverted, wasteful—it was sick.

As organizations focus their attention and efforts on survival, they are apt to fall into the trap of attempting to maintain the present operation unchanged. This conservatism, this inability to adjust to changed circumstances, has its costs. I believe this tendency has already been documented and simply take this opportunity to emphasize it. Bureaucracies tend to be monolithic, unchanging, and inflexible.

Another form of sickness that is built into the system is *linestaff conflicts*. Line and staff represent two different kinds of offices. I will define line as those who are directly engaged in the activity most specifically related to the nominal goals of the organization. Line also includes all those who are supervising or who are responsible for this activity, up the direct chain of command. In the sample organization on page 118, the nominal goal is the production of pumps. Of those shown on the chart, the milling machine operators, who perform manufacturing operations on parts of the pumps, are the first line personnel. In addition, department foreman, line foreman, production superintendent, head of aircraft production, head of manufacture, vice-president of operations, and president are line offices.

I will define staff residually; staff is everybody else. This includes the comptroller, the janitor who sweeps the floor around the milling machines, the person who keeps the typewriter inventory in the office manager's department, salesmen, secretaries, and so on. The activities of staff center around three functions. (1) Staff sustains the organization and provides the setting or framework within which line work proceeds, primarily recruitment, physical plant, and records-keeping functions. (2) Staff coordinates organizational activity. This may involve communication, timing, and the arrangement of work flow. (3) Staff provides information or advice for line decisions. They are experts and specialists who serve the line with ideas.

Some branches of the organization are purely staff; other staff positions or departments may be appended within what is basically a line wing of the organization. If we find line and staff offices at the same level, the incumbents will differ from one another in several respects. The staff person will generally be younger, better educated, more devoted to his professional skill, less loyal to the organization, and will have been with the organization for a shorter time. Some of these characteristics reflect the special expertise required by his position. This same narrow specialization and relatively little experience make the staff person less eligible for promotion within the line. Superior positions, when available, tend to go to line personnel.

The ultimate responsibility and power rest with the line; it is line supervisors who make operative decisions. Special knowledge rests with the staff person, who has no such power. The rivalry between the two groups means that decisions are often made on less than firm grounds. Additionally, much organizational effort is expended in attempts to make the other bunch look bad, in jockeying for position between line and staff. All this exacts a cost on organizational effectiveness.

One final bureaucratic sickness is what I call *weakest-link production*. The notion is simply that the product of an organization is no better than that which could have been produced by the organization's least effective member working alone. As an admittedly oversimplified illustration, let us pretend that the quality of an automobile is strictly determined by the precision of its parts. An automobile in which the parts all fit within .0001 of an inch of perfection would be that much better than one in which the fit is .01, which in turn would be better than one with a fit of .05. Let us add the further condition that an automobile is as bad as its worst part. That is, if a car has four thousand parts and one of these parts fits the rest as poorly as .05, it doesn't matter how much better the rest fit. If .05 parts break down every five hundred miles, this car, this whole car, will be stopped by that part that often.

Now, let us take four thousand machinists. These machinists have varying abilities. A few are expert enough to consistently machine parts to .0001 accuracy, or better. Accuracy decreases from this point with standard human variability, down to the few fumble-fingers who can never do better than .05. If each of these men has a small garage in which he produces cars, each man may turn out a car every other year. There will be a few superb cars produced by the few superb machinists, some good cars, many mediocre cars, and a few truly rotten cars.

If instead we put all four thousand men in a factory, each man produces one part. Each car produced has a part that is made by the worst machinist. Each car produced is likely to break down as often as the worst of the individually-produced cars. There is no point, under these circumstances, in producing a rotten car with a few good parts. The standard of performance for the whole factory will be .05. Again, under the principle of human variability, as more workers are added, the worse will the worst one be. The bigger the organization, the poorer its product.

In defense of the system, we might note one other thing. The four thousand workers in garage shops produced two thousand cars a year. In the factory, they can produce twenty thousand. Under a handicraft system, I could not afford any car. Given my own hierarchy of values, it would be poor consolation to me on foot to know that of the few people who had cars a small portion had good cars. Under bureaucratic production, I can get a mechanical monstrosity rather cheaply, and I like it better when we all ride in bad cars. This brings us back to the starting point of the chapter.

THE SYSTEM HAS GOT YOU, BUT YOU ALSO HAVE GOT THE SYSTEM

Bureaucratic organization is the most efficient means to the accomplishment of a wide variety of goals. Even with the entire set of ailments covered in the last section, this fact is inescapable. Bureaucracy is a powerful enough organizational form that it can carry these handicaps and still serve many functions well. For at least some of these functions there are no alternatives. They will be accomplished bureaucratically or not at all. The performance of these functions and the accomplishment of these goals is fervently desired by man, individually and collectively. Bureaucracy is man's creature, an organizational form designed and cultivated by man for the attainment of these ends.

As a human tool, bureaucracy carries its costs, which were discussed in the previous section. Inefficiencies, nagging frustrations, and the sometime dominance of the organization over the individual. But the profits generally outweigh the costs. Formal organizations deliver benefits and accomplishments to men on terms and conditions that are ultimately determined by those men. Collectively, we will never reject this kind of bargain; we will not knowingly dismantle our bureaucratic structures. Even if we desired, we would probably be unable to do so. The previous section also showed powerful forces within organizations that tend toward their self-preservation. Overcoming this inertial pressure would be difficult, if not impossible.

As an individual actor, then, you had better reconcile yourself to life with bureaucracy. You had better anticipate a world in which your every action is contingent upon and channeled through large formal organizations. The more thoroughly you understand the operations of these systems, the deeper will be your appreciation for them as tools supplementing the human endeavor. The more conversant you are with the sicknesses to which such organizations are prone, the less surprising and more bearable will aberrations of the systems' operations become. The more aware you are of bureaucratic mechanics, the more often will you be the user of the system, rather than its pawn.

FURTHER READING

Bensman, Joseph, *Dollars and Sense*. New York: Macmillan, 1967.

Bensman, Joseph, and Bernard Rosenberg, *Mass, Class, and Bureaucracy: The Evolution of Contemporary Society*. Englewood Cliffs, N.J.: Prentice-Hall, 1963.

Blau, Peter M., *Bureaucracy in Modern Society*. New York: Random House, 1956.* Paperback.

Etzioni, Amitai, *A Comparative Analysis of Complex Organizations*. New York: Free Press, 1961.*

Gouldner, Alvin, *Basic Patterns of Industrial Bureaucracy*. New York: Free Press, 1954. Available in paperback.

Katz, Fred, *Autonomy and Organization: The Limits of Social Control*. New York: Random House, 1968.*

Moore, Wilbert E., *The Conduct of the Corporation*. New York: Random House, 1962. Vintage paperback.

Presthus, Robert, *The Organizational Society*. New York: Random House, 1962. Vintage paperback.

Thompson, James D., *Organizations in Action*. New York: McGraw-Hill, 1967.*

Whyte, William H., Jr., *The Organization Man*. Garden City, N.Y.: Doubleday, 1956. Anchor paperback.

*Difficult, specialized, or technical.

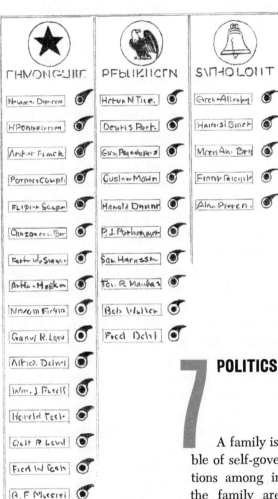

7 POLITICS

A family is apparently capable of self-governance. The relations among individuals within the family are determined by their kin positions. If difficulties arise, they may be settled by referral to another party within the family. Because kin roles are relatively unique, a third party will be available who is not committed to either side. In disagreement between brother and sister, for instance, the appeal may be to cousin, father, grandmother, or some other person. Who should be appealed to may also be set by tradition. If it happened to be grandmother, we may note that she may be somebody's sister—but she is not the quarreling brother's sister. She is also married to a man who may be somebody's brother; she may be a parent of brothers and sisters and has a whole catalog of other kin relationships somehow involving "brotherness" and "sisterness." All these claims more or less cancel out; she can serve as an impartial adjudicator of the quarrel in question.

Two families together form a social unit that is not capable of self-governance. In a two-family society, every person is a member of one family or the other. Quarrels involving members of the two families will find no available disinterested party to whom they can appeal. Everyone has a primary loyalty to one side. Quarrels that cross family lines will inevitably occur. One resolution would be open and total warfare between the two families, but then the two families can no longer be said to form a significant social unit. The other possibility requires the establishment of a social unit other than the two families. We will call such a unit government. In this case, the members of the government will obviously come from the two families, but they will be constrained to act, when they act as government, on behalf of the newly established nonfamilial unit. The new unit must have means to enforce its judgments to make sure that the contesting parties have no appeal besides that to government. In some senses, the government can make war on either family or both, but each family is prohibited from making war on the other. Social order within the unit is maintained; the two families and their government form a society.

To summarize, *a government is a powerful autonomous social unit whose function is the maintenance of social order.* The principles of this definition do not change as we move from a society of two families to a society of many millions of people.

Each of these principles deserves further explanation. *Social order*, as Chapter 4 indicated, follows most fully and directly from the normative order. People go along, routinely compelled by the customs and usages of their own lives, their neighbors, and their ancestors. Informal (again routine and customary) rewards and punishments insure conformity. The various behaviors of many individuals fit together and form an orderly whole that is based on shared values and culture. With all this inducing order, is not government redundant? The answer is no. There are two loopholes in customary order that government may be called on to plug.

The first of these is individual deviation. Every system suffers some occasional lapse or breakdown. The system of customary order is no exception. The action within society of an individual who is not constrained by the norms may pose a threat to the order of that society. Handling such threats may be a charge of government, but other agencies can also assume this responsibility. The situation will vary from society to society. Further exploration of this problem and its solutions will be put off until Chapter 8.

The second loophole is conflicts of interests between individuals or other social units. This is the type of problem that the two-family example posed and which presents serious threats of severe disorder. Because of the need for disinterestedness and for force or threats of force, only government can resolve this problem.

Government's function in maintaining social order is to supplement the normative order, particularly by resolving conflicts of interest between contesting parties within the society.

If government is to intervene successfully in conflicts of interest between other societal agents, some of which themselves may be powerful, the *power* of government must be overwhelming or intimidating. Many texts in sociology and political science suggest that the central characteristic of government is its monopoly of legitimate force. The notion of monopoly is clearly unrealistic; many agencies have and use force within any society. The word "legitimate" also creates some problems. If legitimacy is taken to mean the willing subordination of all the populace and their recognition of the right of the state to wield power, then the power itself would be unnecessary. All the people would voluntarily follow the dictates of the state. If legitimate means according to law, then the concept is redundant, for the state makes the law and is the law. Moral as well as logical contradictions arise from a consideration of issues brought up at the Nuremberg Trials concerning the conduct of the German Third Reich; the draft resistance movement in the contemporary United States presents similar problems. Let's forget, then, about legitimacy and monopoly and stick to the issue of sufficient power for the task at hand.

The government must be powerful, overwhelmingly powerful. If it is not it cannot accomplish the maintenance of order and will not be a government or will find no society to govern.

The final requirement of government is *autonomy*. One possible image is that of a referee, who controls and keeps within bounds the contest between opposing parties; he administers the rules impartially and evenly. Some governments and societies may fit this image. Of course, there are also crooked referees. They alter the rules and bias the decisions to assure victory to the side they favor. Many societies fit this model more closely than the other. In either case, the condition of autonomy still holds. The referee runs the game as a unit that is separate from the contesting teams. Order is still maintained. Only if the referee were to remove his distinctive uniform, don that of the team he favored, and actively participate in the play would our condition of autonomy be violated. These actions would probably cause the game to degenerate into chaos. All this shows that autonomy is not synonymous with neutrality or impartiality. It is only the former that is required of government. The appearance of disinterestedness is useful and may reduce the quotient of power required for order. The reality of disinterest is not part of the essential character of a government.

A government may be a noble proponent of shared ideals, an indifferent dispenser of even-handed justice, or a venal tool of special interest. It is always separate.

PARTY GAMES

Whether government is noble or indifferent or venal is partly determined by who governs. The process of gaining access to political power is called politics. Political parties are mechanisms for gaining such power.

In this sense, the major parties in the United States are better, purer political parties than almost any others anywhere else. In some societies, the dominant political party becomes deeply enmeshed with the governmental system as such. It becomes an instrument through which governmental power is wielded, rather than an instrument for obtaining governmental power. Given our definitional requirement for autonomy of the government, such parties are a part of the autonomous governmental unit. They are therefore not independent agencies in their own right. The Falangists of Spain, the Communists of the USSR, and the Institutional Revolutionary Party of Mexico are good examples. Certainly, this does not mean that there are no struggles for power in these societies. There are. They involve factions of the party, isolated individuals, shifting coalitions, and variable power bases. They are less well organized than is the case when parties are separate units. The bureaucracy of the party belongs to all the competing units and hence can serve as the instrument of none. In another sense, the party bureaucracy belongs to the government and is used for straight governmental functions and is not available at all for political ones. Political functions must then be carried out without the services of a bureaucracy and hence are carried out rather ineffectively.

In some other societies political parties become instruments for the advancement of an ideology. The pursuit of a particular ideology may impose policies that conflict with the pursuit of power; such parties become ambivalent, fragmented, and ineffectual. Arthur B. Tourtellet[1] describes this form of party as being like a sieve. The populace is strained through, and only those of a particular ideological hue are retained. Under such a system, the party does not seek power as power, but power to institute a particular policy that is consistent with its ideology. The ideological purity is retained, even if this means foregoing power. There will be as many separate parties as there are shadings of opinion; none of these will be large enough to muster a majority; government will be carried out by uneasy and ephemeral coalitions of parties. Each party's membership will be so small it cannot support a fully complemented bureaucracy of its own. The political structures of Italy, Belgium, and Chile match this model.

Tourtellet draws an analogy between the type of political party found in the United States and circus tents, an image that gives rise to connotations that are probably intentional. The walls of the tent are expandable, and the party constantly stretches them and drives new stakes so that the tent covers more people, regardless of where they are standing. The object of the party is to achieve power. Members represent power. The party will adopt any ideology that will attract members. The aim of the party is simply to control the government, not to direct it toward some other goal. Australian and West German systems fit this pattern.

These three types of parties—governmental, ideological, and competitive—exhaust our catalog. Some parties and some societies fit the models more neatly than others, but the models will serve for purposes of discussion. The number of parties in a society generally correlates with their type, although there are exceptions. Governmental parties are usually found in one-party systems. In systems with a large number of parties, ideological party patterns usually predominate. Competition ordinarily implies a two-party system. Only the last of these relationships is not self-explanatory. Let us see what it is about party competition that leads to a two-party system.

Power may be used to get other power. This kind of exchange

[1] *An Anatomy of American Politics* (Indianapolis: Bobbs-Merrill, 1950).

was discussed in Chapter 5. In the context here, other kinds of power must be spent to gain control of the government. These other kinds of power may be votes, police force, economic pressure, or any other variety or combination of powers. The task of a political party is to gain and mobilize such forces to propel themselves into government. This requires the party to offer a *quid pro quo* to those who lend power support to the party. What the party has to offer is policy. The competitive party gains its competitive base by trading policy favors for support.

The bargain may be explicit, conscious, and fully two-sided. "Contribute to my campaign, and if I am elected I'll appoint you traffic commissioner." It may be general and weakly contracted. "There are a lot of honest, hard-working, well-qualified men in this town who have never held public office. If I'm elected, I will seek them out and appoint them." The campaigner hopes for the votes of some would-be officeholders who consider themselves honest, hard-working, and qualified. In major political struggles, such as those for national office in sizeable countries, the sources of support are many, varied, and widespread. Even a sophisticated bureaucratic party structure has difficulty establishing firsthand relations with many of these sources. Most bargains are, then, implicit, general, open-ended.

In major political struggles, the range of potential favors the power of government can offer are nearly as diverse as the sources of support they hope to elicit. Most of these favors, the most important ones, hinge around policy. Legislation or administration can be offered that will be considered advantageous to a wide variety of potential sources of support.

Some policies would be considered advantageous by all the constituents. Any competitive party will promise these things. Since they are equally promised by all parties, they offer no competitive edge to any. Competition occurs when a party has opportunities to offer something the other party does not offer. Constituents will support one party rather than another only when they see that one party will serve their policy interests better than the other. Within a society, the policy interests of one group may conflict with the interests of a second group; the nature of government is the control of these conflicting interests. The nature of parties is to turn the conflict into competition for governmental power.

The political process begins when the public is divided on an issue. There are differences of opinion. For any issue, the series of possible positions relative to that issue can be portrayed as a continuum. Whether the issue is national defense, black power, forest conservation, or fluoridation makes no difference. Figure 7–1 is a sample opinion continuum for issue *A* vs. *B*. Although the range of opinion may be infinite, only five points on the continuum for this issue are indicated. Substitute the appropriate rhetoric for any issue at the appropriate point on the line. If you find a position that will not fit, the chances are you have uncovered a different issue. A preference for total integration of the races within the mainstream of American culture, for instance, may not fit anywhere on the continuum for the black power issue. Similarly, a preference for mixing Scotch with water may not be located on the continuum of attitudes for or against mixing fluoride with water.

Fig. 7-1   OPINION CONTINUUM, *A* vs. *B*

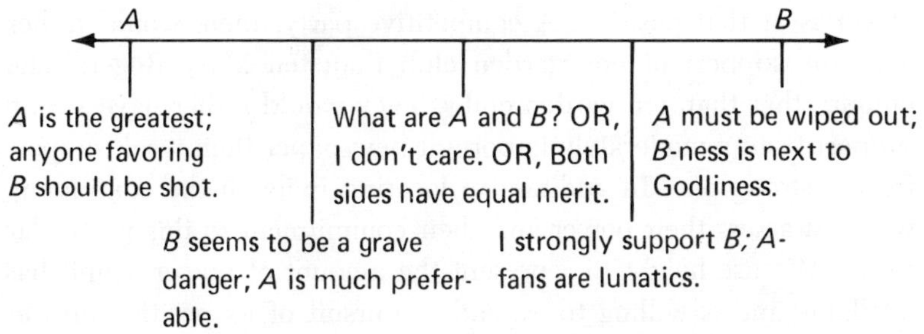

A is the greatest; anyone favoring *B* should be shot.

What are *A* and *B*? OR, I don't care. OR, Both sides have equal merit.

A must be wiped out; *B*-ness is next to Godliness.

B seems to be a grave danger; *A* is much preferable.

I strongly support *B*; *A*-fans are lunatics.

Once a "pure" issue has been defined, we could proceed to mark off more than the five positions portrayed. We could find "mildly-favorably-disposed" and "radically-against-but-somewhat-short-of-the-extreme" positions. We could find, at least theoretically, enough points to make a line. We can then begin placing people at the appropriate points along the line. As our original interest was not in people, but in power, we will likewise place other social units, any unit with power, somewhere along the line. Continuing with black power as an example, the line (drastically oversimplified) might then look like Fig. 7–2. To make the diagram complete, we would have to include additionally: Mr. Arthur Morgan of Harlem, Mrs. Mary Rogers of Cuthbert, Georgia, and the two hundred million other Americans. We would also have to include the San Jose Garden Club, the National Association of Manufacturers, the University of Minnesota, General Electric's Jet Engine Division, the Chattanooga Girl's Choir, *The New York Times*, the Meatcutter's Union, and all other possible power units in American society. When we were done we would have a very confused and crowded diagram.

It would also be politically inadequate. Parties want support,

Fig. 7-2   OPINION CONTINUUM: BLACK POWER

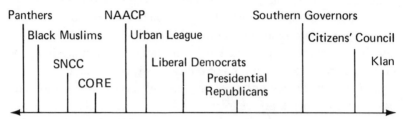

essentially in the form of power. These social units vary in the amount of power they have or will expend on a particular issue. Parties, in their attempt to capture power, will not want to know how many units hold a particular position, but how much available power is at that position. A competitive party, then, would rather have the support of one garden club than ten Mary Rogers, one union rather than ten garden clubs. They would rather have strong support from a moderately important newspaper than weak support from a strong one. In addition to locating units on the continuum, we must assess their power and their commitment to this particular issue.[2] We use height to represent the amount of power a unit has available and is willing to expend in pursuit of its position on this issue. Piling all units with the same position on top of each other and extending the height of available power at that location, our issue continuum now looks like the one shown in Fig. 7–3.

Note that the power distribution resembles a normal curve. Such will not always be the case. It is possible to have a relatively flat distribution on some issues. It is also possible for two, three, or more "humps" to occur or for most of the power to be "loaded" off to one side. The normal distribution is by far the most common. Normality, after all, is not simply a name for the shape of the curve. It implies that more kinds of factors distribute themselves in this fashion than in any other. The laws of probability designate this characteristic distribution as the most likely one for any issue. Moreover, the society will tend to be administered in whatever way is indicated by the dominant powers. If the *status quo* is taken as the center, then the biggest single hump, representing just that kind of concentrated power, is unlikely to be far from the center. Finally, power can be gained and lost. One of the ways in which it can be lost is by plug-

[2]The factors involved in a general consideration of power are found on pages 103–7. The relationship between power and ideology (policy) is explored from another direction on pages 68–71 and in Chapter 11.

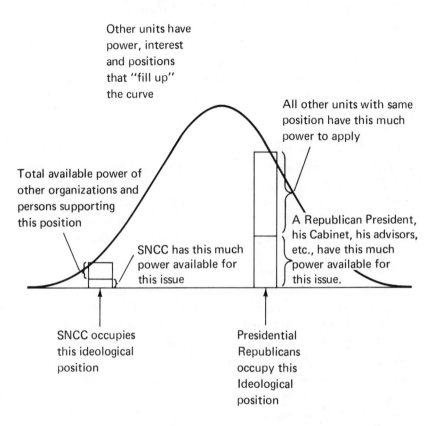

Fig. 7-3   IDEOLOGICAL CONTINUUM: POWER CURVE FOR
            "BLACK POWER" (partial)

Other units have
power, interest
and positions
that "fill up"
the curve

All other units with same
position have this much
power to apply

Total available power of
other organizations and
persons supporting
this position

A Republican President,
his Cabinet, his advisors,
etc., have this much
power available for
this issue.

SNCC has this much
power available for
this issue

SNCC occupies
this ideological
position

Presidential
Republicans
occupy this
Ideological
position

ging too hard for an extremist position. If *The New York Times* were
consistently to push as hard as it could for total black power or total
white power, the newspaper itself would become less powerful. Part
of its present power derives from its reputation for reasoned edi-
torials and balanced reportage. It has a large circulation partly because it seldom stirs violent antagonisms in its subscribers. The same
principle applies to any person or group.

Competitive parties, unlike ideological parties, are not bound
to any one position. They use whatever information is available to
make guesses about the power distribution on an issue, and take
their stand accordingly. They must guess on the basis of inadequate
information, for no precise and complete accountings such as we
have been discussing exist. Parties may be wrong, but they are not
likely to be far wrong often. They are professionals at the politics
game. They maintain their party's existence by accurate guesses.

The system is complicated somewhat by the simultaneous participation of two parties. The party in power can actually institute policy. In this sense, they get first choice of positions. They stake out that choice by their administration. The outs cannot select the same positions; if they did they could offer the constituents no reason for replacing the government. They can have any other position. The contest for control of the government then begins, and the outcome depends on which party's estimate (and consequent stand) was closest to the actual distribution of public support.

If we designate positions numerically, from extreme A (0) to extreme B (100), we can suppose that the ins established themselves at 50. The outs can now have any position other than fifty. They can take 29, 80, or any other number. The optimum strategy, under most conditions, will be for them to take 49 or 51. Compare, for instance, the payoffs for 51 and 80. If the power distribution is perfectly flat and if all units support the party closest to their own position, 80 will win if more than half of the power is between 65 and 100. But 51 will win all of those times and also if the middle is anywhere between 65 and 50.5 The outs have nothing to lose and much to gain by snuggling as close as possible to the ins (see Fig. 7–4).

The advantages of this strategy are increased as the power distribution approaches a normal curve, rather than a flat one. The more peaked the distribution, the greater the chance that the center of power is near the middle of the issue range. The public center is much more likely to be between 50 and 60 than between 70 and 80. The chances of winning are best near the center.

The advantages of this strategy are decreased if some units fail to support the nearest party unless it is close to their own position. Some social units might have extreme positions, say in the 90's. They would offer support to a party close to their position. If they perceived no close party, they might support no party at all. They might lessen their support or drop out entirely as the out party edged below 65. In deciding whether to take a position near the center, the out party must weigh its gains among moderates against its losses among the extreme wing. The more peaked the distribution, the greater the chances that a gain in the center will offset the loss. Further, the in party, by staking a claim near the center, has also lost some extremists at the other end. The losses of the two parties on this ground are likely to offset each other, so the contest is still in the middle.

One more complication is that no contest for governmental control is decided on one issue. Issues may vary in relative importance, hence in relative power potential, but there are always many issues.

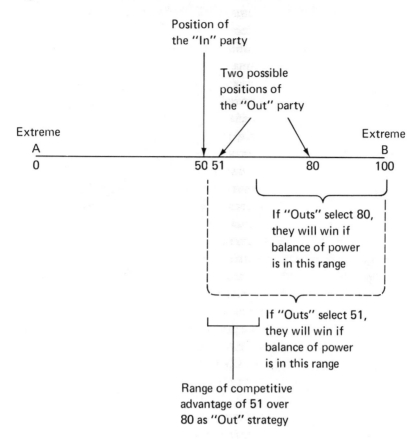

Fig. 7-4   CENTRIST STRATEGY IN TWO-PARTY POLITICS

Position of
the "In" party

Two possible
positions of
the "Out" party

Extreme
A

Extreme
B

0

50 51

80

100

If "Outs" select 80,
they will win if
balance of power
is in this range

If "Outs" select 51,
they will win if
balance of power
is in this range

Range of competitive
advantage of 51 over
80 as "Out" strategy

A party can be wrong on several issues—even most issues—but to win it must somehow be right enough on some combination of issues to gather more power than the other party. The game now gets very complicated. Figure 7–5 shows an issue-power diagram for only two issues.

Suppose the Poetry Party takes position 45 on *AB*, and 52 on *CD*. The Prose Party elects 46 *AB* and 51 *CD*. A moderately powerful pressure group, the Blank Verse Society, stands at 20 *CD* and 44 *AB*. If they are guided by *AB* alone, they lend their support to the Poets. If ruled by *CD*, their support goes to Prose. Will they sit the contest out? Will they give the same support to each group? Will the fact that they are so far out on *CD* make the Poets, who are further from them (though only by a little bit), seem so radical that

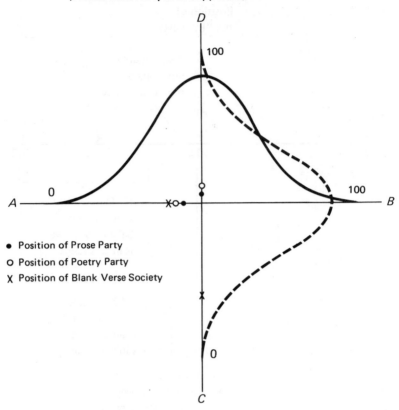

Fig. 7-5   TWO ISSUES, TWO PARTIES, ONE DECISION
(Pressure on Party and Supporter)

● Position of Prose Party
○ Position of Poetry Party
X Position of Blank Verse Society

they vote for the opposition? Or will they be alienated by both parties' stances on this issue, consider it of no salience, and decide solely on *AB* to support Poetry? For this kind of example, we have shown the complicated kind of process that goes into party decision making, particularly if we expand from two to a hundred issues or more. We have also uncovered a dilemma for the decision units to which the party is appealing. Individual or group, all are likely to be subjected to these sorts of *cross-pressures*, where they can find sound motives for supporting both parties or neither.

If we were to change the example so that one party was extreme on one issue, we would uncover another reason why the best party strategy is the snuggle. If Poets stood for 60 *CD*, their net difference from the Blank Versers would be greater than that of the Prose

Party. Even though they would win one issue out of two, they would lose the combination. A party that is extremist on even one issue may totally alienate a number of supporters who would otherwise find it preferable on most issues. It cannot afford to give up that easily on any portion of the public, which it might otherwise capture. The greater the number of salient issues, the greater becomes the tendency for centrist politics in the system.

If we change the example to include more than two parties, we can see why the competitive system usually involves only two. If one party preempts position 50, one of the best strategies for an opposition party is 49. A third party elects 48 or 51. The party in the middle is cut off from support on either side. Multiple issues will lessen this effect; a party that is squeezed out on one issue may get an edge on another. Fairly stable three- or even four-party systems may survive under such conditions, but these possibilities are extremely unlikely; systems with more parties are even rarer. This is the reason why competitive politics are usually two-party politics.

All this has some very important implications for the operation of society as a whole. Picture the issue continuum as a board. The power units are weights placed at their respective positions along the board with weight varying according to committed power. The center that we have been discussing is the point at which the board would balance if a fulcrum were placed underneath. Each party seeks to find that balance point at the same time that it pursues the competitive snuggle strategy and attempts to stay close to the other party. The policy of any government with competitive parties tends to match the moment of power on each issue within that society. Parties and party competition must then be understood as mechanisms that sustain the function of government. Parties cushion and crystallize conflicting interests within a society. From these varying interests they derive governmental policy. Controlling such conflicts and mediating such interests is the function of government; parties are a nearly indispensable part of the operation.

The "fairest"—most accurate—representation of these interests occurs in a competitive party system. I do not imply a moral judgment here. Neither am I saying that such a system is representative of the people, on a one-man, one-vote basis. The system reflects the interests within the society. In a competitive party society where the army is the most powerful unit, governmental policy will be correspondingly militaristic. There will be no guaranteed protection of minorities unless they have some power with which to bargain for that protection. A competitive system may or may not appear to operate through a voting mechanism. It does not matter. What is reflected is power. That is the name of the game the parties play.[3]

Competitive parties, parties in two-party systems, play the game to the utmost. The United States is a near perfect example of a system. You should expect, then, to find little difference between the two major parties in the United States. This is precisely what you will find. You may, if you are a strong partisan of one of the parties, reject this statement. I ask you to consider the evidence a little more fully. List, if you can, the total ideological and policy stand of the two parties. Compare these with the stands of the several parties of France, Japan, or any sizeable mixture of non-American parties. Are not the stands of the Democratic and Republican parties in the United States the most strikingly similar pair of the lot? Compare major American parties with minor ones. The big two appear centrist and identical; the far-out ones are the fractional parties. They are more different from one another and from the major parties than the major parties are from each other. Greenbackers, New Party, Dixiecrat, Farm-Labor, American Independent, Know-nothings, Socialist, Vegetarian, Populist, Progressive, Christian Front, American Nazi, Prohibitionist—here is a garden in which Democrats and Republicans will be recognized as of the same species. Count the leading figures in the two parties. Among Senate Democratic leaders are Eastland and Muskie, among Republican, Thurmond and Javits. Where is the homogeneity; who resembles whom? Both tents expand to cover virtually the same ground. As one final proof I offer the following law. In Presidential elections, each party will nominate the one of its leading candidates who most resembles the candidate of the other party. With small allowance for regional and other kinds of "un-

---

[3]Herbert McClosky, Paul Hoffman, and Rosemary O'Hara measured positions of party leaders and party followers, Democrats and Republicans, on a number of critical issues ("Issue Conflict and Consensus among Party Leaders and Followers," *American Political Science Review*, 54 (1960), 406–27). Their conclusions, generally, were these: Democratic leaders are much like Democratic followers; Republican followers are much like both Democratic leaders and followers; Republican leaders are relatively unlike any of the other three groups. It might seem that the Republican party is, in such a condition, without a constituency. An alternative interpretation is that the study tested only the positions of *individuals*. Constituencies are built, rather, of power units. A few highly powerful individuals and many powerful organizations in the United States have positions that are further right on most issues than the majority of the people. When these power units are added to people as power units, they flesh out the right side of the power curve and explain the position of the Republican leadership. These data, with this interpretation, solidly support the points made in the last few paragraphs.

availability" of an otherwise leading candidate, this law holds up as well as any other for the past fifty years or so. Perhaps the most obvious exception is the Republican nomination of Goldwater to oppose Johnson in 1964, but in this case Goldwater absorbed a defeat that should make Republicans wary of that strategy for another fifty years. The two parties are virtually identical and will remain so.

Several implications that might seem to follow from these points are fallacious and must be laid to rest. (1) That parties change their stands on issues to match their conception of the public stand does not mean that individual politicians, as individuals, are immoral or unopinionated. First, it is certainly possible that an individual will change his mind. Second, one tenable position with regard to public office in a representative system is that the officeholder is indeed a representative—he carries out the public wishes regardless of his own opinions. The third condition is the most important. Although individual politicians are likely to remain steadfast adherents of positions consistent with their own convictions, the party serves as a mechanism for selecting from among its pool of politicians nominees whose positions match the public sentiment. (2) That parties act in this fashion, shifting ideology, embracing a man in one election only to reject him at the next, does not mean that parties are unprincipled. Parties have firm convictions to which they are exceedingly loyal. These are, essentially, that it is better to get elected. They stand by this principle, no matter what it may cost them in other values. Any other posture would make them something other than competitive parties. (3) That the two parties are identical does not mean that the public will is frustrated. Remember, both parties are busily seeking power; they, therefore, advocate a popular policy that will win them this power. Party policy, then, will follow public desires. Both parties will shift to meet any change in public opinion. If they shift together, so what? Toward the end of Chapter 11, I describe the rise of new powers in the United States and the kinds of shifts in party policy that will follow.

The point I want to make here is that competitive party politics are a useful adjunct to government and probably act more "fairly in the public interest" than any other system.

PARTY SYSTEMS

So far, I have spoken of parties as if they were persons. "The party wants." "The party believes." "The party adopts a course of action." Although parties are action units and such usage leads to little confusion of meaning, we must now reemphasize the point that parties, particularly competitive parties, are bureaucratic systems.

They are relatively poorly formed bureaucracies and for this reason are difficult to define or discuss; but they are bureaucracies nonetheless. If we define the party in terms of self-recognized membership, we will have a group, Democrats or Republicans, with forty million or so members. Most of these members will be members only in so labeling themselves and in more or less regularly casting their votes for the party they claim. This kind of behavior fits none of the conditions of offices in formal organizations. We will look instead for individuals who (1) occupy positions that carry prescribed rights and duties within the organization's context; (2) can be placed somewhere within the chain of command; (3) are part of a regularized communications net within the organization. Using these standards, we can isolate the party as bureaucracy from the party in other guises.

Because the party has a rhythm of activities, expanding during election years and contracting at other times, we will still have some definitional difficulties. I will suggest that we include people who meet the above definition at least once every four years. We will then be using rather rigid requirements organizationally, but very liberal ones in terms of time and continuity. By this usage we will include the "hard core" permanent bureaucracy—the full-time party officials and employees. We will also include government officeholders, elected and appointed, who surely belong and who might not be included by some other definitions. Congressmen or members of the President's Cabinet, for instance, may not serve the party bureaucracy for relatively long periods but will become involved at critical times; we will surely want to include them within the party organization. We will also want to include national convention delegates, precinct workers, and chronic members of "Citizens for Somebody."

This way of counting will leave each party with approximately one million people of whom it can, from time to time, make demands with some reasonable expectation of their being met. This is a sizeable organization, even though most of these people are very much occasional or part-time workers. Still, this reservation differs only in degree from the position of any other formal organization. An employer can place only some kinds of demands on his employees, and only under time limitations. The employee may only be obligated for an eight-hour day and a five-day week. The party member may only be obligated for a few afternoons immediately preceding Presidential elections.

With the boundaries at least crudely marked, let us analyze parties as bureaucracies. We have already noted in Chapter 6 that a bureaucracy's first goal is survival. Survival in politics implies election; bureaucratic parties will then seek election. Bureaucratic parties will be competitive parties, and vice versa.

Many segments of the party bureaucracy will be oriented toward mobilizing power-interests to insure election. Under this rubric will be such diverse activities as: collecting funds, driving voters to the polls on election day, coordinating the activities of pressure groups that are working with the party, arranging policy-for-support bargains that are the foundation of the political process, and dispensing favors.

A second function of the party organization is the controlling of information flow. As in all organization, this flow is two-way and imperfect, but important. The party stand on issues must be made known to the public, and diverse segments of this public must be persuaded that these stands are in their interest. The candidates must be similarly exposed, widely and in a favorable light. Special interest groups will receive tailor-made messages that differ from the messages given to the general public. All these flow down from the top and outward from the organization to the public. Messages travel the other way as well. Low-level functionaries feel the "grass roots" and pass their assessments up the line. Shifts in popular stances must be uncovered so that the party position can be altered to match.

The party serves as a broker of governmental services. Sooner or later, the party organization will assist an unemployed steelworker in Pittsburgh in his attempt to get on the welfare rolls. It will also assist a steel executive in his attempt to get a better tax break. Naturally, the party will be more eager to perform this service if the worker and the executive supported their party in the last election. In this sense, the party is simply fulfilling the bargain it made when it elicited the support of these persons. When all these bills are paid, however, we can also notice that more people who are entitled to welfare have it, and more people who deserve tax breaks get them, than would otherwise be the case. The party has, in serving its own ends, also served as an adjunct to government.

The party also serves as a governmental supplement in the guise of placement bureau. At all levels of government, there are nearly a million appointed offices. A new President alone comes to his office faced with the task of appointing several thousand persons. Who shall he appoint? Where will so many qualified people be found?

The party bureaucracy will be glad to recommend party faithful. For the most part and in the long run, the patronage system works. The offices are filled with at least moderately qualified appointees. The government has saved the costs of such things as search and screening. The party does the job free. Of course party workers and party supporters are rewarded by this system. Of course the party in serving the government also serves itself. The point is that it still does serve.

Decisions must be made within the party. Candidates must be nominated; platforms must be developed; coalitions of interests must be welded; policies must be developed and carried out. Here is where the party bureaucracy comes into its own. All the other functions have served to maintain the party, to gather and use nongovernmental power for the purposes of gaining governmental power. Now that power must be harnessed and directed in ways that are consistent with the bargains that were made to obtain the power. The party membership holds this power. Of course they do not hold it equally. The national chairman holds more than the state committeeman who holds more than the county convention delegate. But all of them hold some. After all, the power of the nation—all the people and all their organizations—has been funnelled into two organizations and two million persons. Even the man at the bottom of the party hierarchy has a high power quotient compared to the average citizen. If these men are so important, maybe we ought to take a look at them.

The smallest geographical unit in politics is the territory containing people who vote at a single polling place.[4] Such an area is likely to contain between fifty and two thousand voters and is usually called a precinct. The lowest regularized line office within a party, then, is precinct captain or chairman. These individuals usually serve as delegates to a convention at the next higher level (wards, counties). There, delegates are selected for the next higher level. The process goes on through state and national conventions and committees. The usual mode of selection at any level is election. Conventions may also pass resolutions on policy, which their delegates are bound to propose and support at the next higher convention.

This process sounds like a truly open-ended, broad-based, and representative bureaucracy under control from the bottom. In some

[4]Again I must emphasize that party organizations are poorly defined bureaucracies. Therefore, the organization varies with local custom, state law, and party practice. It is very difficult to make any generalizations that will hold across the board. All descriptions here and following are typical—and typically inaccurate.

ways, it is. In most ways, it is not. Starting again at the bottom, any registered voter within the precinct who belongs to the appropriate party can become a precinct chairman. Precinct chairmen may be selected by ballot during primary elections or at specially-called precinct meetings. In either case, the potential candidate needs only a little initiative and a few friends. In my own experience, I have seen a precinct chairman elected on a primary ballot with seven write-in votes (to three for his combined "opposition") out of a party registration of nine hundred. At precinct meetings, I have seen issues carried by three votes to two in a precinct with five hundred party registrants. From this start the individual can, in time, work his way up the organization. This is not, however, a likely course of events.

If we examine the typical party official, rather than the isolated case, we notice several distinguishing characteristics. He is likely to be slightly better educated and wealthier than the average voter in the area he serves, and will have a slightly better than average job, He is probably a long-term resident. Finally, and most important, he is likely to have a wide circle of acquaintances and be a member of various organizations. Some of these contacts will have provided the impetus for his entrance into politics and will furnish sponsorship as he retains his position or advances. At every level of possible advancement, his way will be blocked by new candidates who are not working up from the bottom, but who offer superior qualifications to his own in terms of wealth, contacts, prestige, and sponsorship.

The seemingly open party organization is in actuality a semi-closed one. It reserves its sensitive positions for the "old pros" and for amateurs who are well-connected with the informal power network of the society. From the party's point of view, such exclusiveness is rational. Its interest is in winning. These are the people who control the resources and have knowledge of how these resources may be utilized—the people who can help the party win.

The stereotyped political machine of the big cities is dead or dying. But the system remains identical in many respects. The composition of the organization formerly included grafting contractors, ethnic frauds, patronage and charity fixers, strong arm boys, election fixers, and industrial monopolists. It now includes corporate executives, pressure-group representatives, welfare specialists, organizers, public relations men, and industrial lobbyists. This change, if it is one, is simply a reflection of changes in the society, not a change in the essential character of parties or their organizations. To the extent that the society's sources of power have changed, the party recruits its organization from different sources. Without seeming closed, or even very organized, each party builds an effective power-seeking bureaucracy and becomes an effective wielder of power as well.

PARTY APPEARANCES

Politics is like an iceberg. Very little of it shows. In the sections on party games and party systems we have looked at the hidden elements: the structure of ice and the bottom and insides of the berg. Let us now have a view from the top: the iceberg as seen from the decks of the *Titanic*. Let's look at politics from the average citizen's viewpoint.

As he grows up, a child absorbs his parents' prejudices and perceptions of the parties and their views on issues. This conception is modified by his peers, his teachers, and the politics of the administrations under which he matures. He reads (a little) and watches TV (a lot). Election time arrives. He goes to the poll or he does not. If he goes, he exercises his franchise by voting for one or another of the candidates. This is democracy in action, at its most sacred and crucial moment. Our mythical voter is likely to select the following:

1. The candidate with the most honest looks, the most straightforward gaze, or the most chaste wife.
2. The candidate of the party his parents supported.
3. The party which, in the traditional mythology of our society, most closely represents the interests of his occupation or class.
4. The candidate who is supported by most of his friends and acquaintances, particularly those one notch higher than he on the prestige ladder; the possibility of influence here is restricted to those of his friends who have been vocal enough to make their choices known.
5. The party supported by some organization to which he belongs and where he feels his membership is important.
6. The party supported by a movie star, athlete, or other hero whom he admires.
7. The party he has always supported.
8. The party whose promises or past performance are closest to his own positions or interests on one particularly salient issue or any combination of issues.
9. The man who happens to be in the same column as someone he really wants to vote for, because straight-ticket voting is easiest.
10. The man with the best background, judgment, or temperament for the job.

At least half of these possibilities are irrational in terms of promoting his own personal well-being or the national welfare. Even the ones that appear rational may not be so on closer inspection.

Take "best man" selection, for instance. Think of someone you know only moderately well: an uncle who lives in a different town, a co-worker whom you do not see socially, a neighbor further down the block. Would he make a good President? Do you know him well-enough to judge? How does he react under stress? How wide is his knowledge about the international situation? Is his feeling for persons sound enough so that he would select appropriate advisors? You must protest, "I don't know him that well." I submit that you know him better than you know the candidates for President. Furthermore, you don't know the office of the Presidency well either. Assuming you have never been President or a close advisor to a President and have not made a life-long career as a scholar of the Presidency, you don't know what the job entails. You don't know what sorts of characteristics a man needs to perform well in the job. Our voter in the booth, if he makes his choice in favor of the best man for the job, is operating in an area of double ignorance where he knows neither the man nor the job. He is actually guided by public images of both. These images flow more from Madison Avenue than from reality.

When most seemingly well informed and rational political choices are dissected, they prove to have been choices of one advertising agency over another, a preference between propaganda pitches. Finally, most choices are not made on the basis of one of the criteria listed above, but on them all. When the voter finds his parents' party to be different from his friends' or the party closest to his positions different from the one offering the best man, he is subject to cross-pressures. Given a list this long, some cross-pressures will probably be operative. The more cross-pressures there are, the greater difficulty he will have making up his mind. Once his mind is made up, however, he finds evidence in support of that position and his mind becomes closed to contrary information.

The voter could, of course, become well-informed. He could work his way past façades and discover the real issues and positions. This would require a major dedication of his time, resources, and intellect. How would a change in the monetary backing requirements of Federal Reserve banks affect you? Where do the major parties and leading figures within these parties stand on this issue? On accelerated trade with Tanzania? On creation of more public-use areas in national forests? On ten thousand other issues? If you knew enough of these things truly, rather than as party propagandists would have you know them, you could cast a rational vote. The odds that your one vote will make any difference in the election are so very small that such effort is scarcely worthwhile.

If a substantial majority of voters were to become informed, the benefits would be enormous. We could expect such things as a sounder government, stronger candidates, and more policy breaks for the majority. Such benefits are for the whole society, including any who remain ignorant. There is no payoff for your becoming an informed voter, unless most others also become informed. If they become informed, you get the payoff even if you remain ignorant. Therefore, it is smart to be dumb. The logic and the conclusion are the same for everyone; as a result, we will continue to operate with an uninformed electorate. Those who do become informed can only receive payoff by placing themselves in positions offering greater leverage than that of mere voter. The logical entry point to such position is the party organization. If you must be smart, join the party.

To whatever extent all of these conditions hold, the ignorant electorate finds its political affairs being managed by the better-informed party organizations. The pressured, propagandized, and passive voter makes a choice that is little better than a coin-toss, but between two parties that are virtually identical anyway. If either party gets too far out of line even he would notice. The uninformed voter is still capable enough to keep the broad principle of party competition in operation. Once that is accomplished the ballot decision is relatively unimportant, which, given the nature of that decision, is fortunate for those of us who live in such a system.

In the early part of this chapter I spoke of parties as mechanisms for gaining power and suggested that two-party competition for that power produced the "fairest" representation of societal interests in the governmental exercise of that power. Competitive parties tend to be bureaucratic parties as well and produce "efficient" administration. Then, dealing more specifically with the system in the United States and other similar systems, I restricted the competition to that based on elections. Elections are a sound basis for competition and tend to create and sustain two-party bureaucratic competitive systems. Hence, elections also tend to produce a "fair" system. The strengths of an election system are not in the election process itself but in the party system it sustains. Such a party system may be supported by other kinds of foundations in other systems and would then carry the same strengths. Politics and elections have, intrinsically, little to do with each other.

GOVERNMENT SYSTEMS

Politics is both crucial to government and interesting. Elections are interesting, but not crucial to government. Administration is crucial to government, but not interesting. Once a party gains access to governmental power it wields that power and puts its policies into practice through the governmental bureaucracy.[5] These bureaucracies are guided, to some extent, by policy considerations already established through the political process. As bureaucracies, they are resistant to this sort of direction. As bureaucracies, they are subject to the intrusion of goals and behaviors of purely organizational origin, as opposed to imposed policy. As bureaucracies, they have inertia, a predilection for continuing to do the same old things in the same old ways. As bureaucracies, work which they accomplish and outputs they produce are marked with a special organizational stamp. In a word, they are just like any other bureaucracies; being governmental doesn't make them any different. They are uninteresting because what we have already said about bureaucratic systems generally says all we can say about government bureaucracies specifically. We said that in Chapter 6. It is important to note this bureaucratic character of government. To do so helps explain why, for instance, policies carried out by the different parties as they succeed each other are even less divergent than the policies the parties advocate. They must try to institute their policies through the same organization, and for the organization tradition *is* policy.

Politics and administration are the halves of government. By giving politics greater attention in this chapter, I do not mean to imply that it is the greater part. It is simply more special. Politics is the gaining of power; administration its exercise. The end of these combined processes is the adjudication of interests within the society, the control of conflict, the governance of society.

---

[5]This bureaucracy is quite distinct from the party bureaucracies; except in monopoly party systems. The governmental bureaucracy, among other things, is likely to be a highly formalized one, full-time, and routine. Some membership between the two may overlap; much will not.

FURTHER READING

Alford, Robert, *Party and Society*. Chicago: Rand-McNally, 1963.*

Banfield, Edward, and James Wilson, *City Politics*. Cambridge, Mass.: Harvard University, 1963. Available in paperback, Random House Vintage Book.

Gamson, William, *Power and Discontent*. Homewood, Ill.: Dorsey, 1968.* Available in paperback.

Horowitz, Irving, *Three Worlds of Development: The Theory and Practice of International Stratification*. New York: Oxford University, 1966. Available in paperback.

Moore, Barrington, Jr., *The Social Origins of Dictatorship and Democracy*. Boston: Beacon, 1966. Available in paperback.

Pranger, Robert J., *The Eclipse of Citizenship*. New York: Holt, 1968. Paperback.

Riemer, Neal, *Representative: Problems in Political Science*. New York: Heath, 1967.

Rose, Arnold M., *The Power Structure: Political Process in American Society*. New York: Oxford University, 1967. Paperback.

Sorauf, Frank J., *Political Parties in the American System*. Boston: Little, Brown, 1968. Paperback.

Zeigler, Harmon, *Interest Groups in American Society*. Englewood Cliffs, N.J.: Prentice-Hall, 1964.*

*Difficult, specialized, or technical.

ELEMENTS OF
INDIVIDUAL
INTEGRATION:
ALIENATION
AND BELONGING

8 ROLES AND ATTITUDES: CONFORMITY AND DEVIANCE

Recent chapters have concerned the ways in which society hangs together. The next few chapters turn to the question of how individuals hang to society. Keeping individuals in society and in viable relationships with society is not a simple process. Individuals must produce the behaviors through which the society operates. They must be able to contemplate themselves with a sense of satisfaction and the society with a sense of belonging.

The individuals must be adjusted to the society.

Adjustment is one of the strangest concepts in the whole socio-logical landscape. If someone is not adjusted, is he recalled by the factory? Does he get his bolts tightened? His timer reset? A complete norm overhaul? A value job? If these don't work, is he junked or traded in? Society and the individual are separate entities, yet human individuality may only be realized in and through society, and society only exists by the agency of human actors. Though separable, the two must work together, or not at all. If they fail to work together, nobody ever talks about an unadjusted society, always about an unadjusted individual.[1] Actually, any failure is a failure of both and for both. If the individual is not comfortably oriented toward the society, neither is the society adequately arranged for the individual. If the society has failed to provide a secure psychic home for the individual, so has the individual failed to render appropriate behaviors for the society. I believe we would be better off to forget adjustment and talk about integration of individual and society with each other.

TYING PEOPLE TO SOCIETY, AND VICE VERSA

The primary mechanism through which such integration can be realized is that of social roles. Roles are pigeonholes in the desk of social organization into which people can be fit. Roles are concrete social identities that individuals can assume. In these twin guises, roles belong both to the individual and to the society and serve to bond the two worlds together.

Roles are bite-sized chunks of society, small enough to be handled by an individual. Not all of the society is contained within the role. Conversely, not all of the individuals in society play any one role. The first requirement in defining a role, then, is to determine who will play it. Each role is associated with a class of individuals who have some distinguishing characteristics. The role applies to old people, sociologists, strong men, unmarried mothers, carpenters, kings, or some other clearly demarcated collection of people. The collection may include only one person at a time, or a majority of the

---

[1] This is true for the general public and for the scholarly and scientific mainstream. Some intellectual descendants of Freud, Marx, and Rousseau (and only a minority of these) may represent exceptions.

society's members, but not all. The label of the class also serves as the name of the role.

Implicit in each role is a set of norms. The norms, in this combination, apply especially to this position. The collection of norms is not a random collection, but a set; it fits together. The role as a bite-sized piece is also a sensible, logically cohering piece. That this set of norms does go together and does apply to this role-position will be agreed upon by those who play the role and by others who may come into interaction with those players. In this agreement rests another conjunct of social and personal orientations.

Roles, like knowledge and values, are subject to the test of significance. A coherent cluster of norms associated with a position will only be considered a role if it carries repercussions further into the person and the society. "Bus rider" designates a social category. We can tell that some people are riding a bus and others are not. There are a set of norms associated with this category. Bus riders are constrained to step to the back of the bus, to remain seated while the vehicle is in motion, and to refrain from smoking and from conversing with the driver. On the test of social significance, this pseudo-role will not rate very highly. If there are some people who are acting like bus riders and some others who are not, the implications for society are minimal. True roles like physician or hippie, in contrast, resonate in the society. That some people act like physicians and others like hippies may cause other people to go to the former for drug prescriptions or to urge banning the latter from public thoroughfares or to act toward them in a wide variety of ways. This mix of hippies and physicians also does more to lend character and definition to the society than does the mix of bus riders. Still, these are fuzzy distinctions of degree; the social significance test does not seem to point up roles nearly as clearly as it did values or knowledge. Again, this simply emphasizes that roles are partly personal and therefore less purely social than were the other elements. In defining roles, we must look for personal significance as well as social. As a matter of fact, the personal test is by far the more decisive. If you know that a person is a "bus rider," what do you know about him? Little more than that he steps to the back of the bus, and so on. If you know, on the other hand, that an individual is a physician, you can describe his probable behavior for next week as well as for now. You can make some shrewd guesses about his age, economic position, personality, political orientation, style of dress, residence, friends, educational background, and many other of his attributes and possessions. You may not be perfectly correct in each guess, but your average will be pretty good. The same would hold true for the hippie. These roles have effect on the individual's personality, attitudes, and other roles.

Some labels are so ambiguous that they may designate a role or may not; further inquiry is demanded. A "surfer" may be simply someone who occasionally goes surfing—label and category and norm cluster, but that's all; a pseudo-role. On the other hand, a surfer may be a sun-bleached, long-haired beach bum who lives only for the big wave. This is a fully developed role. Here are some other ambiguous labels; see if you can recognize both their role and pseudo-role connotations: runner, woman, speaker, upper class, actor, father, traveller, bureaucrat, martyr, drunk. In their true role aspect, these labels go some way toward defining the people to whom the label can be applied, but not all the way.

Make your guesses about a physician, and you will be substantially, but not perfectly, correct. One of the reasons for your areas of uncertainties and for the mistakes you may make in guessing is that people are not restricted to one role. The physician may also be a father, bureaucrat, suburbanite, Lutheran, and a number of other things simultaneously. If you know that he is all of these things, you will be able to anticipate the behaviors and characteristics of the physician much more accurately than you could if you only knew that he was a physician. Each of these roles carries its own implications; one may modify the impact of another.

The total set of roles that an individual plays go far toward defining his behavior, personality, knowledge, attitudes—toward defining the total person. The many roles that make up a person's role complex stand in special relation to each other. Some roles are contingent upon others. No individual may be admitted to the role of college football player unless he simultaneously fills the roles of male and college student. Some role combinations that are not necessary are nonetheless expected or normal. Mothers are ordinarily married women; senators are generally lawyers. Other combinations are so unusual that they are greeted with a surprised reaction on the part of those who encounter them. This response is similar to the one with which deviations from norms are regarded. Though unusual, such combinations can and do occur. A minister's wife may be a prostitute; a banker may be a political radical. Between these two extremes are role combinations that are neither particularly expected or unexpected. It is not especially usual for graduate students to be married; neither is it startling. Salesmen may or may not be Catholic. Finally, some combinations are simply impossible. The role requirements of Marine combat squad leader in Vietnam and of draft resister cannot be met by the same person at the same time.

The differing probabilities and possibilities of various combinations mean that some role complexes will be more or less standard. Whole clusters of roles will be duplicated in the role-baggage of a number of persons. Other complexes will be relatively rare. Essentially, the normative requirements of a role complex are more compatible for some role combinations than for others. The individual with a standard complex will have an easier time meeting the demands of his several roles than will the individual with an odd set. When two or more of his roles place contradictory behavioral demands on the individual, he cannot meet both sets of requirements.

KOOKS AND CROOKS

The person caught in this kind of dilemma will necessarily violate one set of norms or another. He may know the rules perfectly. He may be highly motivated to follow them, but circumstances have placed him in a condition where he cannot. If the term deviant is used to refer to anyone who fails to follow the norm, he becomes a deviant. Let's look at some of the implications of applying this definition of deviance.

In most colleges and universities, C is the normal grade, in all the senses of norm. By this definition, anyone who gets any grade other than C is a deviant. The student who gets all A's will be worse (more deviant) than the one who gets all D's. Although upper-class Ivy League students of a few generations ago strove for the "Gentlemanly C," and some students of today follow a like policy, this is surely not standard. Most students would be pleased to be "deviant" in the sense of doing better than C work; most of the others in their social field would be pleased to see them do it. You can see that this definition of deviance does not correspond to social practice, at least in this case.

Nor will it serve in all cases of "deviance" brought about by conflicting role demands. A student may be involved in a card game at the student union. The time for class approaches. His friends in the game expect him to stay and play. There is a friendship role. Some of the norms within this role demand that he show his regard for the friends as social others by staying with them and sustaining the situation. The friends as others expect these behaviors of him. His instructor, the university administration, and perhaps his parents expect him to go to class. They promote and enforce a set of norms pertaining to his role as student. Here are two roles, two sets of others, and two norms. He cannot go to class and stay and play cards. He will become, no matter which choice he makes, a norm violator and hence a deviant. If you were in this situation, you would not want the harsh label of deviant attached to you. You would not feel it was just. You would hope to escape being labeled deviant, and very well might.

Suppose we change the terms of the example just slightly. A young man is playing knives in the clubhouse. The time for reporting to the probation officer approaches. His friends expect him to stay and play. The officer, the courts, the police, and perhaps his parents expect him to go to the probation office. The gang-friendship and citizen-on-probation norms, others, and roles are in conflict. The young man cannot help but be a deviant. If you were in this situation, you would not feel it was just. You would hope to escape the label, but your chances of doing so would be very slim.

These cases show deviance to be something more than simple violation of the norm. Sometimes norm violations are regarded as deviance, sometimes not. In the case of the grades, students were willing, even anxious, to "violate" the norm. In the cases of role conflict the actors might gladly have followed the norms, but could not. The notion of deviance does not seem to hinge on motives, attitudes, and other things inside the head of the actor. The only area left in these cases is that of the *others*. It is here that we must look for clarification concerning deviance. In these cases, and in all others you could discover or imagine, *deviance* is that which is regarded as deviance by the others in the situation. A *deviant* is any person who is so labeled by the society.

If friends and faculty choose to recognize the dilemma they have placed on the poor student and to excuse him for his failure to live up to their expectations, he is not a deviant, no matter which behavior he chose. If he stays in the card game, but the instructor doesn't take roll that day, he is not a deviant because he was not caught. The individual with the most serious probable fate is the gang member on probation. If he violates the norm of probation he will be more surely labeled more seriously deviant than any of the other examples. This is not because his behavior is more of a violation. It is not because his motives are more antisocial. It is not because he is a more "bad" person. It is because the probation officer, police, and courts are more implacable and powerful others than those supporting the remaining sets of norms. These groups as social others carefully note violations, automatically label violators as deviant, and have the power to enforce their definition.

Kooks and crooks *are* kooks and crooks because they have been so defined by powerful and interested social others. Most important kinds of deviance do not consist simply in violations of norms associated with a particular role. Rather, these deviances become roles in themselves. For them, as for any other social roles, there are sets of norms. If other members of the society label an individual as deviant they expect these behaviors of him. This expectation influences his behavior. He comes to act more deviant because of these expectations. The label may, through these conditions, cause and develop behavioral violations rather than result from them. If the juvenile gangster's probation is revoked (because he is labeled deviant), he will be sent to prison, where he will probably become much more confirmed in deviant behavior and more settled in deviant roles. If the teacher defines the student as a deviant malcontent who is uninterested in the subject matter, he increases the chance that the student will come to feel and act these ways and define himself similarly.

No one is foolish enough to believe that an individual is born a professor, priest, or plumber—or becomes one simply by wishing it. The roles of pickpocket, peyote-eater, and psychopath are no different. They must all be learned through tentative behaviors, which are confirmed by the others in the social situation. This may require a developmental process of months or years. Any case of straightforward, ordinary, confirming, behavior by an individual is predicated on a number of factors. First, there must be a norm. Given a norm, there are a set of conditions for the actor and another set for the social others.

The actor can behave in a pure conforming fashion only if all of a special set of conditions are fulfilled. He must be aware that there is a norm and that it applies to him in his present situation. His definition of the norm must be accurate. He must have a favorable attitude toward the norm. He must have values supporting this attitude. He must be motivated to behave in accord with his definition. Contrary pressures, such as contradictory demands of other norms, must be absent or minimal. He must have the ability and good fortune actually to perform in the fashion the norm, definition, and so on, suggest he should. The absence of any one of these elements may lead to behavior in violation of the norm.

The others can define a purely conforming situation only if all of a special set of conditions are fulfilled. They must recognize the norm and its applicability to this particular person in this particular situation. They must be interested in this situation, actor, and behavior. The behavior must be public or a poorly kept secret. The others must accurately perceive the conforming behavior of the actor. They must attach the label of conformist to the actor. They must present the appropriate reward-sanctions to the actor. The absence of any one of these conditions may lead to labeling the actor deviant.

The considerations of these paragraphs can be condensed into five terms that in proper combination cover any social act and the social response it evokes. They summarize ways in which acts and actors come to be labeled conformist or deviant.

1. *Norms* are the start. It is assumed that the social others know the norm, and that the actor is in a position in which the norm applies to him.

2. The actor, however, may not recognize this. He may or may not accept the norm. His values and attitudes may not encourage conformity. The sum of these circumstances leave the actor with some *impulse* to action, either in conformity with the norm or not.

3. When the actor acts, he may poorly execute whatever *behavior* he intended. He may be intimidated by anticipated sanctions, so that he doesn't do what he wanted to do. He may be detoured by contradictory demands from several sources. In these ways, his behavior may or may not match his impulses.

4. Once the behavior happens, it enters the social world. It may be *perceived* by the others. They may perceive it accurately or inaccurately or fail to note it at all. Distorted perceptions may occur, for instance, when the others already have an emotional disposition toward this particular actor. If they are favorably inclined, they may not "believe their eyes" when they seem to see him acting improperly. If they knew all along that he was rotten, they may distort their perceptions in the opposite direction.

5. The *label*[2] the others attach to the act or the actor may be at variance with their perception. A perceived deviant may escape the penalties of the deviant label through a moral rationalization; he may be excused. The actor who is personally powerful or has accumulated much conformist credit in the past may be exempt. The creation of a scapegoat and similar responses may likewise produce an innocent victim.

Of these five terms, two, impulse (I) and behavior (B), belong to the actor. Perception (P) and label (L) rest with the others. The two pairs are connected by the behavior-perception relationship. Norms (N) more or less stand on their own, but may be involved with the actor's impulse and the labeling process. Placing the terms

[2]The "labeling" concept of deviance has been most successfully advanced by Howard S. Becker, *Outsiders* (New York: The Free Press, 1963). The "behavior ring" follows from my attempts to work with the typology that Becker's book offers (p. 20).

in a way that spatially matches these relations yields the diagram shown in Fig. 8–1.

Fig. 8-1

Each of these terms has only two values: conformist or deviant. We do not want to complicate matters by asking about the content of the norm or the nature of the divergence. Since each has only two values, any two terms that are not equal to a third are equal to each other. In order to keep the circle "true," then, there must always be an even number of inequalities. You can verify this for yourself by substituting the numbers one and zero for the letters, in any combination, and placing equal and not-equal signs to keep the circle mathematically correct.

Figure 8–1 describes the perfectly "straight" normal act and response that occurs if all the conditions listed a few paragraphs ago are met. It is very ordinary and very dull.

The three rings in Fig. 8–2 concern the gang member who was

Fig. 8-2

supposed to meet his probation officer. In Fig. 8–2a, $N \neq L$ indicates that society labels him a deviant because of his failure to keep that appointment. The other inequality is placed between I and B, rather than between N and I, because we described him as wanting (having an impulse) to follow the probation norm, but being unable to meet it and the peer norm simultaneously.

A more hard-core delinquent might have said, right from the start, "Who needs the probation officer [and his norms]." If he then skipped his appointment, his action ring would look like Fig. 8–2b.

If on the other hand he gave in to the system and went to his appointment to avoid a stretch in reform school, his action ring would assume a new form (Fig. 8–2c).

Three more cases and three action rings follow. See if you can pair them up. Correct matches are given in the text.

Case A: A left over: the lucky card-playing college student who didn't go to class on a day the instructor didn't take roll. One of the rings below describes this happening.

Case B: Eliza Dolittle went to a sorority rush party. Eliza was a slob. Her conversation was loud, obscene, and unmannerly. Her table manners were awful. Her clothes were hideous. She was trying her best to make a good impression, but she was totally ignorant of the social niceties by which sorority girls live. After the party was over, the members were laughing about Eliza, recounting her various social atrocities. One girl described Eliza's drinking from the finger bowl. Several others also remembered this; everyone laughed some more. As a matter of fact, this is the one blunder poor Eliza didn't commit. She washed in the finger bowl. She was reaching for the carrots when her hands fell in. Which ring fits Eliza and the finger bowl?

Case C: A popular and successful university president had a special fondness for young redheads. His picture was in the paper with one; she was fifteen years old and was wearing only a slip. The occasion for the picture was a motel fire. Generally, people could not quite bring themselves to believe that he was interviewing her for the early entrance program. Still, they said he had always been good to his wife. They understood that he was working under tremendous pressures and deserved a little relaxation. They said it would be a shame to lose his services over a little scandal like that. He emerged without criminal conviction or social blame, but there is a ring for him below.

Fig. 8-3

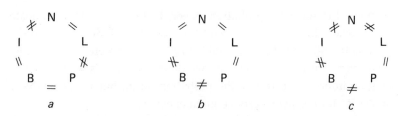

If you have difficulty finding the appropriate rings in Fig. 8–3, remember that you can start with the appropriate relationship between any pair of terms. In *Case C*, for instance, a fondness for young redheads is not normative for university presidents ($N{\neq}I$). When you arrive at some of the obvious relations between pairs, the requirement for an equal number of inequalities in the circle may offer a hint. You can go on and play the game beyond these examples by building the ring for other cases you may know or invent. Alternately, you can arbitrarily create any combination of equalities and inequalities that produce a true ring, then try to imagine a case that it describes. I will caution you that some of the four-inequality forms are pretty far-fetched. In the preceding cases, the card player is described by Fig. 8–3b. Eliza's ring is Fig. 8–3c; the president's is shown in Fig. 8–3a.

The action ring is a simplifying scheme that may be useful to you in interpreting specific events where actor and others come in contact. Mainly, I hope, it will have demonstrated to you that notions of conformity and deviance are actor-other phenomena. The five terms of the ring include some that are rather peculiarly individual, some that inhere in the others in the situation, and the normative one, which is more generally societal. All five and the relations among them are essential parts of the social-psychological process within which behavior occurs and is welded into the society. When this process is repeated a sufficient number of times, the individual is also welded into society. Whether he takes his place as good guy or bad, sane or insane, normal or abnormal depends on society as well as self. In this section, I have tried to deal with conformity and deviance. In so doing, the section has ended up as a special case of the immediately preceding section on tying people and society to each other. Conformity and deviance is settled in the mutual integration of society and individual. This integration, like the action rings we have used to represent it, is as true for the deviant as for the conformist.

SOCIALIZATION

Socialization, literally, is the process of becoming social. Every society is constantly losing, through death, some of its best-trained and most valuable members and acquiring in their place ignorant and useless babies. Most of these babies, in the long run, will become successful operating members of the society, acting at home and in conformity with its norms and values, playing a standard set of its roles. The process through which this occurs is called socialization.

When the process goes awry and the product is a deviant individual, the process, as the preceding section indicated, is still a social one.

For the purposes of social analysis, we can take the biological potential of the human as a given fact, substantially the same for all individuals. If this is not perfectly true—if some newborn babies have greater capacity or different capacities than others—at least the differences are randomly distributed. These inherent differences also pale to insignificance when contrasted to the differences induced later as a consequence of what happens to that baby after he is born. The most influential of these happenings are the social ones.

Organisms are influenced by their environment. Biological potential, when acted upon by the environment, becomes something different than what it once was, and the nature of the differences will depend on that first encounter with the environment. Any second encounter has a special effect also, one determined by the character of the organism at the time of that experience, a character that is the biological potential as modified by the first action of the environment. A steady accretion of specific experiences and the order in which they occur will produce individual personality reflecting these inputs.

Although the logic of this process is simplified, it indicates the possibility of specifying the following "recipe" for producing a standard, conforming, adult, United States citizen.

Take one newborn infant. Bottle-feed regularly. Cuddle three hours a day. Address in English baby talk. Expose to adult females five times as frequently as to adult males. Wean early. Punish physically occasionally; withhold affection frequently. Such a recipe could be spelled out in great detail for the several years of preparation required. If the specifications were adequately followed, the result would be a standard United States adult. It would not matter whether the infant with which the process started were born in New York, Berlin, Lagos, or Tokyo.

Obviously, this formula has not been fully specified and has never been consciously and perfectly followed. Yet most people who grow up in the United States resemble each other rather closely and are much more like one another than they are like most people raised in Berlin, Lagos, or Tokyo. Observing this fact and following the logic of development already set forth, we can deduce that similar individuals must have been formed by similar experiences. The life history of most people brought up in the United States closely approximates the hypothetical recipe.

If a particular individual happens to have had less regular feeding or more exposure to adults than most, it will simply make him a little different from the typical. Some of these peculiarities will be standard for quite a collection of people within the society. Categories of individuals differentiated in this way from the general standard tend to fill some of the specialized role categories within the society. Other differences, more individual, lead to the development of true individuality.

The basic set of experiences generally shared by the children of a society and the special mix of deviations from this standard produce the adult population of the society. A generation is developed with certain kinds of knowledge, values, and identities. As they act these out, they create the social conditions that will be the source of experience for the next generation. The society perpetuates and re-forms itself by this process.

The mechanisms of the process and an inventory of materials that these mechanisms transmit are dealt with in surrounding sections of this chapter and in Chapters 4, 9, and 10. For now, I want to concentrate on two broad categories of social-psychological content and their implications for action.

The materials imparted by socialization experience, to the extent that they have relevance for meaningful social behavior of the individual, may be seen as consisting of value and norm-type material. Crudely, we are considering what an individual wants (goals) and how he goes about getting it (means). If an individual's personal values correspond with the general social values, his goals will be the established ones of his society. The situation of norms is a little more complex. As behavior-ring analysis has already indicated, an individual may accept the norm and yet be unable to act in accordance with it. We will divide the population into those with both the inclination and ability and those failing on one standard or the other.

In the table that follows, a plus sign implies acceptance of the goals or acceptance and actuation of the means. A minus sign means rejection of the goals or rejection or inability concerning the means. The possible permutations of these signs and categories yield four types of adaptation of the individual to the situation.
The types themselves follow the logic of this analysis; the labels are provided afterward. The meaning of each label will give you some feeling for the kind of adaptation likely for an individual with that particular combination of dispositions and conditions.

Because this scheme is more concerned with the orientation of the actor to the situation than with behavior and others in the situation, it forms a useful adjunct to behavior-ring analysis. Different forms of deviance and conformity may be more readily interpreted with one scheme or the other, and the goals-means typology always provides a more psychologically oriented interpretation than the behavior ring.

POSSIBLE ORIENTATIONS TOWARD GOALS AND MEANS[3]

	Goals	Means
Conformity	+	+
Innovation	+	−
Ritualism	−	+
Retreatism	−	−

The goals-means typology contains a social or "other" component in the column headings, which refer to general societal goals and socially approved means. A minus sign in the goals column may indicate, then, that an individual has no goal regarding the situation in question, that he has some goal other than the general social one, or that he actively rejects the societal one. This last possibility opens up a new condition: individuals may rebel against society rather than merely deviate from its dictates.

ALIENATION

Early in this chapter I discarded the term "adjustment." In some ways, I would like to do the same with "alienation." So many magazine articles and television specials have dealt with the problem of alienation in American society, so many meanings have been attached to this term, so many issues have been laid at the door of this concept that I am tempted to let this one slide. Still, the heart of these matters is a war between individual and society. This is a fascinating image and one not nearly so ridiculous as the one conjured up by "adjustment." If we do not call it alienation we would have to call it something else, for it is something we should examine.

Alienation is not the same as deviance. Deviant behavior may

[3]This typology and the discussion surrounding it are adapted with permission of The Macmillan Company from *Social Theory and Social Structure*, rev. ed., by Robert K. Merton. Copyright 1957 by The Free Press, a Corporation. Copyright 1949 by The Free Press.

be caused by an actor's ignorance or awkwardness, by a variety of actor's conditions intervening between norm and behavior, or by others rather than actor. We are on the trail of an individual who, if he acts in a noncomformist fashion, does so because he knows the norm and rejects it. His nonnormative behavior is an act of aggression against the society. Pure cases of withdrawal, likewise, are nonsocial rather than antisocial and are not the same as alienation.

Many acts and actors that are ordinarily termed antisocial are not so in fact. To call the run-of-the-mill professional criminal antisocial is truly libelous. A bank robber does not rob a bank because he hates banks, or the monetary system, or any such thing. He robs the bank because he accepts all these fully. He likes money. In the absence of formal education, upper-class background, inside knowledge of the stock market, or other such means for acquiring money, he uses the skills he has to the best of his ability. His is an American success story, even if not quite a standard one.

Most persons who are called mentally ill must be understood in a similar light. Their attempts to do the right thing or to achieve the right ends may be pathetically twisted or inadequate, but they are almost invariably attempts where the intent would meet general social approval. The mentally ill are not at war with society; they are lost in it.

Deviance revolves around norms and behaviors. Alienation focuses on values. All the forms of deviance given above involve maladroit attempts at acceptable actions with acceptable rationales, the selection of improper means to the fulfillment of eminently proper ends, or, at worst, an occasional stray antisocial value in a basically sound mixture. The alienated individual operates on value premises that are contrary to those of the society in which he operates.

An individual may find himself in a situation where his personal values are different from the social values because he has changed his social residence. If a Japanese moves to the United States, his values will still be those he learned in Japan and which were appropriate for Japanese social life. These will be, to some extent, at variance with those of the United States. When he acts consistently with his personal values, he may be acting contrary to American values. Still, he is not alienated because all Japanese values are not contrary to all American values. His acts will not be predicated on contrary values all the time, nor is he predicating action on them because they are contrary.

What is true of the immigrant will be true to a lesser degree of many purely domestic people who operate in specialized social enclaves. Ethnic groups, religious sects, regions, communities and occupational categories all have their own special cultural milieu. A person whose social experience is largely confined to such a social location will naturally tend to embrace this culture and its somewhat variant values. An individual may also absorb such a culture without truly being a part of it. If he identifies with it or wishes to be part of it, he may mentally project himself there and adopt the appropriate values. He may similarly find negative identities and project values and norms for himself that are opposite those of the reference group in question. "If the Republicans (or Jews or rich people or police or communists) are in favor of it, it must be bad." With membership in a specialty culture, or with positive or negative reference group identification that produces a kind of pretend membership, an individual may acquire some specialty values.

These will be the source of some variation in values in the population and will produce some instances in which a particular value of an individual will be contrary to those of the society. These will be isolated, single values; by and large, the individual and societal values will be in agreement or at least capable of mutual accommodation. Cultural specialties will not universally and consistently produce contrary values. They will not be a source of alienation.

An individual can come to have one or two antisocietal values "by accident." For his whole collection of values to be antisocietal requires some more systematic cause. The only way in which an individual can arrive at a set of values that are totally in conflict with those of the society is by holding the society as a negative reference group. He must consciously and cognitively know the values of the society and adopt contradictory values simply because they are contradictory. Only this kind of individual orientation fulfills the condition of warfare between individual and society. This requires a special sort of person in a special sort of position vis-à-vis society.

Most people are not really in direct contact with the society. Instead, as the next two chapters will indicate, they relate to society through some intervening subsystems. From the point of view of an individual operating within it, society is large, abstract, and remote. Only especially aware and knowledgeable persons operate in relation to their society as well as within it. This kind of consciousness is likely to come with formal education, especially in the humanities and the social sciences, but may also develop in some forms of untutored peasant shrewdness. Whatever the source, only individuals with this consciousness of society can relate to society as society and orient themselves to general societal values.

The fact that an individual can do something does not mean that he will. If he is to orient his beliefs and behaviors to the social whole, he must be cognizant of that whole, and it must be important to him. By analogy to the psychological and interpersonal level, scarcely anyone gets an Oedipus complex regarding Granduncle Jim, who lives in Peoria. Feelings of great strength, based upon intimate and important association, are required to elicit close orientations. For society to become a reference group, the individual must be intimately tied to the society by heavy emotional bonds. Before the alienated individual can become alienated, before he can develop the overriding hostility toward society that alienation requires, he must have been in love with society.

This deep attachment will only turn to hate if the society "done him wrong." The individual's self-perceived relationship with society must become one of frustration or rejection if his strong positive bonds to the society are to be transmuted into those of negative reference. There are at least four ways in which the societal-personal relationship can become frustrating and repelling to the individual. They correspond more or less neatly to four classes of alienated people found in the United States today.

Two of these may be understood as chronic inequalities in the person's action ring. Some people may find that their situation regularly develops inequalities in the self side of the ring. They are constantly unable to bring their impulses into line with the norms or to translate their impulses into behaviors. The individual who is unable to overcome the variant value implications of a specialty culture group to which he belongs would be one example. Many lower-class youths find themselves in this position. They want to succeed but are unable to master the appropriate skills and feelings soon enough to escape rejection. Conflicting demands from various collections of others are part of the same complex. These youths often become alienated and vent their hostility in a special form of crime—destructive delinquency. Vandalism, aggression, and the absence of more "pro-social" profit motives mark this form of crime as the symptom of hostility toward society. In its general form, this malady may be seen to follow from instilling in the individual social desires, without providing the personal means for their achievement. The same terms apply to all impoverished people as consumers and to those in meaningless, routine jobs as workers. This form of alienation is, then, a distinctively lower-class form. This does not imply that all lower-class people suffer alienation. Most lower-class individuals never become knowledgeably conscious of society; many have never been nurtured closely enough by society to develop positive or negative emotional ties to society. Still, this form of alienation, when it occurs, will most frequently appear in the lower-class individual.

If inequalities regularly occur on the other's side of the action ring, alienation may also result. Here we have the individual whose behavior is conformist, but who is perceived or labeled deviant. Clearly, this is a frustrating condition. The person subject to such treatment at the hands of others will naturally feel rejected. Through no flaw or fault of his own, the individual is stigmatized by society. He is relatively blameless in thought and deed. The rationale for his stigmatization is probably physical. (After all, there's not much else left.) Racial and pseudo-racial groups are susceptible to this form of alienation if the conditions of societal consciousness and emotional importance are met. The fulfilling of these last two conditions by the contemporary generation of black Americans is primarily responsible for the rise of militant black alienation. White racism fosters the continued misperception, mislabeling, and stigmatization in which such alienation flourishes.[4]

The first two forms of alienation develop in persons who experience chronically "flawed" action rings, personal frustration or social rejection. They are most likely to occur within a deprived socioeconomic or racial class. The second pair of forms of alienation strikes in the middle class. They develop because of a disjunction between the nurture-agent society and the action-ring society. This disjunction between these two guises of society may be due to differences of time or location; hence the two members of this pair.

If a person is closely identified with his society, adopts all its values, and has strong positive feelings toward the society, he is integrated well with the society. His action ring will be a soothing mass of equal signs. Suppose, then, the society changes? Ordinarily, social change is so slow that an individual has a chance to die before "his" society changes and disappears. In times of extremely rapid social change, this may not be the case. In a very real sense, society has turned against such a person. He may respond by turning against

[4] I would have liked to write a whole chapter on black-white relations in the United States. In the last hundred years, the world has seen few more significant and interesting social phenomena. The situation is changing so rapidly that most of what I could write now would be out of date before you read it. This paragraph and pages 107–13, 195–98, and 240–48 present my efforts to cover the most general and timeless of the issues involved.

society. Swift social change has been taking place in the United States for some time; the America beloved by middle-aged and older people has disappeared. In this age group, those persons of at least marginal middle-class origins were most likely to have had the early personal-social-nurture bonds that induced this love of country. Among these people also, those who have changed social or geographic position—urban dwellers with farm backgrounds, second- or third-generation Americans, and small businessmen—have enjoyed experiences that separate the individual from society and are therefore most likely to have a consciousness of society. By changing, society elicited alienation, a rabidly antisocietal reaction, primarily from these population segments. They are for law and order, God, free enterprise, patriotism, and decency. They find little of any of these in our contemporary world. The John Birch Society, the Minutemen, Wallace-type politics, "Silent Majorityism," and other similar outlets channel their hostility.

The final form of alienation occurs when an individual's entry into the "real world" proves his nurture-society to have been illusion. The society with which he early became integrated was a biased and unrepresentative segment of that society. The social world, as he experiences it, is hopelessly sordid compared to the perceived world in his cushioned early existence. The middle-class American family since the late 1930's provided such cushioning. In this country we have always mouthed a set of ideals that we did not even try to practice. Early and regular contact with what was really happening undeceived several generations. Changes in the family structure, in child-rearing practices, and increased economic security allowed recent parents to prohibit this kind of contact. Some of the people of this young generation, then, grew up actually *believing* all those ideals we say America is about. Their solid formal education and general cultural sophistication developed in them high societal consciousness. When they found that this society didn't have (and maybe even didn't want) freedom, equality, dignity, and individualism, they became bitterly alienated. Yippies, SDS, and similar movements are the central manifestation. The case on hippies, incidentally, remains to be proven. They may be nonsocietal rather than antisocietal and hence represent a form of withdrawal rather than alienation, of retreatism rather than rebellion.

Alienation, in any of these forms, implies that the individual has a solid set of personal values and an established social reference point for their definition and sustenance. The reference group is society and the definition is opposition. The personal values are contrary to those of society. In this sense, the alienated individual is secure. In another sense, he may be called insecure because he lacks positive identifications and a sense of identity. Stating this another way, he is sure about the world but unsure of himself. Absence of a sense of belonging and of self-identity is an inevitable psychological accompaniment of alienation.

Social mechanisms that promote self-identity and a sense of belonging are the topics of the next two chapters.

FURTHER READING

Argyle, Michael, *The Psychology of Interpersonal Behavior*. Baltimore: Penguin, 1967.* Paperback.

Becker, Howard S., *Outsiders: Studies in the Sociology of Deviance*. New York: Free Press, 1963. Available in paperback.

Brim, Orville G., and Stanton Wheeler, *Socialization after Childhood: Two Essays*. New York: Wiley, 1966.* Available in paperback.

Goffman, Erving, *Stigma: Notes on the Management of Spoiled Identity*. Englewood Cliffs, N.J.: Prentice-Hall, 1963. Paperback.

Goodman, Paul, *Growing Up Absurd*. New York: Random House, 1960. Vintage paperback.

Kozol, Jonathan, *Death at an Early Age*. Boston: Houghton-Mifflin, 1967. Also Bantam paperback, 1968.

Liebow, Elliot, *Tally's Corner*. Boston: Little, Brown, 1967. Available in paperback.

Mead, Margaret, *Sex and Temperament in Three Primitive Societies*, rev. ed. New York: Morrow, 1963. Also paperback, Apollo Editions, New York.

Scheff, Thomas, *On Being Mentally Ill: A Sociological Theory*. Chicago: Aldine, 1966.

Simmons, Jerry, *Deviants*. Berkeley, Calif.: Glendessary, 1969.

*Difficult, specialized, or technical.

9 FRIENDSHIP AND ASSOCIATION

The individual guides his own behavior to match his conception of himself. If he considers himself a sex symbol, a wit, a swinger, his conduct at a party will reflect these beliefs about himself. The behavior of such an individual will be quite different from that of some other person who considers himself mystic, quiet, and cold. To be sure, people respond to events around them. The nature of the event partly determines behaviors. But individuals respond as wit, mystic, and so on. The nature of the response depends on the actor's beliefs about what he is, and about how one of what he is is supposed to act.

Some interesting sidelights to this view of behavior are cast by hypnosis phenomena. Individuals under hypnosis can be induced to believe, at some levels of consciousness, that they are military heroes, prostitutes, dogs, or almost anything else. While operating under hypnotic influence and under these beliefs, their behaviors are radically different from their "normal" behaviors. An individual, hypnotized to believe he is a king, will act as he thinks a king should act. This may not be the way *real* kings act. After all, he may not know much about the king business. But he will do his best. The condition under hypnosis is little different from the normal state, except in the normal state the identity the individual accepts will usually be one of which he has considerable knowledge. The individual acts out the appropriate behaviors for his identity and bases his action on some substantial notions about how one of this identity should act.

SUSTAINING THE SELF

If he had no identity, the individual would be at a loss for guides to action. His behavior would be hesitant, unpredictable, fumbling. This unsureness would characterize not only his behavior but also his mental condition. He would be anxiety-ridden, terrorized, confused. To preserve orderly behavior and mental stability, the individual must understand himself. He must be able to label the various roles he plays, appreciate the way these fit together and crystallize with the unique "self" he recognizes, and understand the place of this combination within the world.

These understandings do not come to the individual in a sudden flash of revelation. Self-concept is not acquired through a psychedelic drug trip. No god whispers identity in anyone's ear. Identities are built over an extended period of time, in the interactions between an individual and others. A man sees himself in the social responses he elicits in others. No one is born a humorist. No young child believes himself to be a wit. If, over a period of time and in a variety of situations, people laugh at things he says, he may begin to consider himself a wit. Once he tentatively believes himself to be a wit, he further emphasizes and polishes the kind of behaviors that have drawn laughter from others. The more successfully he manages this, the more often will he get mirthful responses. These responses confirm his tentative self-definition and encourage further behavior along the same lines.

The heart of self-definition, then, is in the social situation. The individual gets his identity from others. Only a very special set of others will serve this function. We suggested that self-identity must include not only roles the individual plays, but the integration of these as total self. Many interactions are one-faceted. Individuals interact with one another purely on the basis of a single role. When you buy a pair of shoes, the salesman treats you as a customer, you treat him as a salesman. Your transaction is conducted entirely on the basis of sizes, styles, and price. You never get an opportunity to react to him as father, lover, Christian, voter, tourist, or all of the other things he may be. He doesn't respond to the many complex aspects of your self. He may learn something about his sales skill; you buy or do not. You may become more insightful concerning your foot or tastes in covering it; neither of you learns much about yourselves as persons. The only interactions where such learning can take place is among persons who know you as a person and who treat you as a person. The interrelationships must be broad enough to encompass the many roles you and the others play. The others must be important to you, otherwise their reflected images of you will fail to have a significant impact. Your self-conception can be built and sustained only by persons whose opinions you value.

The contexts of such interactions have been labeled *primary groups*. Interaction in primary groups provides the individual with a sense of self, with the psychic refueling that is essential to his social operation and psychological balance. Before we go further, we will need to identify *groups* as a special kind of social system, and *primary groups* as a special type of group.

Social systems are built of interrelations. Relations within social groups are the special ones called interaction. The relations within groups are interpersonal, conscious, symbolic, and mutual. A general in North Dakota, by pushing his nuclear button, may unleash a chain of events that will result in your vaporization or your children's genetic disfiguration. This demonstrates the existence of an international military-political system. The general is not aware of your existence. Later, he might not be aware of your nonexistence. That's all right, because you don't spend a lot of time thinking about him either. There is interrelationship but no interaction.

If you were introduced to the general, you would extend your hand; he would extend his; the two would be mutually clasped and waggled up and down; both would release and return to the owner. He would speak; you would reply.[1] His behavior affects you just as it would if he were to push the nuclear button. Each interrelation indicates the presence of a social system. But in this case—hand-shaking—there is a major difference in the relationship. Your behavior also affects him. The relationship is reciprocal. Your behaviors are influenced by the behaviors of the other and by your expectations of future behavior of the other. The central agents in this relationship are all human, in this case just you and the general. Such things as missiles and isotopes do not intrude heavily into the relationship. The medium of your interaction is symbols: words and gestures. You are both aware of each other and of the interrelationship in progress. All these conditions make this a case of interaction.

If interaction among the same persons continues over a relatively long period of time, there are several consequences. The participants grow conscious of one another not simply as being there, but as persons who share something. "Insiders" come to mark themselves off from "outsiders." These boundaries are real. If interaction recurs among the same collection of people, they are set apart from people who do not take part in the interaction. We will look both for boundaries as an operating condition and for conscious recognition of boundaries. A membership can be designated by the disinterested observer and is recognized by the actors at the social scene. As the interaction continues among the same people, they will build "tighter" expectations concerning one another's behavior. Regularization of these expectations results in the evolution of norms that are special to this interaction unit.

The special kind of social system that meets all of these conditions is a group. Interaction, consciousness, boundaries, norms—some social systems may feature one or another of these; groups are characterized by all four. A social unit may be thoroughly normed or only moderately; actors may be fully or only partly conscious of their interactions; boundaries may be clearly marked or fuzzy; and interaction

[1] If you find this style of interaction with a missile commander offensive, consider how much less offensive it is than the earlier interrelationship suggested. Additionally, feel free to substitute picketing and shouting at each other for handshaking and conversation. The point will be illustrated just as well.

may pervade units in varying degrees. Because this is so, the condition of groupness or nongroupness will not be an either-or. Groups will merge gradually with other grouplike organizations, which in turn will merge with more remotely interrelated forms of social system. Still, with these four identifying marks, we can look at any social system and say whether it should be considered a group.

Of those units that are groups, only some will be primary groups. In the term primary group, the qualifier "primary" carries at least three meanings.

(1) Primary groups are primary in terms of their social and psychological importance to the individual. It is only from his interactions in such units that an individual can derive a sense of self. We started this chapter with the idea that individuals needed such support and definition. We began looking at primary groups because they were the place where it all happened

(2) Primary groups are groups in which primary relations take place. These are intimate, face-to-face relations. The actors act toward one another as whole persons, rather than on the level of only one of their segmented roles. The orientation is at least as much to personality as to behavior. The actors are important to one another. The action is engaged in, at least partly, for its own sake, rather than as a means to some other end. All this describes primary relations. Primary relations are a distinguishing feature of primary groups. Only this sort of relationship, we argued earlier, will serve to provide an individual with self-definition and psychological support. This sense of "primary" is therefore perfectly consistent with the first.

(3) Primary groups are the first ones (*primary* meaning first) an individual encounters. Ordinarily, the first contacts of new human beings with the social world take place in the realm of their families. Families are primary groups. Interactions with parents and siblings are an individual's first source of definitions of self. His first psychic supports come with the love, appreciation, and personalization that the family ordinarily provides. This sense of "primary" is likewise consistent with the earlier two, as long as we are dealing with babies and small children. What happens when they grow up? My answer is that when they grow up they identify themselves on the basis of self-concepts learned while they were in the family. The family as primary group may be replaced by such things as peers or clubs, but these are selected by the individual on the basis of self-concepts learned in the family. We already noted that primary relations must be made up of persons who are important to the individual. As he leaves the family, he must build substitute primary groups of impor-

tant others. His notions of who might be important to him will depend on his already established conception of who he is.

When the college-age rebel falls in with a primary group of sexually promiscuous, antiestablishment drug-users, it might seem that he breaks completely from his straight middle-class family. In truth, there is a solid continuity. He does not fall in with this group, he seeks it out. In the college years, he has opportunities for association with fraternity playboys, peaceniks, scholarly grinds, illiterate dropouts, incipient Nazis, and career-oriented operators. In a world peopled with a wildly varied smorgasbord of potential others, he chooses the antiestablishment group as his significant others. They are the ones who meet his psychic needs and respond to the self that he perceives for himself. This perception of self was built in the family and in childhood peer associations. If that is not what the parents intended, it simply shows that this process goes on at several levels, some of which are not conscious. Parents do not spend a lot of time thinking about the kind of self-concepts they are building in their children; even if they did the results would often be wide of the intended mark. Young men do not consciously sort the people they meet: "By God, there's someone who would serve as a significant other for my self, as I see me," but the effect is as if they did. In this way, every new primary group is a direct lineal descendant of the previous ones. *Primary* as first comes to match *primary* as important. The self may evolve, may shift with changes in the character of primary groups, but the converse is also true and continuity is maintained.

Now that the concept of primary group has been explored and the need of individuals for the support of such groups underlined, we can look at the social world for interesting manifestations of these phenomena.

We can notice, now, that a lot of seemingly meaningless human activity is part of this very basic search for the necessities of social and mental life. See the neighborhood housewives gossiping, the students hanging around the union, the businessmen having lunch together, the children playing, the office workers having coffee? You might have thought they were just goofing off. Actually, they are engaged in the vital, essential, perhaps even desperate, search for meaning in their lives. They are reassuring themselves and one another about who they are and what they are doing. They do not realize this. Except in the context of this chapter, you are unlikely to recognize it. Without such interactions, the human actor, on whom all social systems hinge, could not be kept in good "working order."

For human actors to be successful social actors, they must know who they are and what is expected of them. They must have appropriate self-concepts, definitions of roles, and understandings of norms. When all these conditions are realized, the acts of many individuals fit together in a more or less orderly fashion; the society operates. But society is big and complicated. It's tough for an individual even to appreciate the whole, let alone relate to it meaningfully. The individual cannot "take" his norms from society as he would take a daily newspaper. Guides for behavior will not be delivered to your door. Primary groups serve as an intervening agency. They mediate between the individual and the large, unapproachable, incomprehensible social structures within which he must act.

The individual does not possess social-psychological orientations to act within these larger social structures. He operates within, and in relation to, his primary groups. Sociologically, the implications of his actions are operative at the larger structural level. This is the case for society as a whole and is true as well for some of the larger subsystems within that society. In Chapter 1, I mentioned the likelihood of nested social systems: of systems within systems within systems. One of the implications of such nesting is the possibility of a step-by-step lashing together of social units, from small to large. Individuals can relate to primary groups that can relate to larger subsystems, and so on up to the societal level. The group gap is bridged in small steps.

Bureaucracies are prototypically large and complex. In their operation, the mediating function of primary groups should be readily recognizable. Bureaucracies are characterized by formal rules and formal relations. The organization is explicitly formal organization. The successful "fitting together" of the diverse actions of a large number of persons is consequent to this formality. From the point of view of the organization, that is self-sufficient. From the individual point of view, however, this level of organization must be supplemented by one that furnishes a more personalized basis for social action. We may expect to find primary groups within bureaucracies.

Although the norms, the rules of office, derive from the total organization, it is very unusual for an individual to learn these rules through the agency of the bureaucracy. He is far more likely to learn them from his immediate superior, and even more important, from his fellow workers at the same level. Officially, there is no provision for communication between co-workers. Actually, without such communication the bureaucracy would be nearly crippled. The new recruit enters the organization, may have a brief official orientation to his tasks and responsibilities, and is then turned loose within the vast and confusing operation. His real orientation to his work will come from other people who are doing the same work. They will tell him how it is supposed to be done. This they will provide in great detail, on the basis of thorough knowledge, and with repetition over extended time. The official orientation could not offer these strengths.

The primary group orientation will also tell him how the job *is* done. This may differ in substantial respects from the way it is supposed to be done. The real way, the primary group way, is likely to be more flexible and practicable than the official way. Some specific deviations induced by primary group norms may be detrimental, but on the whole, the net effect is advantageous to the larger organization. In a factory situation, for instance, a work group may have an unofficial limitation on production. This is contrary to the corporate ideal of maximum output and would seem to lower productivity, profit, efficiency, and the achievement of other organizational goals. If we look further, we can find ways in which the net gains of such informal impositions exceed the net costs.

Where the primary group imposes a norm of production, this norm serves as a floor as well as a ceiling. Research has shown that as the solidarity of a work group increases (as it becomes more of a primary group) the general effect on production is neither positive or negative. Output will not necessarily rise or fall. What will happen is that the productivity of the individuals within the group will grow more similar. The capacity of the informal group to establish and enforce a norm grows as the group takes on more primary attributes. For the organization, this means that the output of such a group and of the individuals within the group becomes more stable, more predictable. The organization proceeds more smoothly as more of its elements partake of such regularity and can be dealt with in standardized fashions.

As the work group becomes primary, the individuals become attached to the norms the group provides, and to the group itself. They are less likely to leave the group; they develop loyalty and patterns of mutual support and assistance. It is very difficult for an individual to be loyal to a bureaucracy. If he is loyal to a primary group within the organization the effect for the organization may be the same. Perhaps the greatest test of loyalty is the willingness of an individual to risk his life, or even to give it up. Soldiers in combat must offer such sacrifices if the military is to successfully pursue its goals. Soldiers find little motivation toward such sacrifices in the abstractions of duty, country, the service, or the preservation of ideology. They regularly take risks and make sacrifices on the basis of primary ties within the immediate fighting unit. They are brave because their buddies expect it of them. They take risks because all in the group must take such risks if they are to survive collectively. Primary relations sustain the military operation. Less vividly, in a factory situation primary relations encourage lowered turnover rates in employment and some modicum of "pride of workmanship."

In either case or in any case, the primary group meets some basic needs. It does things for the individual and for the complex societal organization that neither could do by themselves. The larger system makes demands of the individual. The primary group translates these into personal terms, so the demands come from a source the individual is less able to turn down. The resulting acts of the individual are in turn filtered back into the organizational context by the agency of the mediating primary group.

The mediating function of primary groups is distinct from the self-defining and self-sustaining function, but only groups with the last two characteristics are close enough to the individual to carry out the first function.

GARDEN CLUBS ARE NOT FOR GARDENS

Things are not always what they seem. This is generally true with regard to social materials and especially true in connection with primary group matters. We remarked a couple of pages ago on the important psychic functions of apparent "goof-off" social interactions like gossiping. With these cautions in mind, I would like to call your attention to a special social form known as voluntary associations.

Voluntary associations are voluntary in the sense that persons may choose to belong to them or not. They are, to some small degree, associations in the sense of formal organization. They are likely to have some official structure, although scarcely a full-blown bureaucracy. They are also by most counts groups. They feature clearly defined membership, norms, interaction, and consciousness of these conditions. Finally, they are implicitly "social leftovers" in the sense that they do not fit neatly into the categories of any of the major social institutions. Unlike insurance agencies, church congregations, and universities—which might fit the other elements of this definition

—they are not charged with meeting one of the standard list of social needs. We can neatly pair off such things as the family and procreation and socialization, economic systems and sustenance, religion and answers to life's basic questions, schools and socialization, government and social order. The organizations that meet any one of these basic requirements are labeled institutions. Many of these may be, literally, voluntary associations, but they are not so called. The term voluntary association is usually reserved for those organizations that do not fit the institutional category.

A sample of such leftovers: the East Berwyn (Ill.) Ladies' Garden Club, the Confederate Air Force, the Baker Street Irregulars, Rotary International, the Tuesday Evening Beer and Poker Society (Syracuse, N.Y.), the Benevolent and Paternal Order of Elks, the Flat Earth Society, and the Edmond (Okla.) Newcomer's Club. The Garden Club is dedicated to the beautification of lawns and gardens in East Berwyn. The Confederate Air Force lobbies to have the United States Capitol building turned to face the south. Baker Street Irregulars promote knowledge and admiration of the world of Sherlock Holmes. Rotary is devoted to international understanding. Beer and Poker Club members drink and play, respectively. The Elks protect the family security of members. The Flat Earth Society extends proof that the world is really table shaped and cautions against falling off the edge. The Newcomer's Club promotes the integration of migrants into the community. None of these could be said to represent the fulfillment of a central need of, or in, the society. There are over a hundred thousand such organizations in the United States.

I have a little difficulty believing that over six hundred Americans are passionately devoted to the adventures of Sherlock Holmes. I'm not at all sure that all the ladies of the East Berwyn Garden Society live for their mulches and hybrids. Most of the druggists and hardware store owners and bank executives I know belong to Rotary and hold political convictions that are diametrically opposed to international understanding. I think we had better ignore what the members say their organizations are about, if we want to find out what they are really about.

One basic need of social life is the need of the individual for self-sustenance, for psychic refueling. That wasn't on the standard list of needs we offered a few paragraphs ago, and there are no institutions nominally devoted to meeting that need. Here we have a collection of organizations that are devoted to meeting un-basic needs or that are only spuriously devoted to anything. Doesn't it make sense to suggest that leftover organizations correspond to leftover needs? Might not voluntary associations be a kind of cover activity for self-sustenance? Certainly this is not the standard institutional form, for voluntary associations, unlike regular institutions, seem ashamed of what they are *really* about.

Perhaps it would weaken the important businessman's self-concept for him to admit that he needs to be reassured by other important businessmen that he is important too. But that is why he really goes to Rotary. Maybe the ladies of East Berwyn feel less guilty about their drive for status and security when it is wrapped in a blanket of flowers. Whatever the reason, voluntary association members use their nominal organizational goals to deceive themselves or others about the goals of their organizations. Any count of the activity, the energy, and the motives involved in voluntary associations will quickly dissolve the front. The important happenings in such organizations are the ones that resemble the unorganized context of the primary group.

Americans have been called a nation of joiners. For at least a generation, scholars have puzzled over our propensity to join. More recently, it has been shown that this trend toward over-organization characterizes other urban industrial societies as well. Urban-industrial society is accompanied by declining importance of peer-primary ties in kin group and neighborhood. People spend less time in a family context. People are mobile to the point that they cannot count on friendships cultivated from childhood through maturity. The community is no longer a meaningful context for interpersonal intimacy. People cannot count on the automatic availability of significant others or primary relations. They solve this problem as they solve most of the other problems of the modern age, with organization.

It may be that the gardens of East Berwyn are more beautiful and the state of international understanding improved as a result of the activities of these organizations, but that is a side effect. There is no reason why an organization may not have several goals and a whole range of unanticipated outcomes in addition to whatever goals are met. The most socially significant impact of voluntary associations is in their service as surrogate primary groups.

So that you won't think I am picking on other people and other people's organizations, let me confess that I am a member of the American Sociological Association. The nominal goals of the Association are the pursuit of knowledge and the advancement of the profession. These goals are surely of interest to practitioners in the field. The Association may be presumed to be engaged in the pursuit of these goals. The publication of journals, the presentations of papers at meetings, lobbying activities in respect to licensing that might affect the profession, compilation of professional directories, and guarding the standards of training in the discipline are some of the diverse means toward these goals. The Association does all these things.

Some other activities are not clearly related to professional goals. The Association's publications include news and notes that in some ways resemble the gossip columns of small town newspapers. The elected officers are sometimes respected symbols, but not necessarily energetic and capable administrators. At the annual conventions, the congregation of participants in the hotel lobby generally exceeds, in numbers and enthusiasm, that at the sessions where scholarly papers are presented. The activity of those in the lobby is greetings, personal conversations, and empathetic display.

The sustenance of primary relationships is a major, if unstated, function of the American Sociological Association.

A bunch of men travel halfway across the country each year to find their primary group support. They are professional sociologists. One of the distinguishing marks of professions, as opposed to other occupations, is their importance to the practitioner. The professional role is basic to the professional; it is a central part of his identity. When a need to be assured of this identity arises, the assurance must come from other professionals. For this aspect of his identity, only other professionals, and of these perhaps only those in the same specialization as the individual, serve as significant others.

If my wife tells me I am a good father and my students indicate that I am a successful teacher, my ego in these areas may be secure. But I think of myself as a sociologist; it is important for me to be a sociologist; I cannot be content to be a father and teacher. My wife, my students, my neighbors may act as if I were a good sociologist, but I must chalk this up to their general positive dispositions toward me and their lack of special expertise in the field. Even my colleagues in my department are working in different specialties. Professionally, my significant others are in places like Bloomington, Indiana; New York; Eugene, Oregon; St. Louis; Boston; Athens, Georgia; Austin, Texas; and Los Angeles. I must exchange small talk and gestures with them. Their needs are the same. We preempt the American Sociological Association for this purpose.

I have not intended to belabor myself or the American Sociological Association. The case is worth covering because it illustrates the situation of many individuals and many voluntary associations. It will come to be true of even more. More and more roles, occupational and otherwise, are becoming specialized and psychically central, like professions. More and more individuals are orienting themselves to a world larger than their local communities. This condition is called cosmopolitanism. One of its implications is a wide spatial scattering of significant others. "Natural" primary groups will fade into relative insignificance. Surrogate primary groups, usually under the guise of voluntary associations, will become a more imposing feature of the social landscape.

WHO'S IN, WHO'S OUT

Groups are characterized by boundaries and consciousness. This entails knowing who is a fellow member of the group and who is not. "We-they" distinctions and feelings are a logical outcome of group existence.

The more people interact with each other, the more similar they become in beliefs and behaviors. The more beliefs and behaviors they share, the more they will like each other. The more they like each other, the more they will interact. All of these dynamics work toward the exclusion of those not within the magic circle. As the beliefs and behaviors of the *ins* become more similar, they stand in ever starker contrast to the different ones of the *outs*. Because these acts and ideas are shared by the good guys they must be good ones; anything different must be bad and those who adhere to them bad guys. This kind of idea becomes part of the in-group milieu. Sharing reinforces it and brings the group still closer together.

One thing that creates group organization and solidarity is hostility toward some others who are not part of the group. There must be a *they* before *we* feelings or behaviors can become operative. Intergroup prejudice, discrimination, and stereotyping evolve from this source.

Of course, out-group hostility is not the only possible source of in-group solidarity. Shared values within the group, recognized interpersonal dependencies, and common acceptance of a normative system serve to cement a group together. These matters were covered more fully in Chapter 4. There is still no denying that prejudice functions to increase group solidarity and to enhance the development of some of these other factors that are also causative agents.

Similarly, in-group solidarity is not the only source of prejudice. At least three other sources can be identified. Cultural mythology is one of these. A tribe may believe that some people on the other side of the mountain grow a second head during the time of crescent moons and devour small children. Such a story may have been handed down from generation to generation. If contact with those other people is minimal, the prejudice will have little salience and little impact on group solidarity, but prejudice it remains. Nobody loves a two-headed babyeater.

A little closer to home, studies of social distance have been conducted periodically in the United States for over a generation. They show the relative disfavor in which the major in-group holds several potential out-groups. One of the consistently most despised national minorities is the Turks. I don't know what the Turks ever did to earn this disfavor. I am not aware of the elements in our culture's myths that bring them to this condition. Whatever the case, I have some difficulty believing that our common antipathy toward Turks is a major factor in American solidarity. I suspect most of you can go for hours at a time without even thinking about Turks. If you wanted a real live one to hate, you might have a tough time finding him. Still, when faced with the hypothetical decision on a multiple choice survey, most Americans say that they would not like to have a Turk move in next door. The prejudice is there, even if it is a shopworn hand-me-down.

Another source of prejudice is ideology. Some ideologies carry strong threads of prejudice as part of their basic fabric. All ideologies are susceptible to extremist fringe interpretations that require that the infidels be punished or exterminated. History is full of examples of ideology gone wild in this fashion.

Rather than consider an extremist version, let us look at everyday prejudice rooted in an everyday ideology. American Christianity carries such prejudice regarding Jews.[2] Not all American Gentiles are prejudiced against Jews, but those who are are most likely to be Christians with strong, orthodox faith and regular devotional practices. This connection begins with blaming ancient Jews for the death of Jesus, transfers the guilt to modern Jews, and broadens from religious guilt to a variety of negative stereotypes and general hostility. Along the way, the part of the Romans in the Crucifixion is forgotten. Judas is considered a Jew, but the other disciples become Christian. A sizeable minority label even Moses and other Hebrew prophets as Christians. Not all anti-Semitism stems from

---

[2]The material in this paragraph is from Charles Y. Glock and Rodney Stark, *Christian Beliefs and Anti-Semitism* (New York: Harper & Row, 1966).

Christian ideology. In some cases individuals may simply rationalize an already existing prejudice by giving it religious trappings. Yet in many cases ideology appears the central cause. Ideologies do contribute a portion of out-group feeling.

Another portion comes as a form of psychopathology. The human need for self-definition, already remarked in this chapter, is powerful. In the face of uncertainty or feelings of inferiority, an individual may assure himself of his own adequacy by projecting inadequacies on others. A psychological need for hate may be part of the mental syndrome of some individuals. Out-groups offer a target on which such hate can be focused. Prejudice serves as a crutch for the crippled personality. Further examination of this variety of prejudice will be left for the psychologists.

Mythological, ideological, and psychopathological prejudice are not the focus of this section. Each of these is in some ways intertwined with, but in other ways distinguishable from, group-generated prejudice. It was necessary to delineate the several forms, but now we can return to the group dynamic in which we are interested.

Group existence implies inside and outside, we and they. The operation of a group tends to lead automatically to out-group hostility. Out-group hostility strengthens in-group ties and promotes stability of the group. This is a two-edged sword. The in-group only becomes more cohesive at the cost of solidarity in the larger social unit that contains both in-group and out-group. Organizationally, a system can only afford prejudice outside the system boundaries.

In concrete terms, anti-Semitism may strengthen the Christian churches in the United States. The country as a whole, where Christians and Jews must act within the same social system, is weakened. Contempt for independents may solidify the fraternity but tends to destroy the university. Class conflict will strengthen the bonds within each class but will rip the society apart.

It might appear that international hate would be organizationally tolerable. If all of us Americans hate Russians or Chinese or Turks or just plain foreigners, we have a national basis for group solidarity and the antagonisms are toward people who aren't part of our social system. However, that simply is not so. With such things as missiles and international trade, the modern world is really one social system. You may not meet a Turk every day, but events in Turkey affect your everyday life.

Race prejudice carries all the disruptive aspects of any other form of prejudice, without offering the small organizational advantages. Race is not a meaningful social category, except where prejudice and discrimination make it so. There are few groups that are purely racial in character. Therefore, there is no social unit whose solidarity is strengthened by racial prejudice, except for groups that grow out of the prejudice and discrimination. There are no in-group racial units to be solidified by racial hostility; there are many multi-racial systems that are weakened by race prejudice.

The result is this: we can't afford to hate anyone except beings from other planets. If in the future we make contact with some, then we won't be able to hate them either. Prejudice is a natural outgrowth of group conditions and is healthy for the social unit from which it emanates. It is decidedly unhealthy for the social unit within which it occurs.

FURTHER READING

Bettelheim, Bruno, *The Empty Fortress: Infantile Autism and the Birth of Self.* New York: Free Press, 1967.*

Gans, Herbert J., *The Levittowners: Ways of Life & Politics in a New Suburban Community.* New York: Pantheon, 1966.

Glaser, William, and David Sills, eds., *The Government of Associations.* Totowa, N.J.: Bedminster, 1966.*

Goffman, Erving, *The Presentation of Self in Everyday Life.* New York: Doubleday, 1959 Anchor paperback.

Keniston, Kenneth, *The Uncommitted: Alienated Youth in American Society.* New York: Harcourt, 1965. Also paperback, Dell.

Lewis, Oscar, *La Vida: A Puerto Rican Family in the Culture of Poverty—San Juan & New York.* New York: Random House, 1966. Available in paperback.

Lofland, John, *Doomsday Cult.* Englewood Cliffs, N.J.: Prentice-Hall, 1966. Paperback.

Newcomb, Theodore M., *The Acquaintance Process.* New York: Holt, 1961.*

Sherif, Muzafer, *The Psychology of Social Norms.* New York: Harper, 1965.

Schachter, Stanley, *The Psychology of Affiliation.* Stanford: Stanford University, 1959.*

*Difficult, specialized, or technical.

10 MASS MEDIA AND MASS MIND

Culture, basically, is the socially significant portion of what people know. Any test of knowledge is a cultural inventory. Finding out how many people—and what people—know a certain thing will tell us something about the culture of that people's society. By selecting the appropriate test questions, we can push inside the mind at selected points and make the inventory specialized. Isolated portions of the culture can be highlighted in this fashion. The resulting profile should offer hints concerning the origins of knowledge and the mechanisms of learning of the society in question. What people know and how they have come to know it are crucial to an understanding of the people themselves and their society.

Please check what *you* know by identifying the following persons.

1. John Falstaff	9. Hoss Cartwright	17. Philip Blaiberg
2. Woodie Guthrie	10. Dana Gibson	18. William Brennan
3. Norman Rockwell	11. Hugh Hefner	19. William Hogarth
4. Lorenzo Jones	12. Golda Meir	20. Guy Gisborne
5. Carl Yastrzemski	13. Béla Bartók	21. Charlie Brown
6. James Forman	14. Maria Martinez	22. Russ Colombo
7. Sancho Panza	15. Diana Ross	23. Charles Manson
8. John Henry	16. Elmer Zilch	24. Richard Daley

Correct identifications will be found at the end of the chapter. Please turn to page 216 and score yourself one point for each correct answer. Keep track, by question number, of the items you missed. Now subdivide your score. Count items 1, 7, 13, and 19. On the basis of number of right answers among these four, assign yourself a score between four and zero. Label this *score A*. Do the same for five other sets: Questions 2, 8, 14, and 20—set *B*; 3, 9, 15, 21—*C*; 4, 10, 16, 22—*D*; 5, 11, 17, 23—*E*; and 6, 12, 18, 24—*F*.

Did your best score come on set *C*? Was your second best score on set *E*? Did you do most poorly on *D*? If so, you are with the majority or, less kindly, the mass.

PERCENT OF STUDENTS WITH PARTICULAR NUMBERS OF CORRECT ANSWERS ON SETS OF ITEMS IN IDENTIFICATION TEST

Number of items correct		A	B	Item Set C	D	E	F
4		2	0	55	0	23	2
3		5	5	40	0	38	27
2		17	29	3	5	28	23
1		36	38	1	20	12	36
0		40	29	0	75	0	11
	TOTAL*	100	101	99	100	101	99

*Totals may not equal 100 percent because of rounding.

I gave a similar test to 146 underclassmen at the University of Florida. The distribution of their scores is shown in the table. The patterns of knowledge and ignorance are obvious and revealing.

I would not use these results to insult my students. Nor do I think you should feel smug or inadequate on the basis of your own score. The general pattern of scores forces an entering wedge into the mass mind rather than into the mind of any individual. That is where we want to go. We will look into the nature of the content of the items and of the knowledge-disseminating system of our society. In these we will attempt to find explanations for the general distribution of knowledge and ignorance, reasons why some things are more likely to be known than others.

THE ARTS

The first four sets of test items call for the identification of persons within the general category of the arts. These sets contain a mixture of performers, creative artists, and fictional characters. Set A includes Falstaff, Panza, Bartók, and Hogarth. This collection could fairly be labeled "classical arts." Set B—Gisborne, Henry, Guthrie, Martinez —can similarly be labeled "folk arts." Set C is just as homogenous, and the basis for their grouping is apparent: Cartwright, Brown, Ross, and Rockwell. It is more difficult to find a suitable title. "Pop arts" will be used; you must take the definition of "pop" from the apparent communality of the set and ignore other connotations that the term might otherwise carry. Other available terms, such as "mass," or "commercial," have the same problem with extraneous meanings. Set D—Jones, Zilch, Colombo, and Gibson—does not differ from the third in artistic type, but only in time. Set D is simply "old pop art." Sets E and F are unrelated to art and will be dealt with later in this chapter.

Time is irrelevant for the classical and folk sets, but becomes important for the pop. The time span between Panza and Bartók or Gisborne and Guthrie is far greater than that between Colombo and Cartwright. The pop clock moves more swiftly; the time dimension is important in this category. The separate classification is justified by the radically different scores obtained on the two sets.

Before we go further in basing analysis on the results of the test, let us make sure that the results were not biased by the test's construction. I have tried to make the test honest. Each set contains two fictional characters, one musician, and one plastic or graphic artist.

Individuals with names departing from the American norm were not offered for identification. This excluded such names as Hamlet, Donovan, Henry VIII, Pogo, and Malcolm X. Also excluded were individuals whose formal names are much more obscure than their popular name, for example Robin Hood (Locksley) and Rembrandt (van Rijn). I also tried to balance popularity within and between categories. Surely several classical artists are more famous than Hogarth; Diana Ross's standing among pop singers may rank about the same. Similar equations can be found across any category line. Differences in scores fairly reflect areas of knowledge and ignorance of the subject matter represented by the several sets.

What these scores indicate, then, is that Americans know new pop art better than classical, classical better than folk, folk better than old pop. If your own scores deviate from this pattern, you have drawn a portrait of yourself as a peculiar American. Ignoring any such deviation, we can learn from the typical distribution something about art and something about knowledge in our society.

Critics tell us that art has something to do with truth and beauty. The variable states of knowledge exposed above would seem to indicate that some art is truer and more beautiful than the remainder; the appeal of the object or creation is more widespread.

I have devised an experiment that would formalize this definition of absolute truth or beauty. If you will send me two hundred thousand dollars (note address on title page of book), I will carry out the research. I will get a big bag and fill it up with art objects—pictures, statues, recordings—from the several categories of pop, folk, and classical. I will then go around the world, stopping off in London, Moscow, Bombay, the Himalaya slopes of Nepal, the Brazilian jungle, the upper Zambezi valley, and a thousand other places, a fair sample of the world's societies. At each stop, I will rummage in my bag, pull out an object, display it, and ask a native "Do you like it?" His reaction to each bit of art in the bag will be recorded, and I will move on to the next stop. When I return home I will total up a "worldwide appreciation score" for each art object. I expect, if you sent me the money and I were able to carry through this procedure, that the scores of objects would show high variability. I expect that the scores of classical and folk arts would average much higher than those of pop. I would be prepared to call beautiful those objects that received high scores, regardless of their origin, and to assert that they portrayed a high level of truth.

The logic for calling art with high scores better art rests in the notion that universal acceptance indicates superiority. I argue that an object that elicits aesthetic appreciation from nearly everyone (regardless of personal experience, language, cultural standards of beauty, values, or prejudices) must have inherent aesthetic quality. The appeal is to a universal human quality.

The logic for predicting that classical and folk arts will score better than pop art rests in the fact that approximations of this experiment already exist. Conditions of formality and control have not been met, but the indications are there. The classical and folk items from the test list have endured the trial of both space and time. Elizabethan London, where Falstaff was created and first appreciated, is not the same society as the contemporary United States, but Falstaff is still appreciated here, and has been appreciated in the societies of most of the intervening generations. If his popularity in this generation is not as high as Cartwright's, that is purely a temporary phenomenon, as the fate of Lorenzo Jones demonstrates. Thirty years ago Jones's recognition was greater than Falstaff's. Thirty years from now Cartwright will have faded into the same limbo, while Falstaff plugs along. (How many of you have already forgotten Napoleon Solo?) Falstaff's cross-cultural appreciation score is high; longevity equals universality equals quality. Hence the timelessness of folk and classical art versus the time-bounded nature of pop art, noted earlier in this chapter, becomes a point of aesthetic difference as well.

Now we have established that classical and folk arts are generally superior to pop arts. This is a general principle, a tendency, not a universal. I am simply saying that the average appreciation scores vary between categories, and therefore the average participation in truth and beauty varies. Some pop art, and indeed some natural objects, such as an occasional sand-eroded rock on the beach, may have high "beauty-quotients." When it is a question of averages, we are inquiring, in a sense, into the batting averages of artists. We are asking how it happens that some kinds of artists succeed in putting beauty and truth into their products more often than others.

For the classical artist, the answer must rest in his classical training. The classical musician learns a complex and quasi-mathematical set of rules concerning harmonic resolution and chord progressions. These are now so formalized that a properly programmed computer can produce a passable symphonic movement. The classical composer also develops an intimate familiarity with his artistic ancestry, with the several schools and traditions of the art form. This is likely to include exposure to other times and places, developing a cross-cultural frame of reference. He becomes, in effect, a rational and knowledgeable scholar of truth and beauty as expressed in sound. He will not slavishly follow traditions or formulas, but his violations will be conscious and purposeful ones, his creation a logical extension of established truths and beauties. Success is not guaranteed, but is more probable than if creation is random.

Artistic quality may occur as an intellectual outgrowth of a tradition of artistic quality, and this is what classical art is all about. The principles set forth here for music apply as well to artists working in any other medium.

Folk artists are clearly not of this sort; folk arts' quality can not be explained on these grounds. Folklorists disagree among themselves concerning what folk art is. A definition accepted by some, and rejected violently by others, is that folk art is any art that has been passed on through common people (the folk) long enough that its original creator is unknown. Without entering the argument concerning the merits of this definition, as definition, we can use it as a signpost directing us toward understanding creativity and quality in folk art.

The original creator of any item of folk art is unlikely to be tutored in an intellectual tradition of creativity, but he surely is steeped in a tradition of folk performance. He creates within this tradition and with cultural roots deeply in the soil of his people. What he creates may or may not have high artistic value, but, by the definition with which we started, it is not yet folk art. It must be passed on through the hands of the artist's fellowmen until he has receded from sight. Such a process may require several generations or the crossing of several geographical frontiers. Each of the folk who serves as a medium must remember the performance and appreciate it enough to repeat it. This condition must hold for several such steps. Works lacking the quality that induces such continuing transmission will die, will disappear. During the transmission process alterations may be made by any medium-performer, alterations that bring the art work more in line with that person's aesthetic sense. Through enough such steps, it may often be that the alterations form more of the work than did the original creator. In such a case "the folk" have collectively become the creator.[1]

When we examine folk art, we find, then, only that which has already passed the survival, or cross-cultural appreciation, test. Folk creators have no intrinsic edge in production of quality art. The

---

[1] This process is only possible for oral arts. Plastic or graphic creations do not lend themselves to such alteration. In consequence, these latter forms are under-represented in folk art, compared to oral contributions.

quality of the final product comes with selection and remolding by the transmission process. Folk art achieves high artistic value as it comes to reflect the human and societal conditions in which it circulates.

Pop art has the advantages of neither folk nor classical. It is a conscious creation, but not an intellectual one. It is transmitted to, but not through, the folk. Its appeal is a peculiar result of special training among its audience, not among its creators. Appreciation for pop art is an acquired taste and is likely to hold only for one society and one short period of time. These arts are created to meet that taste. They are produced (and perhaps this is a better term than created) for that market. Like other commodities, they are vended to that market until the market won't take any more. This point is reached when the consumer's exposure to the bit of art reaches satiation, a point not very far away when the frequency of exposure is maximized.

This torrential exposure rate is the first factor that helps account for the short-lived character of pop art. A second is the market orientation, rather than aesthetic orientation, of the creators. A third is in the market nature of the audience. Acquired tastes, the taste of fashion, are not enduring or universally human. As the society changes, tastes change. Lacking any more substantial base, pop art fades from the scene and is replaced by another generation of the same category but a different kind.

Meanwhile, there is one purely artistic explanation to cover. It is a sort of Grisham's Law of art: bad drives out good. Classical art has been portrayed as a rational creative act. Rationally, why should an individual spend years of arduous study in preparation for classical productivity, when the prestige and economic rewards for untutored pop production are so much greater? How is an individual to acquire the original motivation to a classical career when in his formative years he is bombarded with works that violate all the classical precepts and is trained to regard this material as good? Conditions of modern society imply that only a small proportion of those with artistic potential will enter the classical arena.

The fate of folk art is worse. Those same conditions of modern society transform the folk into an audience. In a society of individuals with transistor radios at their ears, no man is troubadour. There is nobody left to create a folksong, nobody to hear, nobody to transmit. The population lives off the pop produce to such an extent that it may become their world. They no longer have a grass roots appreciation of their society or community, and are consequently unable to judge art as good or bad reflections of that social reality. The pop image has become their reality. Field workers in Latin America report that rural peasants' perceptions of the United States are based almost entirely on our movies. The extent to which our own perceptions of our society are similarly based has been severely underestimated.

Once bad art, pop art, has currency, it is easy to see how it becomes the dominant art. In summary, the art that most Americans know is bad art; the art to which they are exposed is bad art. This summary also points to the places where an explanation of these conditions may be sought. In the heads of the knowers and in the systems of the exposers, in minds and in media, lie the explanations. When our search takes this twist we have moved away from the world of art; we are dealing with more general categories of knowledge and information flow. Such inquiry must wait until after we have examined the nonartistic portion of the test with which this chapter started.

THE NEWS

"The news" is a funny term. If I were to simply slide it in at this time without discussion, most of you would let it pass, never realizing you had been intellectually taken. Yet the meaning and import of the term is open to serious question.

Operationally, "the news" is what is presented in the news media. Read your newspaper; watch your TV newscast. What do you find there? A murder. Yesterday's activity in America's quasiwar. Border clashes in somebody else's quasiwar. Marriage of two movie stars (his third, her fourth). Divorces of some other movie stars. Testimony from a Congressional investigation. An Asian Prime Minister visits a European capital. Another murder. A Detroit automaker announces a new model. A Senator urges a new policy. Riots at a university. A pro ball club manager explains his team's loss. Someone charges $17,468.11 worth of goods and services on an American Express credit card before the owner reports the card missing. A space launch is postponed. An Undersecretary of Health is appointed. An armored car robbery. An actor likes his new series. The city council of a small town in Ohio repeals an ordinance (unenforced for forty years) prohibiting autos from the city streets. The defense attorney in last month's famous trial files an appeal. The President goes for a walk. An airplane crash in South America.

If this is the news, what is it? Studies of metropolitan areas during newspaper strikes show that residents really miss this stuff. They go to great lengths to find substitute sources. This information is part of their security. But what is it that they need; what is it that they gain? The chaotic collection of materials from the representative list above does not answer this question. An operational answer does not settle our problem.

Let us try, then, an analytic answer. Toward the end of Chapter 3, I suggested that man's psychological security in modern society was derived in part from his conception of his place in that society, from his understanding of the network of interrelationships and interdependencies within the world and his function in that network. Psychologically, then, it might be said that man needs the news, to whatever extent the news helped him to build these conceptions. In a democracy, a social need parallels this psychological one. Voter-citizens need critical information on which to base their political decisions. Democracy requires an informed populace. These arguments indicate that the utilitarian and essential portions of the news are those reporting on significant happenings. The news allows man to keep abreast of the societal operation and to assess its impact on him, and vice versa. Theoretically, this is a tight answer. Sadly, it will not hold evidential water.

The two remaining sets of identifications from the test with which this chapter began can be labeled "names in the news." Set F—James Forman, Golda Meir, Richard Daley, and William Brennan —represents news content consistent with the explanation in the last paragraph. These people are socially significant. Their conduct today may affect your life and mine tomorrow. Our understanding of that world will be enhanced by our knowledge of these people. But, if you check the knowledge results on the identification test, these are not the men of whom we are knowledgeable. We know set E better: Carl Yastrzemski, Hugh Hefner, Philip Blaiberg, and Charles Manson. These are not socially significant, they are simply well known. They are celebrities. They are a major part of the news that is sent, and virtually the only portion that is received and retained. Obviously, our selective retention disproves any notion of man as a utilitarian-information seeking animal and denies that the news media are substantially venders of such material.

"The news," baldly, is what we get. Analysis on any other basis would represent empty theorizing at best and pathetic dream-dealing at worst. We get that news through communication processes. Such communication processes can be conceived as starting with a set of potential messages, passing through a series of selective filters at several stages of message emission, transmission, reception, and assimilation.

The potential news contains all the varied happenings and opinions of the world. The actual news is the limited and confused portion of this that ends up in the mind of everyman. "The news" is the content of the mass mind. I label it the mass mind only in the sense that it is the product of mass communication processes. That is, at this point we are not interested in the knowledge and sentiments individuals have through contact with their mothers, brothers, neighbors, and fellow workers. We are only interested in those sentiments and knowledge that result from exposure to newspapers, television, radio, movies, magazines, and books. The selective narrowing and rejection of potential news at world source to yield actual news in the mass mind will be understood to follow from several filtration processes. We will examine some of these filters.

Starting from the happening end, the first filter encountered is that of secrecy or privacy. Many events fail to become news because individuals or groups make more or less conscious attempts to prevent the event from coming to public view. If the attempt is successful, such events are never subject to judgments concerning their appropriateness or news value; they have the same public value as non-happenings. Diverse examples of this class of event would include: sexual relations of most married couples, a variety of business dealings (corporate secrets), many cases of sexual assault, successful crime and fraud, and official government secrets. These "messages" are simply not available.

The second filter is law. Although these messages are available in a sense in which secrets are not, they have been officially labeled "do not transmit." Libelous, pornographic, and seditious messages form the main content here. Legal sanctions stand as threat to those who fail to apply this filter. Such filtration is held to be justifiable on the grounds of general welfare or public good.

News is "made" at least twice—once by the actors who bring the event into being and once by the newsman who uncovers and reports it. The third filter is in the decisions and actions of that newsman. There is more police news than welfare news. One might take this as an indication that there are more police than welfare activities, or more crime than need. Rather, I think, the explanation rests in the fact that reporters are regularly assigned to the precinct house but not to the welfare agency. Reporters report what they see; what they see is contingent upon where they are looking. The decision concerning where to look is part of the filtration process. Moreover, the reporter does not report all that he sees. He selects, omits, organizes. Ultimately, much of this filtering power does not rest with the individual newsman. He takes orders from the supervisor, the editor, and others in the hierarchy of his media organization. He also follows the dictates of tradition in a profession that has been defining, perhaps even creating, news for several generations. The editors and other supervisors are simply successful newsmen grown older, more steeped in the same traditions, so their supervision does not add a new element. For reasons that may become apparent later in the analysis, this journalistic filter is sociologically uninteresting in its effect on content.

Further filtration does occur at this level, however, when nonjournalistic definitions of news and limitations on news appear. This filtration is at the hands of "interest-power." A wide variety of controls fall under this heading. The most obvious ones are the direct commercial interests of the media. The newspapers most Americans read, if they read one at all, cater to the wishes of their local merchant-advertisers. Potential news that might be bad for business or for the town's image is suppressed. Material with the opposite effect, which by other standards would be non-news, is elevated in importance. The influence of radio and television sponsors on content in those media is, if anything, even more drastic and blatant. Media publishers, owners, and stockholders who have political or economic interests other than the media exert similar and extremely effective pressures on behalf of these other special interests. In this respect also the situation is particularly serious in the case of television. Over a third of all TV franchises have national political figures among their major stockholders. From the other viewpoint and for a more select group, over half of all United States senators own stock in broadcasting corporations. Further power-interest control is in the hands of formally organized pressure groups, for whom censorship pressure represents a major investment of their power and effort. Included here would be such strange bedfellows as the League of Decency, Italian Anti-Defamation League, Liberty Lobby, American Bar Association, United States Army Corps of Engineers, Society for the Prevention of Cruelty to Animals, Paul Newman Fan Club, and Chicago Chamber of Commerce.

One final power-interest influence is that exercised by the sources of the news. Some individuals are automatically newsworthy in themselves, others occupy strategic positions with respect to news activity. The newsman is dependent on these individuals as sources and is consequently subject to manipulation by them. During President Lyndon Johnson's administration it was public knowledge that a reporter who depicted the President or his policies unfavorably would miss out on subsequent news breaks from the White House. For such a practice of reprisal to become widely known is unusual and must be ascribed to Johnson's general unpopularity with the press and his blunter use of the weapon. The practice of reprisal is universal among all Presidents, all politicians, and all other persons who are regular sources for reporters. Policemen and crime reporters regularly have this easy sort of understanding: the newsman has special access to police business and in return portrays the police as efficient, honest, and dedicated. Worthy of special note here is the long-term symbiosis between the entire news establishment and the FBI.

The several forms of power-interest filters represent a wide variety of interests and a broad range of power levers. Collectively, they eliminate an enormous amount of news on criteria unrelated to public interests or welfare and equally unrelated to journalistic standards. In this sense they represent censorship rather than merely filtration and are damaging to freedom of information, which is part of a free society.

Further filtration occurs with the transmission process itself. Even if the medium is not truly the message, it defines the message or limits the message. Newspaper headlines are rigidly circumscribed messages. Number of words, length of words, and grammatical construction are determined by considerations of space and form. For those who read no further than the headline, this is the only message they get. Television, similarly, makes editorial decisions on the basis of format. A certain portion of each show's material must be accompanied by attention-holding pictures. TV is a visual medium; the show must have a show. The question, "What is news?" is converted into the question "Which are our best films?" Each medium, and to a lesser degree each organization, falls heir to, and elaborates, a form, a style, an approach. The news they survey is that which is compatible with, and has been adapted to, that package.

The other aspect of transmission is distribution. Dollar magazines and fifteen-cent magazines find their way to different reading publics. Even if the price is the same, magazines sold only in bookstores and large newsstands reach different portions of the mass than those that are widely distributed in drugstores, groceries, and corner newsstands. Still different in distribution are those that sell mainly by subscription. Radio broadcasts at 2:00 P.M. and 4:00 P.M. have radically different audiences. Few residents of Indiana read the Denver Post. Even fewer Coloradans regularly watch WISH-TV, Indianapolis. In this sense our "mass mind" is made up of numerous small and sharply differentiated segments. The differentiation is in different exposures to similarly agglomerated but bounded elements of the "mass media."

The final filters are in the almost limitless void between printed page or spoken word and individual's mind. Between speaker and ear? Print and eye? Or between sensory apparatus and brain? Selective perception and selective memory may both be at work here, and I do not think we need inquire into the relative effect of one versus the other. Rather, we can refer once more to the quiz materials with which this chapter started. The American population generally is more familiar with Hugh Hefner than with Richard Daley. Richard Daley is a mover and shaker. He is one of the most powerful politicians in the United States. He rules Chicago and the Illinois Democratic Party with a grip that is as firm as that held by any individual in the country over units of this magnitude. Hefner is the publisher of a slightly thoughtful and slightly risqué and very ordinary magazine. He has very ordinary ideas and some slight power to further them. Yet more Americans are familiar with Hefner than with Daley. At this point one might indict the mass media for their emphasis on the unimportant, the dilettante. It is very fashionable to flagellate the mass media, particularly television. The media, particularly television, deserve all the abuse they can receive. I will try to get in some licks a little later. But not here, for the simple fact is that the media are not to blame for the perverse knowledge of Hefner and ignorance of Daley that the masses display. I have not measured the news communications relative to these two men. I am sure, however, that by any conceivable measure and for any recent time span, Daley has been the topic of more and larger messages than Hefner. The indictment of misplaced importance must be brought against the public rather than against the media. Ignoring the weight the media places on these two individuals, the public prefers to remember Hefner and forget Daley. The individual psychological filter is the final one, and a drastic one indeed.

Each of the millions of individuals who make up the mass has his own personal biases, interests, and psychological sets. The filtering process occurs individually and uniquely for each of these persons. The "average effect" of the filtering is nonetheless strikingly clear and similar for a very large portion of these persons. In this similarity we are able to consider our topic still a mass phenomenon.

That mass effect is precisely opposite to the prediction that the rational information-seeking model offered a few pages back. The mass preference is for the bizarre over the basic, the glamorous over the significant, the frivolous over the portentous.

By any evidence, "pop" news is as pervasive as pop art and drives out the competing forms just as effectively.

In this sense it does not matter what news messages the media make available to the public. The public receives and absorbs only the pop portion. This preference is evidenced by the filtering at the psychological level and by the fact that individuals seek out preferred messages, a behavioral factor. In this sense it is not necessary to do a knowledge inventory test on the population to discover the kinds of knowledges they prefer. Instead, one could merely check ratings of broadcasts or sales of publications.

Because this is true, the psychological filter influences filtration at some of the other levels. Earlier, I spoke of the canons of journalism—the guidelines that newsmen use to decide what is the news. These guidelines are deeply influenced by the public definitions, at least inasmuch as these public definitions are expressed in consumption patterns. Laws are created, repealed, and interpreted at least in part in terms of public definitions. Obscenity laws, for instance, change with public morality. One would do less than total violence to reality, then, if he were to ignore the several levels of filters that we have examined and treat the media as nonintervening transmitters. They simply and uncritically deliver to the mass the goods that the mass desires. The filter of which this is not true is the one that was previously referred to invidiously—pressure-interest. The power units that exert special, independent, selfish, often unrecognized, and usually damaging influence on news message content are economic and political power units with special access. They prevent the mass media from conforming very closely to a free market operation.

One other deviation from the ordinary free market operation is that mass communication is always a mass market and sometimes a monopoly market. Here, I think, lies a great unresolved issue. Television is the most nearly monopolistic of the media, so I will rest this argument mostly on the condition of television. Much of the argument applies to some degree to the several other media. Television is basically monopolistic because of the limited broadcasting range, the high unit-cost of the message, and the quasi-monopolistic effect of station licensing by the government. (Incidentally, politicians' personal investments in TV are greater than in the other media.) The exorbitant profits of television operations (averaging over forty percent on investments and over twenty percent on gross income) is evidence of their monopolistic position.

Monopoly implies that there is only one purveyor of the product. Communication mechanics demand that only one product be purveyed at a time. Market exigencies require that at all times the product be the one with the widest possible market. There can be no catering to minority interests, to smaller segments of the potential audience who might have special wishes or needs. The attempt must constantly be to reach the mass. This is one more force that serves to make the concept of mass so very appropriate to the kinds of materials with which this chapter deals. In a free market, a variety of goods are offered at appropriate prices for a variety of consumers. In a mass market such as that which applies to communication, to the news and the arts, only one product, the least common denominator, is offered to the mass.

Earlier I argued that communication institution filters were simply reflections of the psychological filters of individuals, and that the media, therefore, could not be faulted for the evisceration of the news. Now, however, it should be apparent that the media do not simply reflect the mass, they create it.

Critics decry the pandering to low tastes that is so characteristic of mass communications. The media apologists defend themselves by saying that the public tastes are low. Our analysis shows that this is indeed the case, but the public tastes are to some extent creations of the communicators. By failing to take into account the diversity of the publics that they serve, the communicators have created a mass at the level of the worst of those publics.

In concrete terms and in a utopian world, the rectification of this situation would not be difficult. If the franchised air of TV wavelengths is seen as a privilege granted for public service, then that air's use should serve those publics. If we imagine a hypothetical market of one million people and one thousand broadcast minutes per day, then every individual is entitled to six-hundredths of a second of program to his wishes. Eight thousand opera buffs could pool their time, entitling them to fifty-six minutes a week. Under such a system the majority would still be allocated the majority of the time and most programming would be the same mush that is on the air now. But this would be just the major portion, not the whole. Television would offer serious news commentary proportionate to the percent of the population who would consume such material. Carried to its logical extreme, this practice might give us an occasional

"Fun with Model Ship Building" and "Sado-Masochists Review," as well as significant news. But why not? The option of turning the set off would still be there, but under this plan the option of leaving it on is an option for entertaining a wider variety of messages than are currently offered.

INTELLECTUAL EFFORT, MEDIA CONTENT, AND LEISURE

We have seen that the media are at least partly responsible for creating the tastes they serve. The pop taste in art and pop definitions of news develop in the mass as a result of media exposure of these contents under these labels. Still, one wonders if the causation is all one-way, or if there is some substance to the media spokesmen's defense. One wonders if the selective retention of consumers is purely reflective of media training, or if some other independent factor gives the pop taste ascendancy. Most generally, one wonders to what extent the shift from publics to mass is complete so that there is no market for any but a pop product. Perhaps a system of dividing broadcast time in a way that would serve the desires of all consumers, such as that proposed at the end of the last section, would not serve to decrease the hold of pop messages. It may be that the condition of modern man not only supplies the means for the transmission of pop messages but also creates a need for such messages.

To discover such a condition, we must first observe that audience time is leisure time and then turn our analysis to leisure. Leisure is non-work. It is more than that which is not work; it is the opposite of work. It is the contrast time, the recuperation and preparation for reentry into work time. To effectively serve these functions it must be radically different from work. It must rest man in the same respects in which work tires him and must exercise those facilities that lie dormant during work time. Leisure, then, must be intellectual when work is dulling. It must be physical when work is mental. It must be active when work is passive. It must contrast.

Studies have shown that white-collar workers are more likely to participate in active sports than are laborers; laborers' leisure is more likely to be lethargic.[2] In specific terms, he who exercises his body all day as work has no desire to exercise it afterward as play. Similarly, may we not expect individuals who exercise their minds at

---

[2]Thomas Lasswell, *Class and Stratum* (Boston: Houghton-Mifflin, 1965), pp. 258–64.

work to be willing to rest them during their leisure hours? May we not expect such persons to seek nonintellectual pastimes for their leisure and to avoid the intellectually demanding ones?

Modern society's work places intellectual demands on an ever-increasing portion of the work force. No wonder, then, that pop messages are so attractive to that work force—pop is an inviting mental mattress. The de-intellectualization of mass media content is a natural and inescapable consequence of the condition of work in modern society.

M ASS AND SOCIETY

If these factors explain why the media assume their present con-figuration, they do not totally discover the effect of the mass media on contemporary society. Although mass communication may operate as it does because of the audience's "need" for intellectual ease, the messages and the learning that follow have other consequences.

The leisure need exists primarily among working adults, yet patterns of transmission established to meet this need present the same materials to children who are in the same audience. The aver-age child watches TV several hours a day, more hours than he spends in direct interaction with his parents or friends of the same age, nearly as many as he spends in school. Naturally, his under-standing of the social world is greatly colored by what he sees on TV. Much of his understanding of occupational and social class differences, for instance, follows from what is portrayed in family "situation comedies" and similar shows. When the child grows up and acts toward the world as he has learned on his TV set, the real world comes to more closely resemble that of television. The full impact of this change will be felt in the next few years, as the first true TV generation reaches maturity and comes to assume positions of power within the society.

The situation of adults is only different in their relatively late first exposure to television. Emphasis here must be placed on tele-vision for no media of the past occupied as large a portion of the waking hours of any society's people as television does now. The same sort of statement could have been made of radio in the pre-World War II period and of newspapers following the Civil War. This progression points to increasing leisure time and increasingly available and engaging mass media with which to fill it.

One long-term trend, for adults as well as children, is the increasing homogenization of culture. Regional and ethnic distinctions in style, customs, and speech all fade more and more before the universal and increasing influence of identical exposure to identical experience through the media. The mass society, in which life imitates art, has already begun to appear.

Answers to Identification Quiz

1. John Falstaff *(1600)* Fictional comic character in Shakespeare's *Henry IV* and *Merry Wives of Windsor.*

2. Woodie Guthrie *(1940)* American musician—singer, guitarist, composer; wrote "This Land is Your Land," a series of songs known collectively as "Dust Bowl Ballads," and others; father of Arlo ("Alice's Restaurant") Guthrie.

3. Norman Rockwell *(1950)* American artist; known for *Collier's* and *Post* magazine covers, Boy Scout calendars, and military recruiting posters; portrays wholesome Americana, usually with freckle-faced boys and shaggy dogs.

4. Lorenzo Jones *(1940)* Fictional character in radio soap opera; small-town philosopher.

5. Carl Yastrzemski *(1967)* Outfielder for the Boston Red Sox; sometime league leader in batting average, home runs, runs batted in.

6. James Forman *(1969)* Black American leader; once head of SNCC; spokesman for group seeking reparations from organized religious bodies (National Black Economic Development Corporation).

7. Sancho Panza *(1605)* Fictional character in Cervantes' *Don Quixote;* Quixote's manservant.

8. John Henry *(1870)* Fictional, mythological character in song; a steel-driving man.

9. Hoss Cartwright *(1966)* Fictional character in TV series; largest and most stupid of the brothers in "Bonanza."

10. Dana Gibson *(1910)* American artist; principally magazine illustrations; creator of the "Gibson girl."

11. Hugh Hefner *(1965)* American publisher, writer, businessman; *Playboy* magazine, clubs, philosophy.

12. Golda Meir *(1970)* Prime Minister of Israel.

13. Béla Bartók *(1930)* Hungarian composer; *The Miraculous Mandarin, Te Deum.*

14. Maria Martinez *(1960)* American potter, "The Potter of San Ildefonso"; work within Pueblo traditions, but with a special flair.

15. Diana Ross *(1968)* American singer; former leader and star of "The Supremes"; modified Mo-town.

16. Elmer Zilch *(1932)* Fictional cartoon character; figurehead-host of *Ballyhoo* magazine; similar in many respects to *Mad's* Alfred E. Neuman.

17. Philip Blaiberg *(1968)* South African dentist; one of the world's first heart transplant patients; holder of record for postoperative longevity.

18. William Brennan *(1969)* American jurist; Associate Justice of U.S. Supreme Court since 1956.

19. William Hogarth *(1740)* English artist; engravings and paintings.

20. Guy Gisborne *(1400)* Fictional character; good-bad knight in *Robin Hood* myth.

21. Charlie Brown *(1967)* Fictional character in *Peanuts* comic strip; a round-headed kid.

22. Russ Colombo *(1925)* American singer; he and Bing Crosby were the original "crooners."

23. Charles Manson *(1970)* Mystic and commune leader; alleged murderer in Sharon Tate slayings, Los Angeles.

24. Richard Daley *(1968)* American politician; long-time mayor of Chicago and Democratic Party boss.

FURTHER READING

Charlesworth, James C., ed., *Leisure in America: Blessing or Curse?* Philadelphia: American Academy of Political and Social Science, Monograph 4 (April 1964).

Denney, Reuel, *The Astonished Muse.* Chicago: University of Chicago, 1957.

Dorfles, Gillo, *Kitsch.* New York: Universal Books, 1969.

Dumazedier, Joffree, *Toward a Society of Leisure,* trans. Stewart McClure. New York: Free Press, 1966.*

Ellul, Jacques, *Propaganda.* New York: Knopf, 1965.

Friendly, Fred W., *Due to Circumstances Beyond Our Control.* New York: Random House, 1967.

McLuhan, Marshall, *The Gutenberg Galaxy.* Toronto: University of Toronto, 1962. Available in paperback.

"Mass Culture and Mass Media," Daedalus (Spring 1960).

Rosenberg, Bernard, and David Manning White, eds., *Mass Culture.* New York: Free Press, 1957. Available in paperback.

Stephenson, William, *The Play Theory of Mass Communication.* Chicago: University of Chicago, 1966.*

*Difficult, specialized, or technical.

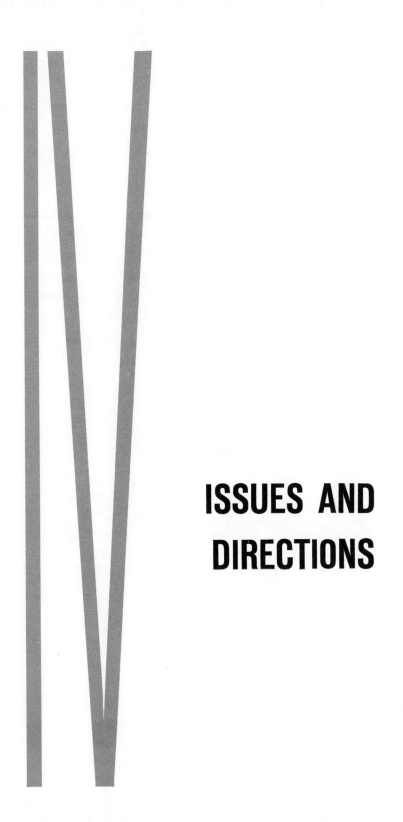

IV

**ISSUES AND
DIRECTIONS**

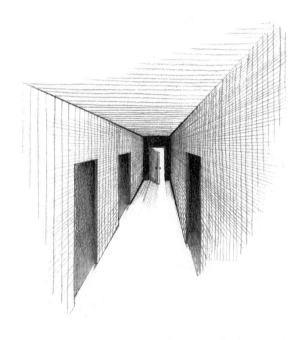

11 PICTURES OF SOME PLAUSIBLE NEAR FUTURES

No man may know the future, but each man is free to guess. Some guesses may be random or based on wish-fulfillment; others may be magical in character. Some may follow evidence and reason. As the future unfolds, some may prove accurate, some inaccurate, some irrelevant; for some the assessment of accuracy may be impossible even after the event. In this chapter we will try to see what lies ahead for man in the near future, basing our study on trends of the recent past surveyed in Chapter 3 and on the insights into social operations covered in Chapters 4 through 10.

The field of social prognostication is strewn with the bodies of scholarly warriors who had more valor than discretion. Good prediction regarding social events is possible, but bad prediction is usual. On the other hand, too much discretion makes apparent prediction meaningless. Often the most interesting predictions come from those who go out on a limb. We must note, however, how far out on the limb a given predictor is, keeping in mind the fact that the turn of events may saw the limb off behind him.

PLAUSIBLE NEAR FUTURES AS PREDICTIONS

The remainder of this chapter will be devoted to three different pictures of some plausible near futures—the next fifty years—of societies like our own. By plausible I mean that the canons of prediction have been adhered to at least moderately well. I also mean this word to imply that the predictions are relatively dangerous and uncertain, that they venture into questions that rate relatively poorly in accuracy-inducing conditions. They deal with relatively "unique" events; they involve a moderately long time span; they leave little margin for error. I will at this time present two conditional hedges. First, the freedom of the world from total nuclear war is assumed. Second, I assume that population pressures will not become extreme enough to bring about a radical alteration in human social life as we know it. Although these may be major conditions in themselves, they are not so very large in the prediction context. Should either assumption fail, the surviving social life, if any, would be rather uninteresting from a sociological point of view. In a sense, if these predictions fail for these reasons, all social predictions before the failure will become irrelevant.

Should neither exempting catastrophe occur and the predictions still fail, as well they might, perhaps the preceding paragraphs represent my excuses offered in advance. It is a failure I could avoid by filling the remainder of this chapter with high-probability predictions: mathematically elegant, embedded in solid evidence, logically precise without strain. This would require restricting the subjects of prediction to such matters as birth rates in rural Michigan in 1985 and content of conversation of pairs of college students who are strangers to each other until they meet in an observation room under laboratory conditions. Instead, I choose to try to describe the shape of whole societies. I will take my chances on being wrong later, in the hope that I will not be boring now.

ANOMIA: THE END OF IDEOLOGY

Humans are *self*-conscious. Each individual's personal sense of well-being comes from understanding who he is, his place in the world, and from some degree of satisfaction with those conditions.[1] He acquires these by coming to understand the world through his experience in it, and by coming to understand himself through the understandings of him held by other persons with whom he comes in contact.

When the world in which the individual lives is a relatively small and circumscribed one, when the portion of the world with which he comes in contact is virtually all of the world that affects him, the problem of knowing the world is simple. When the persons with whom an individual interacts are known to him and know him, when they respond to him as a person, it is easy for him to draw a definition of self from the reflected images that those others offer. Such conditions are found only in tribal life. The tribal group lives in virtual isolation from the rest of the world. The life of any individual is affected only by the behaviors of the other fifty or so persons in that group, and by physical-environment forces that act on the immediate preceptual field of the individual.

Similarly, in a group that small every individual knows every other individual on a personal, face-to-face, basis. Each knows the life history, ancestry, personality quirks, and social condition of all the others. Each person has lived his entire life within the confines of the group. To this extent, the people are all the same—they know the same things, do the same things, have had the same experiences. One can get his sense of self first on the basis of personalized interaction with those who are as familiar with him as it is possible to be. Second, he who understands any other in the society also understands himself, because all are identical.

With the rise of urban-industrial society, the conditions that allow this easy self-knowledge disappear. The ordinary population unit includes large numbers of highly varied people who are strangers to each other. Many, perhaps most, of an individual's interactions will be with people who are unlike him in significant respects, and to whom he is unknown.

[1] Elaborations of these matters are to be found in Chapters 3, 8, and 9.

In parallel fashion, the world becomes less comprehensible. Each person's life is affected by a variety of complex forces. Decisions and fortuitous events occurring in dusty corners of the world may have great impact on the life circumstance of the individual. His world, the world that can affect him, expands beyond any local community boundary to become almost coterminous with the entire world. It is impossible for him to assimilate all the facts about this world, let alone organize them or discern which among them has significance for his life.

Many of these same points about the social-psychological implications of urban and industrial trends were made toward the close of Chapter 3. There the emphasis was on the erosion of traditional religion, which occurs with such development. The rise of ideology, a modernized version of religious faith, was seen as a response to this erosion. There are obvious connections between the social-psychological problems of identity and the problems implicated in the original rise of religion. Naturally, ideology offers a functional substitute for knowledge in providing social-psychological support to the individual.

Ideologies differ from traditional religion in two respects. They are logically coherent and have some empirical anchorages. These conditions give force to ideas and make them credible to man as he enters the urban age. In previous times the monolithic acceptance of a traditional religion within an isolated community was sufficient to induce belief. Cultural diversity, individual sophistication, and a loss of community altered the situation and demanded answers in an ideological form. The same urban propensities, when carried far enough, render ideology obsolete.

If some modest sophistication is required before a man needs ideology or can assimilate it, greater sophistication may render him again skeptical of ideological oversimplification and immune to its appeal. All ideology is oversimplified. If this were not the case, it would not be needed. Ideologies claim to explain the world. If the world were simple enough to understand, such explanation would be unnecessary. As the world becomes vast, intricate, and amorphous, alleged explanation must gloss over detail and reduce the focus. A more sophisticated man recognizes these flaws and grows disenchanted.

Another source of disenchantment is in the ties of elements of the ideology to the empirical world. As the preceding paragraph suggests, the correspondence is far less than perfect. The more successful ideologies have been those that "touched" the real world at relatively few points. The logical structure and fabric of the ideology holds together best if most of its content is purely ideational. Facts are an awkward stumbling block. Since the whole structure is so much of a piece, refutation at one point means rejection of the whole. Yet some empirical referent is necessary. The solution of this problem in most successful ideologies, again, has been to minimize the contacts with reality and to make relatively inaccessible those contacts that are included. For instance, an ideology may offer any internally consistent and plausible set of otherworldly explanations, deny their applicability to the empirical here and now, but hold their eventual historical fulfillment. Most ideologies hinge their empirical reference most solidly in the future. They are either utopian or apocalyptic.

Believers may be put off for some years, perhaps even for some generations, but sooner or later they will get tired of waiting for the promised times and the promised proofs. Ideologies tend to wear out. No population can embrace an ideology forever.

The logical interconnectedness of an ideology demands that it have a few central themes or organizing principles. When boiled down to the minimum, there are only a few such basic propositions on which any ideology may be based. The number of possible different ideologies, then, is severely limited. A people who has lost its faith in a given ideology may shift to a different one, but before long the entire set will be exhausted. No alternatives will then be available.

For these reasons, the age of ideology is waning. Acceptance of ideology is declining and cannot rise again. If a sense of self-identity and place in the world is essential to man, he must begin looking to some other source for it.

The cultural diversity of urban life helps to give rise to ideology and then undercut it, thereby depriving man of a source of identity. This same diversity also robs him of guides to action. When all men are the same, man may look anywhere around him for a model to guide his own behavior. He should do what the others are doing. No matter where he happens to look, he will get the same guidance; it will be uncontradicted, for all men behave in the same way. The conditions of modern society change all this. Complex urban societies display a bewildering variety of behavioral models, with no clear signposts to indicate which are the proper ones. The individual is unsure how he should act. He may act in doubt, or fail to act, with equal uncertainty.

This condition is serious enough for the large, important matters

225

of human behavior, but its impact becomes even more severe when it applies as well to the most minor and routine kinds of situations. Simply, the very notion of routine disappears. This trend accelerates as more and more behavioral issues move from the arena of habit or custom into that of problematic decision-making, and there are no clear standards on which such decisions should be made. Modern society fails to provide norms. This is true in matters ranging from selecting a mate to selecting a meal, from deciding on a life's career to deciding on today's clothing.

In all four of these areas, the choice is more wide open now than it was five hundred, or one hundred, or even ten years ago. Unmarried people travel more widely and engage in interaction in a wider variety of situations than ever before. Earlier I pointed out that more of our interactions occur with diverse strangers. It is a corollary of this that more of the heterosexual interaction of unmarried people will be with diverse strangers. Although most marriages are between members of some relatively homogeneous ethnic and religious class, examples of marriages with other compositions are readily noticed. Growing acceptance of homosexual mating or none at all further compounds the confusion.

One very special monument of this generation is the pizza place. Twenty-five years ago if one did not live in a major metropolitan community, or one with a large Italian population, he was forced to survive without pizza. Although the pizza explosion may be the largest, similar trends are evidenced for bagels, chow mein, stroganoff, pastrami, tacos, gumbo, tempura, submarine sandwiches, and hundreds of other dishes. The number of specific food items available in the average supermarket has multiplied tenfold in the last two decades. Restaurants come in magnificent (and bewildering) varieties of specialty and style. If these changes are most noticeable in small-towns in the Southern and Midwestern United States, it simply demonstrates the impact of urbanism on even the least urban of places. The psychic burdens of life are increased, three times a day, every day. The decision concerning what to eat offers more room for uncertainty than ever before. Every one of life's decisions is similarly rendered more complex by the conditions of urban life.

In pre-industrial times every boy knew that he would grow up to the occupation held by his father. Farmers' sons became farmers, blacksmiths' sons blacksmiths, and so on. Even in situations where this pattern was not perfectly followed, some pattern was discernible and the choices were limited. English noble families, for instance, could offer a job as earl only to the earl's oldest son. The second son, in effect, had his choice between the church and the military. These were the only careers considered suitable for one of his station. The situation now is different. The constant changes of urban-industrial society so alter the occupational structure that the number of chemists needed twenty-five years ago is little related to the number needed now. If all sons of blacksmiths in the last three generations had become blacksmiths, there would now be a legion of blacksmiths on the welfare roles. If only sons of atomic physicists became atomic physicists, there would now be none; the job did not exist three generations ago. Even where occupational inheritance is possible, it is not widely practiced. When the modern youth is still in his preschool years, relatives and neighbors and department store Santas begin to put on the pressure: "What are you going to be when you grow up?" If he makes a decision then and sticks to it, he is binding an adult to a lifetime's servitude on the interests and inclinations of a child. If he postpones the decision or changes, he may become a junior in college who is still unable to decide what to major in. Still later, settled in an occupation for some years, he may regret the choice or be uncertain. The key is uncertainty. The choices are myriad; the guidelines for choice nonexistent; the anxiety endures for many years.

This is also the age of the mini, midi, and maxi, of the button-down collar and the ruffled cuff, of the furry, frilly, leather, tailored, busy, severe, natural, hard, formal, bright, casual, covered, subdued, bare, boxy looks. I am a university professor. In the relatively safe and clear-cut times of even thirty years ago, I would have taught my classes in tweed or gabardine suits of modified Ivy cut, white shirt and tie (paisley, stripe, or solid color). The colors would have been subdued blues, browns, greys, or blacks. Every now and then this might have been varied with a modestly patterned sport coat and complementary solid-color slacks. Same cut, same colors, same shirt and tie. Instead I came a generation (or half a generation, anyway) too late. Instead of rising and automatically donning the professorial uniform, I must stand in the closet and wonder what to wear. It is not a terribly important decision to me. I do not think that I will ever burst into tears because I am unable to decide. But it is another small erosion of certainty, piled on the many other erosions that herald the modern age. I own some of those professorial uniforms and teach in them occasionally. I also teach in wheat jeans, Bermuda shorts, sandals, turtlenecks, Italian silks, and a miscellany of less distinctive body coverings. This may add some small uncertainty to my students' lives as well as my own.

What has been said for these four areas of behavior is just as true of all others.

Men must act; they need guides to action; city life fails to provide them. The failure lies in the form or condition of the society itself. Such a condition—when the societal guides to action are unclear, contradictory, or absent, where the system norms are underdeveloped—is called *anomie*. This condition is a property of the social order. Obviously, it will have its psychological impact. Individuals attempting to operate in such a system and under such condition will be confused and anxiety-ridden. Their actions will become more and more hesitant and erratic. Their mental state will degenerate correspondingly with more doubts. They may suffer mental illness, commit suicide, undergo severe withdrawal, or turn to radically antisocial behavior. This psychological or individual concomitant of anomie is called *anomia*. The two go together.

In an anomic society, we can expect individuals to develop anomia. As anomic individuals attempt to sustain a social system through their uncertain and vagrant behavior, the system becomes more confused, less systematic, and furthers the condition of anomie.

The conditions of the city, it is argued, inevitably set up precisely this spiral of cause. At the end of the urban era, past the age of ideology, lies a future of chaos. Social order must degenerate to disorder. Individual conviction and motivation must dissolve to confusion, terror, and insanity. The future, then, is a non-future.

Presumably, death and destruction would run their course until mankind was extinct or was reduced to a population of cavemen with caveman cultural levels. Social disintegration would proceed until there was no society. This future is plausible, if unpleasant. Many of the points from which it is projected are unimpeachable in fact or argument. There may be a couple of possible "outs," one of which will be explored in the next section.

SUBURBIA: THE END OF URBANISM

We have noted that cities are heterogeneous, segmentalized, anonymous, massive, changing, and potentially chaotic. These conditions, it was asserted, are painful and are destructive of individual personality. Can we not, then, expect persons to avoid these conditions? Humans, like most other relatively advanced organisms, seek gratification and avoid pain. Let us look for evidences that urban man seeks to avoid the conditions of urbanism.

228

As we riffle the chronicles of recent urbanism, there are a number of different behaviors that characterize some of the people in some times and some places. This sort of variety is, after all, the mark of urbanism itself. That this sort of variety is endemic makes our search that much easier: any uniformity in such diversity should be indeed striking. We find such uniformity in the suburban trend.

Suburbs are growing many times faster than the central cities with which they are associated. Indeed, in the years since 1960, several of the largest cities have decreased in population, if only the core of the metropolis is considered. The population table gives some indication of this trend. The fact is even more extreme than these figures. Our concern is with suburbia as a way of life, not as a political or geographic entity, and for many of these cities "suburban" neighborhoods are found within the legal boundaries of the city itself. For places like Los Angeles and Houston, the suburban movement is drastically underestimated by the table. Areas such as Anaheim are virtually entirely suburban with reference to some other city (see table, Central City and Suburban Populations).

Beyond the raw figures are some other indications. Movement to the suburbs comes almost entirely from the central city. The central city's population is only holding up as well as it is because it is constantly being replenished by excess births and migrants from small-town and rural areas. Analysis of the social characteristics of the population segments involved shows that those who move to suburbs are predominantly white, employed in high-status occupations, well educated, and financially secure—four characteristics that generally do not apply to those who move to destinations other than the suburbs, or who do not move at all.

The implications are clear. The people who avoid the city are those who have experienced it. Of those who have experienced the city, those with the greatest resources, and consequent discretionary power, predominate among those who escape. Those who have experienced the pain of the city avoid it if possible, but those who have not experienced it step unwarily into the situation. When migration trends for American cities are viewed in this light, it becomes apparent that the city is a pain-inducing location. The conception of the relation between urbanism, anomie, and anomia is sustained. There is further indication that suburbia offers an escape from the pain, and hence from anomia. We can look to the characteristics of suburbs for "un-urbanism," for conditions that suppress anomia, for orderly rather than anomic social organization.

We find precisely that. The suburb is homogeneous. Any one

CENTRAL CITY AND SUBURBAN POPULATIONS, 1940–1970 (thousands of persons): METROPOLITAN AREAS IN THE U.S. WITH OVER ONE MILLION PERSONS, 1970*

Year	New York City	New York Suburb	Los Angeles† City	Los Angeles† Suburb	Chicago† City	Chicago† Suburb	Philadelphia City	Philadelphia Suburb	Detroit City	Detroit Suburb
1970	7772	3980‡	3129	3845	3325	3568	1927	2850	1493	2671
1960	7782	2913	2823	3920	3550	2671	2003	2340	1670	2092
1950	7892	1664	2221	2147	3621	1557	2072	1599	1850	1167
1940	7455	1252	1669	1248	3397	1173	1931	1268	1623	754

Year	San Francisco† City	San Francisco† Suburb	Washington† City	Washington† Suburb	Boston City	Boston Suburb	St. Louis† City	St. Louis† Suburb	Pittsburgh City	Pittsburgh Suburb
1970	1063	2172	746	1922	628	2102	608	1733	513	1871
1960	1108	1675	764	1238	697	1892	750	1310	604	1801
1950	1160	1081	802	662	801	1609	857	862	677	1536
1940	937	525	663	305	771	1439	816	648	672	1411

Year	Baltimore† City	Baltimore† Suburb	Cleveland† City	Cleveland† Suburb	Newark City	Newark Suburb	Houston† City	Houston† Suburb	Minneapolis-St. Paul City	Minneapolis-St. Paul Suburb
1970	895	1150	739	1304	378	1460	1213	745	741	1064
1960	939	788	876	921	405	1284	938	305	796	686
1950	950	456	915	551	439	1030	596	211	833	318
1940	859	280	878	389	430	862	385	144	780	187

Year	Dallas† City	Dallas† Suburb	Atlanta City	Atlanta Suburb	Anaheim-Santa Ana-Garden Grove City	Anaheim-Santa Ana-Garden Grove Suburb	Cincinnati† City	Cincinnati† Suburb	Paterson-Clifton-Passaic City	Paterson-Clifton-Passaic Suburb
1970	836	703	488	886	441	968	488	885	279	1063
1960	680	404	487	530	289	415	503	569	280	907
1950	434	309	331	396	118	98	504	400	262	615
1940	295	232	302	257	56	75	456	331	250	469

Milwaukee† / Buffalo / Seattle / Kansas City† / San Diego

Year	City	Suburb†	City	Suburb	City	Suburb	City	Suburb†	City	Suburb
	Milwaukee†		Buffalo		Seattle		Kansas City†		San Diego	
1970	710	684	458	831‡	524	880	495	745	676	642
1960	741	453	533	774	557	550	476	564	573	460
1950	637	320	509	468	468	377	457	358	334	222
1940	587	242	383	368	368	225	399	287	203	86

San Bernardino-Riverside-Ontario / Miami / Denver† / San Jose / New Orleans†

Year	City	Suburb	City	Suburb	City	Suburb	City	Suburb	City	Suburb
	San Bernardino-Riverside-Ontario		Miami		Denver†		San Jose		New Orleans†	
1970	310	812	332	928	513	709	437	620	586	499
1960	223	587	292	643	494	435	204	438	628	241
1950	133	319	249	246	416	196	95	195	570	115
1940	91	174	172	96	332	123	68	106	495	58

Indianapolis† / Tampa-St. Petersburg

Year	City	Suburb	City	Suburb
	Indianapolis†		Tampa-St. Petersburg	
1970	743	357	488	512
1960	476	221	456	316
1950	427	125	221	188
1940	387	74	169	103

*Data derived in part from United States Bureau of the Census, Statistical Abstract of the United States: 1968; County and City Data Book: 1967; Census of Population: 1960; Census of Population: 1970, Preliminary Reports.

†1970 figures are not strictly comparable to 1960 and earlier owing to changes in territory enclosed in central city, metropolitan area, or both.

‡Author's estimate; census figure was not available when we went to press.

suburban neighborhood is likely to be made up of some dozens or hundreds of houses with a single style and a narrow price range. The characteristic curving and cul-de-sac street patterns are likely to provide some degree of isolation from the surroundings. The location provides easy access to some places of employment but not others. All the homes were built at the same time. The promotion and sales were handled through one set of institutional channels. All of these tend toward a grinding homogeneity in the residents of this physical setting.

The price range restricts the residents to those who can afford at least that much, and snobbery and the consumer ethic eliminate those who can afford much better. The style and setting further homogenize by attracting only individuals with a special taste and similar needs. The location draws on persons employed in only a few organizations. Families in similar career-stages and of similar ages simultaneously enter the simultaneously completed homes. The developer reaches and attracts a narrow segment of the possible market.

Similarities begun by these automatic mechanisms are finished by conscious social ones. Para-legal or merely customary convenants may keep out Jews, Gentiles, Mexicans, Poles, Catholics, blacks, government workers, or what-have-you. Potential residents look for "nice, compatible, neighbors"—by which they mean people very much like themselves. They want a neighborhood where their kids will have someone their own age to play with, where the husband will find other husbands who have the same interests, where he can make contacts that may be useful in his work. They want a place where the clubs, churches, schools, and other supporting institutions are compatible with the needs and interests of their family, and therefore only with those of families exactly like theirs.

The suburb neighborhood is made up of individuals who do the same things, know the same things, have the same things, and believe the same things. A suburbanite need only look around him to find straightforward and uncontradicted signposts directing him toward appropriate behavior.

The neighbors are not mere passive providers of patterns, they offer conscientious encouragements and pressures toward conformity. Suburban neighborhoods are relatively small collections of similar individuals; they come to know each other personally and intimately. They thrust their friendship on each other. They bare their souls to each other. Their leisure hours are spent in one another's company. To an escapee from city anonymity, this enforced camaraderie may be welcome relief. The pressure toward participation and conformity may be candy-coated. They are nonetheless real and effective.

Suburban life is organized and integrated by its women. The husbands have their work, the children their school. The women are more fully captive of the suburb. They find identity and meaning by weaving a social web within the community. Across the driveways, down the streets, of coffee shared in the kitchen and common participation in clubs, the web of interest and involvement is woven. Children, already enrolled in a neighborhood school and playing with neighborhood peers, are easily caught up. Husbands are trapped last but without struggle. The only alternative they have to offer is their work associations and these represent the quality of association that characterizes the uneasy urban-industrial world; husbands slip compliantly or eagerly into the suburban web.

The following statement about New York City, made by a commuting resident of Mount Arlington, N.J., sums up the orientation of suburbanites to the central cities:

> I feel I'm a citizen where I live. The only reason I've been coming here [New York City] for 20 years is because of my occupation. I don't like the place—downtown is dirty, people are impolite. I don't see anything similar in our problems at all. The minute I get out of the city I don't think of it at all.[2]

The speaker is the mayor of his commuter town, an actively involved public-spirited citizen—on a local basis.

All the waking hours of these people, except work and school hours, are spent in the company of the suburbs. Cocktail hour, weekends at the beach, cards or charades in the evening, Little League, bowling, PTA, backyard barbecue, ski weekends, Neighborhood Improvement Association, parties, golf at the club: no one need wonder what to do; it has all been organized in advance. Each suburb develops a style, concentrates on some limited number of leisure interests, enforces participation on the residents, and drives out those who are unable or unwilling to conform.

This culture perpetuates itself. Newly arriving residents, already preselected for similarity, are retrained to virtual identity. Change, representing as it must a source of diversity, is abhorred. Children may grow up and leave their retired parents, but this happens for the community-suburb-neighborhood as a whole, for

---

[2]Quoted in Richard Reeves, "The Changing City: Power Is Limited," *The New York Times* (June 8, 1969). Copyright © 1969 by The New York Times Company. Reprinted by permission.

each family in it, at the same time. If it does not, if the neighborhood is invaded by numbers of families in a different stage of the life cycle, the retirees beat a retreat and find a community that is homogeneously of their kind.[3]

Summing up, the suburb is characterized by the following:

Small population	No (free) leisure time
Personalized social relations	Homogeneity
Isolation	Neotraditionalism
A minimal division of labor	An unchanging life

The correspondence between this list and the list of characteristics that were offered as typical of pre-agricultural bands is striking, if not quite complete (see pp. 44–47). That list was offered in an attempt to explain why social change had been so rare and slow for all the aeons of early human society and why change began to accelerate so rapidly with the end of these conditions in agriculture and urbanism. The features of life in bands and suburbs are not conducive to innovation. The features of urban life do stimulate invention. If people find this life painful and seek to escape the pain, they also give up the potential for invention. A nonurban, *suburban*, society will become a stultified and unchanging one. The argument for the necessity of urban conditions as prerequisite for inventiveness was offered in Chapter 3 and will not be repeated here. Leisure, anonymity, heterogeneity, and the several other circumstances that promote innovation do not characterize the suburbs. To whatever extent suburbanism characterizes a society, that society will be uncreative and unchanging.

If the escape from urban anomia becomes universal, we might then suspect that the future will be very much like the present—that things will go on pretty much the same as they are now. If this were a prediction it would be a very dull one. It would suggest a societal epoch for contemporary society that would be unchanging. Current urban-industrial society would perpetuate itself like tribal society. We would be on the threshold of an era concerning which a historian of the far future could say, as I have said of the tribal era, "nothing much happened for a long time."

---

[3] Some sociologists and journalists have vastly exaggerated the homogeneity of the suburb. Later and more careful research has corrected this picture. Still, the contrast with truly urban communities is striking enough to permit the thematic generalization of the following paragraph. The reservations about the "end-of-urbanism" prediction are comments on some of the remaining threads of urban, heterogeneous influence.

This is not a sensible prediction, because urban society is not like tribal society and cannot sustain itself in the way in which tribal society did. Urbanism is a changing form and cannot endure under conditions of no change. There are many reasons why this is so. Let us examine at least one of these. The suburb, although band-like in many respects, is not a self-sufficient unit. No matter how psychologically unimportant work might become to the suburbanite, it remains important economically. At least the adult male suburbanite must keep one foot in the urban world, and that urban world must continue to operate as the work world, although it is not a residential or psychic location. The groceries and barbecue pit and picture windows and TV sets of suburbia generally originate in the urban world.

If all the operators of the urban work system are psychologically committed only to the suburban community system in which they hold simultaneous membership, performance in the work system will obviously degenerate.

The work system will clearly be unchanging, because there will be no innovative individuals. This means that the number of kinds of jobs available within the system will be unchanging. Assuming similar fertility for the several occupational groups, each group will produce its own successors for the next generation. No person can have realistic expectations of advancing within the system, of improving his work tasks or his rewards. Motivation and incentives to competent performance will suffer grievously. Under such conditions, productivity will decline. Even with competent performance, in the absence of innovation it would have done no better than remain constant. The urban-industrial system will go into decline and decay. We return to the cave by a different route. The implications of the suburban trend are that urbanism will end "not with a bang but a whimper."

Here we have another basically sound but pessimistic prediction. If there is a flaw in this one, it rests in the possibility that escape from urbanism may not be that easy or complete. With mass communication, travel, and the hard fact of the interdependencies of all aspects of modern life, the suburb and even the farm must partake of some of the characteristics of urbanism. Human mentality is not adjustable enough that people who work in urban settings can close that part of their minds off from the rest. Still, the prediction is sound, most of the argument convincing.

In the two preceding sections two plausible futures have been offered. The decline and fall of progressive, urban society has been asserted to follow urban anomia or suburban stultification. These two outcomes are echoes of the end of the first urban epoch. Urban chaos roughly parallels the demise of cities in the West; suburban decay is similar to the decline of Eastern urbanism.

If some more hopeful plausible future is to be found, it must be one that offers variety without chaos, vigor without frenzy, and security without suffocation. The final possible future discussed in this chapter meets these qualifications. It is offered not because it is pleasing, but because it is plausible.

REDEMOCRATIZATION: THE END OF STATISM

Statism is a political and social system in which the central government imposes social order on the populace. The people have little power over the form of this order and no power to resist its imposition. Centralization grew out of the economic and ideological circumstances of early industrialism. With the development of the instruments of modern warfare, it became a centralism from which there could be no appeal.

The cornerstone of statism is this superior military might. Might makes right. In any warfare, between individuals or nations, the winners write the history books and define the morality. The ability to impose specified forms of behavior becomes in the long run the ability to specify right and wrong.

This view will be morally repugnant to many of you. You will surely cry that the treatment the Nazis accorded European Jews was absolutely wrong and would have been just as wrong had Germany won World War II. But the absoluteness of this sense of morality, its very life, follows from the fact that we have survived that war. The major proponents of the alternative view have not. The power to hold the Nuremberg trials confirmed this morality. The lack of such power prohibited any San Francisco trials concerning the United State's treatment of American Japanese. That policy escaped a fair measure of shame. The outcome of World War II did not, of course, create our common sense of justice afresh—it simply reaffirmed the morality already evolved with Caesar, Charlemagne, Grant, Harold, Pericles, Pershing, Washington, and Wellington.

By this listing of rulers and generals no proximation of a "great man" theory of history is intended. The names are used merely to stand for the victories at arms. The victories are more attributable to the military technologies, organizational and mechanical, than to the leaders. To prove this point one need look no further than the inclusion of Grant on the list. Grant is not ordinarily considered as good a general as Lee or others among the Southerners, but he commanded a superior force. Therefore, and thenceforth, slavery was wrong in the United States.

Bertrand Russell once said that "the superiority of Western culture over the Chinese does not consist in the fact that Dante, Shakespeare, and Goethe have triumphed over Confucious and Lao-Tse, over the poetic and mantic gifts of China, but rather in the fact that by and large, a Westerner can kill a Chinese more easily than a Chinese can kill a Westerner."[4] Since Russell made this statement, the political situation has changed in at least two respects. The ease-of-killing gap has been reduced by Chinese technological advances. The kill-need ratio has been increased by Asiatic population growth. Western ideas are therefore less superior to those of China, but Russell's principle is timeless. Power is truth.

In every society, the ruling class or the ruling system imposes its will on the mass so long as it has the ability. For most of history this ability has been held by a minority or by the state as an impersonal mechanism. Power has been subject to monopolization or gross inequities. The powerful ruled the powerless. Two exceptions worthy of note are the power conditions of primitive hunting and gathering folk and the power conditions of the early years of guns. In these circumstances, the majority held the power and made the state, if any, an extention of their own wishes and beliefs. Both of those periods are irretrievably lost and the present is, as was noted in Chapter 3, a period of statism.

The state is a formal organization with no purpose but survival and hence no interest but maintenance of the *status quo*. It rules impersonally but oppressively. The instruments of oppression are ones that no individual citizen or any combination of citizens can match. Technically there are tanks, machine guns, airplanes, atom bombs, and other instruments of war. Organizationally there are sophisticated administrative structures, surveillance techniques, and security measures.

Urbanization, industrialization, and bureaucratization—the basic themes in the metamorphoses of society—are responsible for the rise of statism but also carry other implications that have not yet been manifested. These developments are commonplace, but their impli-

[4]Quoted in Emil Lederer and Emy Lederer-Seidler, *Japan in Transition* (New Haven: Yale University Press, 1938), p. 177.

cations portend another future. These trends, repeated so often in this book, are here summed up once more. Man lives in larger, denser population concentrations than ever before. He is supported by a complex, interlocking, and interdependent technology that is essential not simply to his present life-style but to his very existence. This technology is managed and its produce rendered effective by an equally complex, interwoven, and essential human relations network.

Like all complicated machines, these are delicate. Small dislocations may have magnified effect. Uniquely tooled parts are seldom interchangeable, often irreplaceable. Stoppage at one point incapacitates the entire chain. Despite this mechanistic analogy, all parts are, or are controlled by, or are vulnerable to, individual human actors. Social thinkers for generations have enunciated the increasing interdependence of persons with increasing modernization of human society. That interdependence has now reached a point where it has implications for the realm of force. Society is a complicated machine, vulnerable to destruction at the hands of any one of its parts.

Massive deterrence is the term orginally applied to the strategy of nuclear threat. "If your country doesn't behave, we will destroy it." Such threats can now be made meaningfully by an individual against the society; the strategy is reduced from the international to the personal level. It is surely not now articulated by the man in the streets, but it need not be articulated to be put in practice. Its practice has scarcely begun, but some tentative operations have occurred. Others have been proposed, and experiment and imitation will bring it to full fruition.

Let us briefly review some of the real and potential applications of the new force.

The New York garbage strike, in its short duration, posed a threat to the aesthetic, commercial, and physical well-being of one of the world's great cities. The issue may seem laughable, but what would happen, in the long run, to seven and a half million closely-packed people and their trash? They cannot eat it, nor destroy it, nor hide it. It must be taken away or they will bury themselves. Actually, long before that it will breed enough disease to kill them. Some, as a last resort, can bundle their garbage up, load it in their cars, and haul it to New Jersey. Gasoline, tolls, depreciation, and lost time make this an impracticable solution. Others (many among New Yorkers) have no cars. Throwing trash in a neighbor's yard when he is asleep is an individual, but not a collective, solution. Garbage can institute an urban crisis.

In New York, it did. Governor Rockefeller refused to send in troops as garbage collectors on the grounds that the cost to the state would be greater than the price of any settlement and that soldiers were not competent to operate the sophisticated collection equipment. The Governor may have had other unstated grounds for his decision, but the stated grounds are real enough and correct.

It is precisely my point that all occupational niches are becoming so esoteric that it is impossible to replace their occupants quickly. Similarly, all functions are becoming as critical to the general welfare as garbage collection. In the New York case, the workers were seeking only small improvements in wages and working conditions. Suppose instead they had been dedicated to having Congress recalled or demanded war against Cuba?

Strikes by longshoremen, transit workers, firemen, policemen, mailmen, teamsters, teachers, newsmen, telephone workers, and others replicate the above analysis. Strikes by auto workers, carpenters, and others in less "public" positions are almost as harmful in effect, although the damage may be more purely economic and less directly noticeable. It becomes ever more difficult to find unsensitive areas in the total social fabric. The Taft-Hartley Labor Act contains a clause permitting injunction of a ninety-day cooling-off period in cases where work stoppage would adversely affect the national welfare. This clause has been invoked in a wide variety of cases, and logically could be invoked in any. Any employed collection of people have the national welfare in their hands.

Actions other than strikes are more variable. General strikes and shapeless mob violence are an occasional mark of the present. The best example from the recent past is the anti-Gaulist rioting in France in the spring of 1968. Chicago (1968), Watts (1965), Detroit (1967), Mexico City (1968), and other more or less major incidents could be added to the list. These bear a superficial resemblance to old-fashioned riots or to the beginnings of old-fashioned revolutionary uprisings. They are not the former because they are explicitly protestant and purposely disruptive and destructive. They are not the latter because they are short-lived, sustain no solution to the problems they protest against, and offer no alternative order to the one they interrupt. They are not likely to be effective because they are old-fashioned.

They fail to use the new weapon, the societal weapon. They are space-bound. They endure through time. They outrage the mass of citizenry in every respect. Participants are easily marked. These characteristics make them easy for the traditional state to counter with traditional force, with guns, armies, and all the state's naked power. These forms mean that such countermeasures will meet with the approval of the general populace. These conditions demand considerable dedication and sacrifice of the participant. Kidnapping and assassination as political blackmail similarly violate the basic values and incite revulsion, not concession.

Modern forces are shrewder instruments than strikes, mobs, or violence. A movement to drain New York dry during a drought by simply leaving water taps running was begun by CORE and others a few years ago, but was unsuccessful. Draft resistance groups are steadily experimenting with acts disruptive of military procedure, and with destruction of the files on which such procedure feeds. It is rumored that some scholarly black militants have become experts on the 1966 East Coast blackout and are currently seeking engineering information on crucial electrical linkages while they stockpile dynamite. Others have formulated a plan for hit-and-run delayed arson that would destroy hundreds of miles of grass, crops, and forests along major highways. Air traffic control officers have seriously and deliberately disrupted the airways by slavishly following regulations. Yippies have made a farce of Congressional investigative hearings with similar forms of obedience. Hippies muse over the possibility of introducing LSD into a city water supply, knowing that an effective dosage is chemically feasible. Some civil rights groups have made modest but disorganized attempts at traffic snarls. This list scarcely touches the possibilities. I will stop here nonetheless, partly because I do not intend to write a how-to manual for protestors, and partly so you can add a few variations of your own and prove how easy the game is.

The rules are simple. The action must cause serious disruption, long or short term, for the society. It should not involve direct violation of the most sacred ideals. Elaborate preparation, special access, great resources, complex skills, refined teamwork, and large numbers of participants should be unnecessary. The instigators should escape identification or capture.

Let us take just one example and see how effective this kind of force can be. Suppose a small group of men were unhappy with the present form of American society. If petition and conventional political action failed to move the society, they might choose to exercise the new weapon. Suppose they lived in Boston and selected the traffic jam as their instrument of protest. Depending on their inclinations and abilities they could steal trucks or rent them with forged credentials.

Four trucks will effectively seal off a busy but restricted artery, as shown in Fig. 11–1. Trucks A and B must be crashed and wedged

Fig. 11-1   TRAFFIC JAM FOR A TWO-LANE, ONE-WAY HIGHWAY

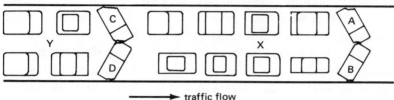

→ traffic flow

firmly enough to require an hour or so for removal; some distance behind, trucks C and D have a simultaneous accident. The wreckers can only approach A and B from the "wrong" direction, after leading traffic has been cleared. This elapsed time will be enough for some drivers in location X, trapped between two wrecks, to grow tired, get out, and walk away, leaving their cars. Other cars in this location will overheat, run out of gas, develop dead batteries, or suffer other mechanical difficulty. They must be cleared in order to get to trucks C and D, which need not be crashed as hard as A and B. Meanwhile, and it will be a much longer meanwhile, cars in location Y, held in by backed-up traffic, will experience the same difficulties as those in location X. It is safe to say that twelve to twenty-four hours will elapse before any traffic moves through this artery.

With sixteen men and sixteen trucks, the dissidents in Boston could block off the Callahan and Sumner tunnels and the Mystic Bridge in both directions, at five o'clock on a weekday afternoon. These are the only major north-south auto routes from the city to the northern towns and suburbs. Those of you who have experienced rush-hour traffic in large cities can imagine something of the chaos to be created by a traffic jam like this. Even then, you are likely to seriously underestimate the disruption and cost.

The 1970 population of Boston was approximately six hundred and thirty thousand. At the same time, the commuter area outside the city included over two million people. Over one and a quarter million trips are made to, from, or through the central city daily. Over one hundred and twenty-five thousand of these trips are made over the bridge and tunnels mentioned. Most of these are North

Shore suburb residents who work in Boston. These routes offer the only easy auto connections.

There are alternative routes. The other highway exits are circuitous and overloaded. Public transit, train and subway, carries fifty thousand commuters daily to and from the North Shore and can handle only a few more at rush hour.[5]

As the first effect of a traffic jam such as I have described, a minimum of thirty thousand people would be late getting home from work, or would not get home at all, on the "target day." Some of these, through exhaustion, loss of vehicle in the jam, or remaining transportation confusion, would not get to work the next day. Although they are only crude estimates, I offer below some of the economic costs, to the citizens and to the society itself, of such an event.

FINANCIAL LOSSES CAUSED BY TRAFFIC JAM

Source	Estimated Cost
Work hours lost by those caught in jam	$500,000
Overtime to city workers clearing jam	30,000
Meals and lodging of those kept away from home by jam	400,000
Delays in delivery of goods, etc.	80,000
Clerkage cost processing absentee records, insurance claims, etc.	130,000
Telephone overloads, etc., caused by emergency inquiries	20,000
Other	60,000
TOTAL	$1,220,000

In addition to economic costs, there would be other consequences less subject to accounting. Several brides-to-be would be left at the church. Some babies would be born, and some sick people die, relatively unattended, in the middle of the jam. Theater tickets would not be used. Deals would remain unclosed. Thousands of human dramas would develop or alter their plot lines.[6]

---

[5]Most of these figures are from *Transportation Facts for the Boston Region, 1968/1969 Edition* (Boston: Transportation Planning Department/Boston Redevelopment Authority, 1969).

[6]On the "human" costs of disruption, one of my favorite examples occurred because of an airplane hijacking. A New York to Miami flight was hijacked to Cuba. When the list of

A million dollar price, then could be exacted on the city of Boston, on the whole society. At what cost to the protestors? If they used fake driver's licenses, rented the trucks, and bought the gasoline, the total expenditure could not exceed a thousand dollars. With elaborate and probably unnecessary rehearsal, the entire operation could not require a week's preparation. The manpower requirement is sixteen persons capable of driving and telling time. With luck, they could crash the trucks delicately enough to escape injury, get out, and walk away undetected in the confusion.

If power is understood as the ability of one side to effect penalties on the other, the advantage in this equation is to the individuals against the society. I have gone into detail on this one case to demonstrate the magnitude of this power. It is a power held by the individual, as I indicated earlier, because of the complex and delicate nature of modern society. What is true of the traffic jam is just as true of dozens of similar strategies.

What sort of defense does the state have against this kind of attack? The tools of order for the recent state have been identical with those of warfare, but the increasing power and complexity of these weapons, the same power and complexity that took them out of the hands of the citizens, now prevents the state from exercising them at home. A government can scarcely bomb its own cities. The rhetoric of Vietnam ("We had to destroy the city to save it,") will not serve. Many city police forces are acting as if it will. They are equipping themselves with tanks, cannon, and other tools of international warfare. In all probability some blundering and searing use will be made of these. But not much and not for long. The public outrage occasioned by the killings at Kent State and Jackson State will tend to inhibit repetitions of this warfare against protestors. Washington (1968) did not become wreckage thanks to restraint—restraint learned from the wreckage of Detroit (1967). Prague (1968) was handled by the Soviets in ways learned from their earlier experience in Warsaw. Governments, even impersonal statist govern-

---

passengers was released, it included "Mr. and Mrs. Mack Roberts, of Miami." (The name is fictitious, but the incident described actually occurred in 1969.) The release of this list disturbed Mr. Roberts, for the woman with him was his secretary, rather than his wife. When the list was made public, it disturbed the real Mrs. Roberts, at home in Miami, for she had understood her husband was making a business trip to New York by himself. The uncovering of the incident disturbed the airline, for Mr. Roberts had paid a reduced family fare for his "wife." The discovery of presumed adultery and fraud, and their wide publication, fell on the unfortunate Mr. Roberts as he was (more or less innocently) caught in the consequences of an act of civil disruption.

ments, can learn. One lesson they will learn is this: no one can consistently rid his person of fleas with a sledge hammer or napalm.

If military methods are no longer feasible for internal control, what about policing? First, police control is based on the apprehension and punishment of a culprit after his violation. This will not retrieve the damage done the society by the act. It may protect society from further harm at the hands of the same person, but with society's new delicacy, the one-time offense can have serious and society-wide consequences. Still, society can absorb, must learn to absorb, an occasional attack by an isolated individual with idiosyncratic motives. As long as the violation is individual, policing will prevent recurrence and be moderately effective.

If, on the other hand, the offender is one member of a significant class of persons who have reason to be disgruntled with the society, the problem is quite different. Let us look at the implications of this statement.

The potential offender is *one*. He does not represent any others. He is an individual acting as an individual. There need be no advance communications and plots, which might be uncovered in time to forestall the action.

There is a *class* of such persons. Not a cell, or a group, but a collection of people who have some characteristic in common. They themselves may not be aware of this communality, but an observer can note it as distinguishing this collection from other persons in the population.

They *have reason to be disgruntled.* This disgruntlement was the motive for the one offender's attack on society. Not all members of the class will feel disgruntled; not all those disgruntled will act aggressively toward society on that basis. Nonetheless, one of the common attributes that defines the class is systematic discrimination, frustration, and deprivation visited on the members by the society. Ordinarily, this visitation will be in consequence of some other of the attributes of the class.

The class becomes *significant* if the serial probability of antisocietal action by individuals of that class reaches a level that endangers the survival of the system. This will be a joint function of the size of the class, the degree of alienation, the relative sensitivity of the members' positions, and the activity-aggression level of their subcultural predisposition.

Society's fate at the hands of such a class is grim. One offender after another can be snatched up, but only after he has done his damage. The class represents a pool of potential offenders and the

244

potential for repeated damage, which can result in the ultimate downfall of the society.

Total surveillance is the next logical police strategy; keep an eye on all the members of the disgruntled class. But when the class of potential offenders is large and free and scattered and when the vulnerable points are ubiquitous, such a policy is impracticable. There remains only incarceration or extermination of all potential offenders: all blacks, union members, communists, farm laborers, atheists, potheads, college students, bachelors, or whatever the alienated class. The specter of a genocidal strategy, of escalated statism, of the class war of most against some, is real but not probable. It fades for three reasons.

First, use of force on this scale would be a change of state policy and practice not merely in degree but in kind. For the state to preserve its rule and itself by changing both is a contradiction in terms. Such a policy would itself be a radical change. Before embarking on such a policy a state would surely consider the alternatives. Changing itself in ways that would accommodate rather than annihilate the revolutionary class would surely be the more conservative course, and governmental statism is essentially conservative.

Second, if the dissident class could somehow be exterminated without any other change, the niche that they had filled would have to be occupied. Some other segment of the population would have to perform the functions of the departed. The conditions inducing antisocietal action by the extinct group would now fall upon the replacements and build in them the same response. The substitutes would form a disgruntled and potentially disruptive class. The process could continue until there was no one left to man the instruments of suppression.

The third reason is that total terror is too far from the values urban-industrial society has evolved over the generations, values that may be necessary to its sustenance. We can stand some measure of cruelty and terror, but would not tolerate these if they became unrestrained. The United States, for instance, is a society that may condone the shooting of looters or even bystanders who may seem involved with looters in the heat of the moment. The United States would not tolerate, I believe, the systematic seeking out and murder of all urban poor because it is known that most looters are urban poor. In this or similar cases, totalitarian suppression of a disaffected class becomes a source of disaffection for other classes; more opponents of the system would be created than would be destroyed.

The avenues explored so far have shown several reasons why

statism cannot survive. Modern society cannot stand antagonistic action by classes of individuals, cannot prevent the actions, and cannot eliminate the classes. It must therefore eliminate the sources of the antagonism. Modern society must adjust its operation so that no sizeable segment of the population reaches the point of disgruntlement. Uncompromising and contrary stances of any class must be modified, accommodations arrived at, heterodoxy tolerated. Statism must disappear as government becomes no more than the instrument of each person's will and the adjudicator between persons. These things must happen, or any faction among us can destroy us all. These lessons we must learn if society is to survive. It may take a generation of wounding offenses against society and of clumsy and terrifying and ineffective attempts at suppression. Perhaps rational calculation of self-interest will minimize the spasm of violence, perhaps not. But I believe the lesson will be learned. Liberty, equality, opportunity, and self-determination will be extended to each person in all the urban-industrial nations. This is our most probable near future. It cannot be otherwise when each person is hostage to the other, when societal power is wielded by all.

Several kinds of policy thrust that can cultivate such conditions will be outlined in the closing paragraphs of this chapter.

There are some "goods" that are generally desired; these must be made available to every segment of the population. A portion of these are economic: quality housing and nutrition and the standard suburban American package of durables and leisures. The direction of programs that will provide this material well-being is already a part of every national politician's platform. The possible mechanisms for its actualization include extension of present welfare efforts, community bootstrap operations, state socialism, guaranteed annual wage, and negative income tax proposals. The directions may have been marked, but few have recognized the distances involved. Traditional welfare practices are motivated by altruistic concern for the well-being of the individual and seek to insure that each person gets enough of the proper foods to maintain health. With the amendments following from the power analysis above, there must be a pragmatic concern for the *sense* of well-being of the individual and insurance that each person gets what he considers enough of what he wants to eat. Specifically, this may mean a steak, rather than adequate protein. It implies that present government concern with subsistence, poverty levels, minimum housing, and other floors is misplaced. These could be reached without lowering the general level of discontent. Truly radically raised goals for such programs are imperative. Yet, provision of these economic goods to all the people is possible with the resources of any economically developed nation. It would involve added effort and dedication and some altered priorities but no basic change.

Some social "goods" are as universally desired as are the economic ones and present greater problems. Insuring to every man such commodities as equal access to public and quasi-public facilities, respect and fairness in his contacts with other persons and the state, and human dignity is not a simple task. Some portion can be managed, again, with further steps down already-traveled roads. Civil rights legislation and court rulings such as the United States has recently seen in the areas of race relations and criminal proceedings mark a beginning. Escalated coverage and vigorous enforcement must follow, but the way is already indicated in existing trends. This case differs from that concerning economic goods, however, in that interpersonal behavior, on which so much of the social good rests, is not an inert and deliverable commodity. State dedication and action must be much more actively supported and supplemented by the general populace. Custom may follow law in large part and in the long run, but not soon enough or surely enough to prevent the impending crisis. The remaining portion must come in altered attitudes and actions of individuals. The possibilities of such alteration through political resocialization will be discussed shortly.

Subgroups within the population may have unique desires in addition to those for the general goods that are desired by almost all members of the society. This is the second issue. It is not necessary to consider purely individual desires, for remember that the concern is with potential disgruntlement of a significant segment of the population, a portion large enough to have potent disruptive effect. Any major nation has such segments in large number: communities, regions, classes, occupations, ethnic groups, and other collectivities.

Any such collection of people will have a set of goals, beliefs, and attitudes that are especially their own. They will have had some special social experiences that have engendered these. As the group's unique experience happened to the individuals, they did not think to themselves, "Here is an experience unique to my people: I must not let the values it engenders become confounded with the general societal values following from experiences that everyone shares." Their special values, then, are not special to them, but rather coexist in their minds with the general values, attract the same adherence, and engender desires that are of equal salience. It does not matter that their special "good" may seem irrelevant, perverse, or immoral to the majority. Their disaffection, if deprived of that good, will carry the same bitter consequence for society as if it had been general.

Each population segment must then be assured not only of the general goods, but of the chance to do or have their own thing. Such assurance will require policies more abruptly divergent from present trends than those discussed above. It may require a more libertarian approach to government generally and batteries of class legislation specifically.

Class legislation has been used by rulers as an instrument of suppression. It seems antithetical to libertarianism because historically it has meant unequal access to generally desired privilege. Traditionally, some people get more of what everyone wants. Class legislation can provide as well a system of equal access to specific portions of varied privileges. Its use to deliver to all people the same satisfaction in different currencies has not been explored. Class legislation implies a complex of law that extends special privileges to designated portions of the population, privileges not available to the remainder. In this special application, each individual would be free to choose his own class membership. It is to be expected that he will do so in terms of the privilege situation of each class and his own partly special but partly shared values. In addition to the general goods already assured by the programs described, class legislation would provide a smorgasbord of subsidiary goods. The individual would elect a position that would give him legal access to some combination chosen from among pot, admissions to country clubs or colleges, stereo sets, winter vacations, pornography, stable marriages, and so on.

In addition to legal mechanisms, this program would require a social and psychological reconditioning of the population to (a) limit the variety of goods demanded to a range that the system could offer and (b) broaden tolerance to the point where people would acquiesce to others who pursued goals divergent from, and even contradictory to, their own. This leads us back to the resocialization problem.

The third thrust, then, is resocialization of the population. There must be public commitment to the state programs suggested in the first two points and a private actualization of the behaviors they imply. Elaborate propaganda aimed at mass subversion of the mass mind may play a small part. It will not play a large part for several reasons. The state is the only instrument for coordinating such a campaign, but in its present form is too conservative to do so. Further, with the passing of the age of ideology, mass propaganda will not be terribly persuasive.

The personal change will come, rather, with the experiences of everyday life. The streets and work and leisure of urban-industrial society will provide the lessons. The individual encounters of the victims with the new power will furnish the stimulus. On occasions of social disruption people will get smaller paychecks, gain fewer goods, enjoy less anxiety-free hours, and receive less benefit from the system. This reduction in contentment will shake the old values, will make them more receptive to alteration. Intolerance values are second-order values; the values concerning the preservation of life, security, and well-being are of the first order. When experience shows the two to be incompatible, it is the former that will be altered. The requisite psychological changes then tend simultaneously toward realization of the greater selfish good and toward rationality. Tradition may slow the victory of this powerful combination but cannot prevent it.

The near future offers a society that systematically prevents any collection of its peoples from becoming actively unhappy. Assurance of the general goods and of discretionary opportunities to seek special goods is the base of this system. The state becomes nothing more than an instrument for the provision of these goods; statism disappears. An open society emerges.

The role of prophet is always an uneasy one. Optimistic prophecies are always most academically suspect. Still, I offer this prediction not because it is optimistic but because I believe it will be realized. Finally, if I am wrong, if this is not our future, I suspect there will be nobody left to say "I told you so."

FURTHER READING

Bell, Daniel, *The End of Ideology.* New York: Free Press, 1959. Available in paperback.

Cox, Harvey, *The Secular City.* New York: Macmillan, 1965. Available in paperback.

Drucker, Peter, *Recent Future: Guidelines to Our Changing Society.* New York: Harper, 1968.*

Etzioni, Amitai, *The Active Society.* New York: Free Press, 1968.*

Jacobs, Jane, *The Death and Life of Great American Cities.* New York: Random House, 1961. Vintage paperback.

Keller, Suzanne, *The Urban Neighborhood.* New York: Random House, 1968. Paperback.

Marcuse, Herbert, *Reason and Revolution.* Boston: Beacon, 1960. Paperback.

Riesman, David, *The Lonely Crowd.* New Haven: Yale University, 1950. Available in paperback.

Sykes, Gerald, ed., *Alienation: The Cultural Climate of Our Time,* 2 vols. New York: Braziller, 1964.*

"Toward the Year 2000: Work in Progress," *Daedalus* (Summer 1967).

*Difficult, specialized, or technical.

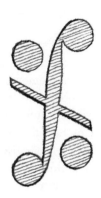

12 REPRISE

In Chapter 1, I promised a book that would be intellectually suited to the amateur and would provide something of an introduction to society. If you have come this far, well and good. My intent was to provide explanations of the social world that would be useful to any individual in his attempt to live in that world. If you accept these explanations and find them useful, again, well and good. They are sound explanations and should have utility. They are sound because they are solidly based on sociology, which offers the best available basis for the explanation of social phenomena.

If the book has shown some of the ways in which sociological explanation can illuminate society, it has not yet said much about sociology as such. I would now like to take a few pages to examine the field.

WHAT SOCIOLOGY IS MADE OF

I have defined sociology as the science whose special province is social systems. Another way of defining the field is to say that sociology is what sociologists do. This definition supplements the other without replacing it and is not as silly as it looks. Any scientific field can be defined in this fashion, as, indeed, can any field of endeavor. Similarly, scientific knowledge is perhaps best defined as that explanation within a field that is accepted by the scientists of that field. Carrying this form of definition one step further, sociologists are those persons who are recognized as sociologists by other people who call themselves sociologists.

If sociology is what sociologists do, then it is a rich and varied field, for sociologists engage in a marked variety of professional behaviors. Some examples might serve to indicate the scope of sociological activity.

On a given day, we might find a sociologist testifying before a Senate committee. As an expert witness, he explains to the Senators some of the cultural sources of resistance to birth control practices that will be encountered should they decide to take particular approaches to this measure in a foreign aid bill.

Another sociologist is advising a market research firm regarding a new product of their clients. The sociologist has designed interviews, supervised their administration in the field, and analyzed the result. He is now in a position to tell the manufacturers what they should name the product, what color packages it should come in, and how wide a market it is likely to find.

Another sociologist is busy assessing the results of a similar survey procedure—the 1970 census. He has already begun to think about technique for improving the 1980 census on the basis of this experience.

In order to collect data with still another questionnaire, a sociologist is tracking down men who attended Job Corps training schools five years ago. He will find out what sorts of employment these men have now and the ways in which their training was effective or ineffective.

The administrator of an inner city youth program is a sociologist. Although his duties are strictly administrative, his direction of his staff and establishment of tactics for meeting the welfare goals of the program are based on his sociological insights into the community.

Another sociologist is in a computer center. He is engaged in computer simulation of international relations. He has programmed the computer with the personality characteristics of world leaders, policy guidelines of the nations, and prevailing legal, military, and economic conditions. The computer will then offer probable national actions, responses of other nations to those actions, further reactions of the original nation, and so on for as many steps as desired. Several years of future history can be compressed into a few minutes of computer time. The results can be used to promote world peace (or world war, for that matter). Nations with access to the simulated results can avoid actions that led to undesirable outcomes.

A sociologist teaches. There may be five students or five hundred. They may be college freshmen, graduate students, student nurses, army colonels, social workers, Peace Corps trainees, high schoolers, agricultural agents, or sex offenders. The subject may be general sociology or any specialized area within the field. The aim may be general education, enhancement of expertise, or eradication of pathology.

Another sociologist consults with couples who are having marital problems. He is a licensed marriage counselor, offering diagnosis and prescription for interpersonal ills in much the same fashion as does a physician for bodily ailments.

Playing the part, blending with his surroundings, a sociologist becomes a member of a hippy commune. He lives there for months, all the while observing, taking notes, or even making tape recordings if this can be done without disturbing the ongoing social processes of the group. The data he gathers, mostly impressionistic, will later be organized with the intent of understanding such communes, or perhaps group life generally.

Another researcher performs his observation of group processes through one-way glass in a laboratory. The conditions under which the group operates are rigidly and artificially manipulated. The data obtained are neater, if less fun, than that from the commune. The goals of the two researchers may be the same.

These and many more are the activities of sociologists. No sociologist does all these things, although most do more than one. The common core of all such activities is the scientific search for explanation. The sample activities above include some of these searches and efforts to disseminate or apply the obtained knowledge.

Another way of exploring the field of sociology goes back to notions in Chapter 1 concerning a scientific division of labor. Because sociologists are all specialists in social systems, we may expect to find sub-specialties. Although each is in some measure distinctive, there is considerable overlap. Some, such as sociological theory and statistics, are core areas that are used by most sociologists in their pursuit of knowledge in any other kind of specialized area. Still, there are individuals who specialize in statistics, and theory. They service the more substantive areas.

Passing over the service specializations, there are two types of substantive specialty. Fields such as the family, complex organizations, religion, and suicide have focused on a *concrete* segment of the larger social system. The subject matter is relatively easy to identify and to isolate. Other specialization is *analytic* rather than concrete. A list of analytic specialties would include stratification, values, roles, and social structure. These subject matters permeate the several concrete elements of society and are only conceptually separable. Analytic and concrete kinds of specialties follow from two different approaches to the problem of narrowing the focus on subject matter. Concrete specializations are basically restricted to classes of similar subsystems. Analytic specialties deal with a subsystem marked by unique relational bonds. Obviously, these two types will overlap; one sociologist might be studying ministers' and parishioners' roles as part of a study of analytic role systems; another might study such roles as part of the concrete church institution.

Another kind of overlap occurs when several specialities represent different levels of specialization. Religion, family, industrial, political, and others can all be seen as sub-subfields within the "institution" subfield. Crowds, mass communication, and public opinion are subfields of collective behavior, which itself may be a subfield of social psychology or interaction. Such specification could be carried much further. A sociologist who specialized in the effect of television on the attitudes of children ages 0–5 in the United States would be working in a sub-sub-sub-sub-sub-sub-subfield of sociology. His narrowing is this: of social systems only the social psychological; of social psychology only collective behavior; of collective behavior only mass communications; of mass communications only television;

of television only impact on audience; of audiences only children; of children only American; of impacts only attitude change.

I am not sure that this rich and textured variety of specializations is entirely justifiable. It may be that some neater division of labor would produce fewer specialties on more homogeneous grounds, ones that would cover the field with less overlap. So channeled, sociologist's efforts might produce explanation more efficiently. If such an effect were possible, I suspect it would follow a purely analytic division of the field. Such reorganization is not likely and I am not prepared to guarantee the benefits. We will probably go along with the jumble of specialties we have now, adding some new ones, but never eliminating any. The subject system is, at any rate, covered—exhaustively, from many angles, and perhaps redundantly. The shape, the scope, and the disarray of the sociological endeavor is revealed in the naming of its subfields. That revelation was the intent of this section.

THE CASE FOR JARGON, MINUTIAE, COMPUTERS, AND OTHER ESOTERIC STUFF

It is possible to "know" a thing at several different levels. The moon, for instance, is pretty obvious. The first thinking man surely gave some thought to the moon. If he ever stayed up after dark, he would have noticed it. If it is really true that wolves howl at the moon, they also "know" it. But wolves do not know the moon as well as did the first man. That man, in turn, knew the moon less well than later hunting tribes who kept time by its phases. After the invention of the telescope the moon was still better known, and still more fully known after the Apollo mission returned with samples. This is not a simple time-line trend; there are some people on earth now who are less knowledgeable about the moon than those hunting tribesmen.

One's level of knowledge regarding anything is set by several contingencies. Effort expended in attempts to know is one of these. People who spend a great deal of time studying the moon know more about it than those who spend less. A second variable is the character of the study attempted. Contemplation unaided by data would make folly of any amount of study time. What we mean here by knowledge requires both data and contemplation. The most effective form of study has already been marked; it is that prescribed in science. The third contingency is the power of the tools with which the study is conducted. With regard to the moon, the telescope, rocket technology, and the mathematics of orbits are examples of powerful tools. The employment of each led to much expanded knowledge about the moon, for those who were able to employ it.

Some tools, such as the telescope, are mechanical; others, such as orbit mathematics, are purely conceptual. Generally, the more sophisticated the tools, the greater the knowledge they produce. Ultimately, this means that the greatest knowledge concerning anything will be in the possession of experts in that field. Experts are those who master the tools of the trade and who devote much time to effectively focusing these tools on the subject.

What has been said so far in general terms and about the moon is just as true of social systems as objects of study. You have lived within social systems all your life. Surely you were not totally oblivious; surely your experience left you with some knowledge of social systems. Some of the shortcomings of this knowledge were discussed in Chapter 1. Your studies in social science areas, including the reading of this book, may have increased and strengthened your knowledge. There are many levels of knowledge about social systems beyond this point, but they are available only to those who have some mastery of the tools to understanding that mark sociology as a scientific discipline.

The main constraint upon this book has been to keep it available to the amateur. This means that its explanations have been simplified and are in some respects less than complete. If you want to know much more, you must make some start toward being a professional. You must acquire the tools that are essential to further knowledge. Again, I must emphasize that there are several levels. You may work a little bit, become slightly professional, and learn a little bit more, or increase all the factors proportionately. I hope that the "sample" that this book offered encourages you to try at least one more step toward expertise. I must warn you that it is hard work, that the learning process itself is often tedious. I promise you that the understandings that the learning uncovers are satisfying.

At this point I would like to offer a few pages of professional sociology, the kind of thing your backgrounds do not prepare you to understand, the kind of material I have striven to avoid in this book. I hope you don't understand it—if you do I will have disproven my point and demonstrated this book to be unnecessary. If, as I believe, you do not understand it, its inclusion here will demonstrate that a book like this one may be a useful start toward understanding society, but only a start. Before the specimens are displayed, let me offer a few guarantees.

First, the excerpts below are real. They are not put-ons; I am not faking them. Although I did select for difficulty, I did not go out of my way to find obscurity. These represent the leading-edge of sophisticated sociological attempts to place more accurate interpretations on social reality.

Second, to some extent, at least, they are successful. They contain sounder and more precise explanations of social reality than the commonsense, common-language substance of amateur sociology like this book.

Third, they are not translatable. Attempts to render them in commonsense, common-language form would involve loss of precision or logic or some other explanatory value.

Example A: Morris Friedell on Organizations.[1]

Appendix II: A Theorem

Theorem: A congruence class, C, of a semilattice is closed, convex, and contains a maximal element.

(1) C is closed. Asssume $a \in C$ and $b \in C$. Then $ab \in CC$.
Now, $a = aa \in CC$, so $C = CC$.

(2) C contains a maximal element. By closure the product, p, of all elements in C is in C, and by idempotence $pc = p$ for an arbitrary $c \in C$. Hence p is a maximal element of C.

(3) C is convex. Let $a \in C$, $b \in C$, $a \geq x \geq b$, $x \in X$, $xa = a$ so $XC = X$, $xb = x$ so $XC = X$. Thus $X = C$.

Appendix III: Miscellaneous Results

(1) If two members have a common subordinate they have a greatest common subordinate.

(2) Any semilattice may be made into a lattice by adjoining an element ("nobody") which is a lower bond of all elements. Conversely, if the minimal element is removed from a lattice a semilattice is obtained.

(3) Let $\bar{x}$ be the endomorphism of a semilattice given by $a \to ax$, let $\overline{xy}$ be $a \to axy$. The semilattice formed by such endomorphisms is isomorphic to the original semilattice and is isomorphic to a semilattice of the lattice of canonical homomorphisms of the original semilatttice. (It follows that an organization has at least as many possible office-structures as members.)

[1]Morris F. Friedell, "Organizations as Semilattices," *American Sociological Review*, 32 (1967), 54.

Example B: Andre Modigliani on Embarrassment.[2]

A person's general identity, or "total self," consists of many overlapping sets of attributes which are relevant to, and grounded in, all the various segments of his social environment. A person's situational identity, or "immediate self," consists only of that limited set of attributes which is relevant to, and made salient by, current interaction. Paralleling the terminology Miller uses in his discussion of general identity, we label the individual's own conception of his situational identity his *situational-self-identity,* the conception which others present have of his situational identity his situational-public-identity, and his own preception of his situational-public-identity his *situational-subjective-public-identity.* In referring to the level of adequacy which the individual and others present impute to his situational identity, we use the corresponding terms: *situational-self-esteem, situational-public-esteem,* and *situational-subjective-public-esteem.* These last three terms must be clearly distinguished from their counterparts at the level of general identity, i.e., general-self-esteem, general-public-esteem, and general-subjective-public-esteem. Since these counterparts are based on a much larger set of attributes—on the adequacy of a person's total self—they are necessarily much more stable evaluations and unlikely to be much affected by the loss of a few valued attributes. Thus, the individual may suffer the relatively severe loss of situational-self-esteem associated with embarrassment by failing to manifest situationally appropriate demeanor. At the same time, after disengaging himself from the interaction, he is likely to find that his general-self-esteem has been little affected by the experience.

We may summarize this discussion with the following basic proposition: *embarrassment is the psychological state associated with a loss in situational-self-esteem that is caused by loss in situational-subjective-public-esteem.*

Example C: Blau and Duncan on Occupational Inheritance.[3]

The "Guttman-Lingoes Smallest Space Analysis I" provides a technique suited for [ascertaining factors that influence social distance between occupational groupings] . . . although it is still in the experimental stage and not all its properties are fully known. The triangular matrix of distance measures . . . is used as input in a computer program employing this technique, the output of which defines underlying dimensions of distance. In our case two dimensions appeared to be sufficient. The results of the analysis are presented in [Fig. 12–1]. The scale on the two coordinates is arbitrary, provided that their relative value is preserved. The distance on a straight line between any two occupations can be ascertained. These distances supplied by the model can then be compared with the observed distances, and the relationship between the two indicates the goodness of fit of the model. The measure used to determine the fit of the derived model is called the coefficient of alienation, which approaches zero as the solution im-

---

[2]Andre Modigliani, "Embarrassment and Embarrassability," *Sociometry,* 31 (1968), 315–16.

[3]Peter M. Blau and Otis Dudley Duncan, *The American Occupational Structure* (New York: John Wiley, 1967), pp. 69–73.

proves. . . . For our model in [Fig. 12–1], the coefficient of alienation is .07, an appreciable improvement over the one-dimensional solution with a coefficient of .15. It is highly questionable whether additional dimensions would be meaningful. Rotation is permissible, as the orientation of the axes as well as the scale of distances is arbitrary.

. . . The first dimension in [Fig. 12–1] evidently represents the socio-economic status of occupations. . . . The meaning of the second dimension is not easily discernible, but . . . . A possible interpretation of the distinction between the two extremes is in terms of the principles that govern the organization of work and the acquisition of skills necessary to perform it. On the one hand, work may be organized on the basis of rational principles explicitly formulated; the performance of individuals is expected to conform to these universalistic standards. Such conformance is brought about either by placing individuals into circumscribed roles in complex structures that are organized in accordance with rational principles or by training them to acquire abstract rational standards of performance . . . . On the other hand, general principles for dealing with the diverse, idiosyncratic problems encountered at work may not have been formulated, and individuals must acquire the so-called intuitive knowledge required for dealing with these problems through apprenticeship and trial and error.

Fig. 12-1   TWO-DIMENSIONAL GUTTMAN-LINGOES SOLUTION
Distances between Fathers' Occupations with respect to 1962 occupations (outflow)

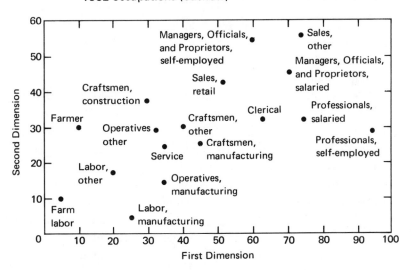

The point I am making by this display is that as explanation becomes more powerful it is likely to become more esoteric. Before Einstein could develop his explanation of the physical world, he had to invent a special calculus by which it could be expressed. The explanation was, and is, truly accessible only to those who learn that calculus. You and I can talk about "relativity," but without the conceptual equipment our knowledge will remain very low-level. Although none of the examples of sociological explanation above can pretend to the power of Einstein's physical explanation, neither do any of them present the intellectual density of tensor calculus. Should social science ever arrive at such powerful explanation, I suspect it will be in equally esoteric vehicles.

Surely there is much to be said for ordinary everyday English. It communicates. But it communicates ordinary everyday ideas, often fuzzily and imprecisely. The word "class," for instance, has been used in this book in perhaps a half a dozen different senses. Some of these meanings are general, some of special sociological derivation. If you read further in sociology you may find at least another dozen meanings for the same term. A communication that baldly used the word "class" ("Class membership in the United States is determined by occupation") might communicate different things to different people. Before communication can afford the precision of designation that leads to powerful explanations, a definition of the term must be specified. This could be done by appending a second communication to the first. ("By 'class,' I mean. . . .") But what if the words in the definition are as variable in meaning as the original? Such a process could extend ad infinitum. The only way out is to invent new terms that are not already burdened with meanings, define them once and unambiguously, and reserve their use for that meaning alone.

This solution implies that any specialized field of explanation is likely to have a large catalog of special words. It will be very large indeed, for, after all, we will need a score of new terms for the subdivided meanings of "class" alone. It is fashionable to criticize academic disciplines for their excessive use of jargon. The argument here would suggest that such elaborations of language are not excessive. Rather, it may be that the number of esoteric terms in currency in a discipline is directly related to its scientific sophistication. There are of course dangers in this direction; multiplication of terms without meaning or with duplicate meanings is not merely useless but confusing. Still, "class" will probably be a less potent term than "anomia," which is purely sociological and only has three or four meanings. "Semilattice" and "situational-subjective-public-esteem" may be even better.

Still, we may have nagging doubts. Are these terms ambiguous? Are they precise? Do they hold duplicate meanings with other terms?

As the number of terms grows larger the process of checking grows more voluminous. The multiplication of terms creates a problem at the same time that it solves another. If we remember that our defense of jargon was really a defense of clarity, we may find a way out.

There is available a system of terms where identity of definition is easily checked. Principles of definition are rigorous and unambiguous. The grammar under which these terms are assembled into communications is highly formalized and offers no possibility of misinterpretation. The name of this system is mathematics. Jargon, a special terminology for the field, will still be necessary. Its primary function, however, should not be to provide explanation, but rather to mediate between the reality system under study and the mathematical symbols in which explanation is to be conceived and communicated. The degree to which a field casts its explanation in mathematics is a better index of its explanatory power than is the volume of its jargon.

I must warn you against overacceptance of mathematics as I earlier warned you against overacceptance of science. Nonsense *can* be offered in mathematical form. Indeed, it often is. The special advantage of mathematics over other symbol-systems rests in the fact that it is easier for one conversant with that form to detect the communication as nonsense. The special danger lies in the fact that mathematical presentation may convince the non-expert by its imposing form. Much of the work in the field of sociology is precisely this sort of humbug. One more point: anything that can be expressed mathematically can also be expressed in literary or any other symbolic form. The advantage of mathematics is that complex explanation is more efficiently expressed mathematically. Explanation of any given problem in less precise symbols would take more effort in the conception and more bulk of communication. This does not mean that such explanation should be ignored.

In Chapter 3 I outlined the necessary relationship between thought and symbols. Here I will simply remind you of that and suggest that the utilization of precise and unambiguous symbols renders precise and unambiguous thought more probable. Sociological explanation will improve as it leans more heavily on such symbols. These cannot be the symbols of everyday discourse; they will tend to be mathematics and jargon. Sociological concepts will therefore be esoteric and to some degree inaccessible to the amateur.

A second form of alienation from everyday understanding is in technical instruments. Earlier I mentioned Newton's concepts and

Galileo's telescope. Newton's concepts are esoteric concepts cast in special languages including that of mathematics; this material we have already covered. This sort of conceptual tool serves the cause of efficiency in organizing data and developing explanation. Let's think a little bit about the telescope. The telescope is not conceptual. It is not directly concerned with explanation. Rather, it is a tool that helps to obtain data. With its use, man can get data he could not otherwise obtain or get it in a more usable form than would be otherwise available. Technical instrumentation may be as esoteric as conceptual instrumentation. The technical instruments of sociology are many and varied. I do not intend to go through a catalog of them here. If we take simple, verbal responses of people as a form of data, we can briefly sketch the point. You might say "You ask some questions and you get some answers, big deal!" Such a response is analogous to describing the use of a telescope as "looking through a piece of glass." Telescopes come in a variety of powers, resolutions, focus areas. They may be equipped with filters. The image may be recorded visually, photographically, or in tele-dots. Radar, radio, lasers, and other variations may be added. What you see is as much a function of what you look through as it is of what's on the other end. Precisely the same point may be made about questioning. Interview and questionnaire technology is at least as critical for sociologists as the telescope is for astronomers. Appreciation of this has led sociologists to the development of many variations, highly stylized designs, special utilizations, and cognizance of the effect of each on the data obtained. The amateur who fails to recognize this will grow impatient with such emphasis on details of technique.

The third way in which sociology frustrates the amateur who approaches it is with its subject-matter focus. As you went through the series of examples in the last section, you may have asked "Who gives a damn about semilattices?" The other examples dealt with whether salesmen's sons are likely to become salesmen and who might blush when he spilled his drink. Such topics are, admittedly, of less than earth-shaking importance. With a whole world full of grave issues facing mankind, why are sociologists spending their time on unimportant minutiae? The charge is at least partly justified and gives the non-sociologist reason to censure the professional. The key that will win acquittal from the charge is in the definition of *unimportant*. Grave issues are likely to involve many social elements and complicated relationships. They are likely to be the sort of subject that is most troublesome to investigate. Investigation in these areas is least likely to produce powerful explanation. In Chapter 11,

I suggested that some questions are more easily answered than others. Sadly, unimportant questions are usually easy, important ones difficult.

A man might spend a lifetime seeking explanation in a major problem-area without tangible results. If, instead, he chooses to narrow the problem, to limit the number of variables and cases with which he will deal, he may attack and solve a small problem. If the choice, then, is between some small answers to small questions and no answers to large questions, the weight of science will surely fall with the first alternative. The goal of science is explanation; some is better than none. Furthermore, small answers may be accumulated to yield large ones, or small solutions may offer analogies helpful in solving great questions.

A physicist friend of mine spends much of his time studying superheated gases. He explores the characteristics and behavior of submicroscopic particles in a small chamber and under conditions different from any nature provides. His interest in this pickey little problem-area is subsidiary to his main interest: the properties of interstellar space. Let molecules equal stars; the particles and spaces between are proportionate for heated chamber and the universe. Little answers may be extensible to big. He studies superheated gases rather than the universe directly because it is easier. The universe will not fit into his laboratory; it is not susceptible to experimental manipulation.

So it is with the sociologist. It is easier to develop and codify knowledge about semilattices than about the operation of federal bureaucracies. But federal bureaucracies are made up, in part, of semilattices. Once adequate explanation of semilattices is available, it may be possible for sociologists to offer a design for a bureaucracy that would permit greater adjustment in organizational behavior following policy shifts. The net effect would be a government more responsive to the electorate. To expect such large oaks from our inconsistent acorns requires an act of faith, but I hope you will bear with sociology as it cultivates its spindly saplings of knowledge.

I have shown you three ways in which sociology is esoteric: concepts, tools, and topics. Exotic language and mathematics may tend to alienate the casual investigator of the field but are essential to sound and precise conceptualization. Formalized and elaborate instrumentation—observational and interview techniques—may seem arbitrary and overblown but develops more data in more usable forms than would otherwise be available. Concentration on minutiae is easily mistaken for frivolity or a misplaced sense of importance but leads to the development of models offering the only route to larger issues. The very strengths of the field appear as weaknesses to the amateur and make difficult his attempt to become less amateurish.

POSTURES FOR THE AMATEUR

If you did not understand the examples a few pages back, you are still a sociological amateur. As an amateur, faced with these alienating features of sociology, you may write off the field. I hope you reject this course. I promise you that we will not go away even if you ignore us. I assure you that you must continue to live in a problematic social world. I warn you that folk, theological, and artistic bases for dealing with these problematic issues are less sound than sociological ones.

If you are willing to give sociology this due, you still have a serious problem. I spent some time earlier persuading you, as an amateur, that you "need" sociology and the last few pages persuading you that you, as an amateur, cannot "have" sociology. One way out would be for you to become a professional. I hope some of you decide to enter into sociology as a career, to give the rest of your lives to learning and practice of the sociological discipline. Still, most of you will not.

Another possibility, open to even the grossest amateur, is to place yourself in the hands of the professional when the occasion warrants. Most of you are anxious to accept physician's advice when you are ill and attorney's counsel when you have legal difficulties. Why not, then, the social equivalent? When social issues, personal or national, grow too complex, call on the expert. When societal matters remain stubbornly problematic in the face of amateur attempts at solution, call on the sociologist. I cannot guarantee that he won't botch the job, but his chances of failure are as much smaller as his explanations are better.

This stance on the part of the amateur, of yielding to expertise, does not involve an abdication of freedom or individual power of decision. It simply implies a more rational actor, one who makes his decisions on the basis of the best available grounds. All considerations of ends are reserved to personal or popular-collective autonomy; sociology can be consulted regarding surest means to their attainment. Should you decide to go to the moon, you could insist on riding in a rocket you understood. You would be better advised to make the trip in a rocket that is beyond your engineering under-standing, but up to the engineering requirements of the trip. Leave the design to experts.

A further option may be pursued in tandem with this one. The amateur can become a semipro. Understanding is available in small chunks. You can bite off a few more than you have now. The more knowledgeable you become about sociology, the more rational your actions in subjecting yourself to sociological expertise when you choose to do so. The more sociology you know, the more likely it is that you will recognize the situations that call for bowing to the expert. Additionally, you operate in social situations most of the time. All of these situations are rife with problematic aspects. Sociological consultants are not likely always to be available. On such occasions you will need to serve as your own sociologist, however inadequate your qualifications. You will be well advised to reduce your inade-quacy, to become just a little more cognizant of sociological mate-rials. Social operations and consequent opportunities for social mal-functions occur in greater volume than automobile operations, yet the number of social technicians available for assistance is much smaller than the number of auto repairmen. Every citizen must, then, be more ready for do-it-yourself work in the social arena. Without becoming a professional sociologist, you should become a conversant amateur. You should learn more sociology than this book contains. You should venture at least to the edges of the esoteric content of the discipline. You should be prepared to put in some hard work for every measure of additional understanding, for the esoteric content is resistant to amateurish approaches.

There are several works available which will serve as a next step beyond this one. Some of them are listed as recommended readings at the end of this chapter. The further pursuit of social explanation demands labor and patience, but it also offers challenge and reward.

"Power to the people" is a slogan. It is also an invitation that can be accepted only by those who have the knowledge to become effective action agents in their own and their society's fate.

FURTHER READING

Further Introductions to Society

Faris, R. E., ed., *Handbook of Modern Sociology*. Chicago: Rand-McNally, 1964.*
Sills, David L., ed., *International Encyclopedia of the Social Sciences* (17 vols.): New York: Macmillan-Free Press, 1968.

Standard introductory texts by Broom, Chinoy, Johnson, Lenski, Leslie, Lundberg, and Smelser.

Sociology: The Field and the Practitioners

Cuzzort, R. P., *Humanity and Modern Sociological Thought*. New York: Holt, 1969. Available in paperback.

DiRenzo, Gordon, ed., *Concepts, Theory, and Explanation in the Behavioral Sciences*. New York: Random House, 1966.*

Quine, Willard V., *Word and Object*. Cambridge, Mass.: Massachusetts Institute of Technology, 1960. Available in paperback.

Sjoberg, Gideon, ed., *Ethics, Politics, and Social Research*. San Francisco: Schenkman, 1967. Available in paperback.

The Uses of Sociology

Deutsch, Steven, and John Howard, eds., *Where It's At: Radical Perspectives in Sociology*. New York: Harper, 1969. Available in paperback.

Heidt, Sarajane, and Amitai Etzioni, eds., *Societal Guidance: A New Approach to Social Problems*. New York: Crowell, 1969. Available in paperback.

Shostak, Arthur, ed., *Sociology in Action: Case Studies in Social Problems and Directed Social Change*. Homewood, Ill.: Dorsey, 1966.* Available in paperback.

*Difficult, specialized, or technical.

Greece, classical, 70
Group:
  attachment (biblio.), 198
  biological sources of, 34-35, 42-43
  classes as, 112-113
  in, 195-198
  loyalty, 190-191
  mediating function of, 189-191
  out, 195-198
  primary, 185-195
    surrogates, 191-195
  reference, 178
  solidarity, 195-198
Guthrie, Woodie, 200, 201, 216
Guttman, Louis, 256

HEFNER, HUGH, 200, 207, 211, 216
Heidt, Sarajane, 265
Henry, John, 200, 201, 216
Heterogeneity of population, 54
Heterogeneity, social, in urbanism, 225-228
Hippies, 181
History (biblio.), 71-72
Hodge, Robert, 99
Hodgson, R. E., 32
Hoffman, Paul, 150
Hogarth, William, 200, 201, 202, 217
Homogeneity, social, 46, 223
  as consequence of mass media, 215-216
  in suburbs, 228-234
Horowitz, Irving, 160
Howard, John, 266
Howell, F. Clark, 32
Howton, William, 14
Huff, Darell, 14
Hull, Raymond, 128
Hulse, Frederick, 32
Human nature, 32, 34-39, 42-43, 169, 183-185
  (biblio.), 32

IDENTITY, INDIVIDUAL, 183-188
Ideology, 67-69
  decline of, 224-225
  in prejudice, 196-197
Immigrants, 177-178
Incest taboo, 39-42
India, early social development, 49, 53
India, traditional caste system, 111
Individual:
  alienation, 176-182
  anomia, 223-228

conformity, 176
goal orientations, 176
human potential, 174
identity, 183-188
motives, 170
and society, 163-167, 223-228
variation in values, 86
(see also Self)
Industrial revolution, 62-63, 67
Infant dependency, 20, 25-26
In-group, 195-198
Inheritance of occupation, 226-227, 258-259
Inheritance of prestige, 107-108
Inkeles, Alex, 14
Innovation, 44-47, 59-60, 176
Institutions, 191-193
Instruments in science, 262
Intelligence, 19-20, 23-24
Interaction, 80-82, 184-186
Intergroup relations, 2, 180, 195-198
  (see also Minorities)
Italian Anti-Defamation League, 209
Italy, religion, 64
Italy, politics, 141

JACOBS, JANE, 249
Jackson State University, police riot, 243
Japan, politics, 150
Japan, stratification, 114
Japanese-American's values, 177
Japanese Americans, World War II, 236
Javits, Jacob, 150
Jaw, physiology of, 21
Jews, European, World War II, 236
Jews as minority, 196-197
John Birch Society, 181
Johnson, Harry, 266
Johnson, Lyndon, 151, 210
Jones, James, 128
Jones, Lorenzo, 200, 201, 203, 216
Judgments of prestige, 96-100

KAHL, JOSEPH, 114
Katz, Fred, 135
Keller, Suzanne, 249
Keniston, Kenneth, 198
Kent State University, National Guard riot, 243
Kidnapping, political blackmail, 240
Klan, Ku Klux, 144
Klapp, Orrin E., 14